BURMA

BURMA
A PROFILE

Norma Bixler

PRAEGER PUBLISHERS
New York • Washington • London

PRAEGER PUBLISHERS
111 Fourth Avenue, New York, N.Y. 10003, U.S.A.
5, Cromwell Place, London S.W.7, England

Published in the United States of America in 1971
by Praeger Publishers, Inc.

© 1971 by Praeger Publishers, Inc.

Library of Congress Catalog Card Number: 77–118047

Printed in the United States of America

Contents

A SECTION OF PHOTOGRAPHS FOLLOWS PAGE 84.

Maps

Foreword

Other people share in the forming of a book besides the author and the editor who first believes it can be written. In addition to authors and scholars listed in the bibliography, many Burmese— my friends and others, whose names I never knew—taught me about their country's history and culture. Quotations from Bogyoke Aung San come from a 1946 collection of his speeches called *Burma's Challenge,* which has not been published in English. My English-language manuscript copy was a gift from Dr. Maung Maung, for which I have always been grateful. The supportive interest of Helen and Frank Trager has been an encouragement. I owe a great deal to my husband, Paul Bixler, who read and reread the various drafts of the manuscript. Many of the photographs are the work of Phillip F. Thomas. Suzanne Clauser voluntarily abandoned her own writing to return to an earlier craft; as draftsman, she is responsible for the book's maps. I am happy to acknowledge her contribution.

Of course, all interpretations and opinions expressed in the book remain my own responsibility.

Yellow Springs, Ohio
August, 1970

Introduction

The American is lucky whose first overseas assignment is in a land with a culture alien to his own. Our country is so large that we can travel for thousands of miles and never leave home, as many Europeans, Asians, and Africans cannot. We lack experience with the barrier of a foreign language, let alone an alien religion, except as tourists.

But as tourists we still travel in the shell of our own culture, safe in the shadow of our embassies, our traveler's checks, the hotelkeepers and taxi drivers who have carefully learned our language and are anxious to please us.

An American who is living and working abroad will register at his embassy; he may still keep some traveler's checks locked away for an emergency exit. But he lives under another nation's laws and, if the culture is truly alien, with people who worship differently, work differently, and cherish different values. That they speak in another tongue may be the least important of the differences.

If the worker is patient and reasonably open-minded, he begins to learn what shapes that alien culture and, by contrast, what shapes his own. He discovers that the American, or the Western, life pattern is not something handed down from on high, that it results from a particular conjunction of history, geography, and religion, that other people can be virtuous, cultivated, and full of self-respect in quite a different life pattern. This learning can occur whether or not the American develops any liking for the people among whom he lives.

But the greatest boon of all for that American on his first

foreign assignment is to find himself in a country whose people he learns to love. This emotion doesn't develop overnight. Six or eight months aren't long enough. He must live through and survive his initial culture shock, a common ailment. He must even live through his first wave of undiscriminating affection which verges on infatuation, when everything is good even if it's bad and he brings no judgment to his viewing or his learning.

After culture shock, after infatuation, he begins to reach out, tentatively, over what he now knows are the real cultural differences, to find that his neighbors and fellow workers are reaching out to him, past courtesy, past even respect, to trust and affection.

From talking to permanent foreign service personnel, I gather that this can happen only once and usually on the first assignment. After that, strangeness is never as strange again, the American is never again as aware and sensitized. He will learn about new countries; he knows now how to go about it. He will curb his impatience by habit, not an effort of will. He will learn respect and affection for other peoples.

But those first people will be a part of him as no other people but his own can ever be. They were the ones who taught him to love and respect an alien country and, oddly enough, to love and cherish his own with a larger spirit than he had known before. For him, the world shrinks immeasurably because of them. He brings a continent home with him, not one single, small nation. Even though he may not know other continents, he doesn't ignore odd, unpronounceable date lines in his newspaper. The people who live there, as different as his people, with their odd, unpronounceable names now grown so familiar, are a real people. He accepts that without thought.

Such an American becomes vulnerable in the shrunken world where he now lives. He owns two citizenships. The second is not in the marrow of his bones as is that of his own birth-nation, for intimacy with all the small nuances of a culture is not reached in a couple of years. But that second citizenship is there, irrevocably. With it he has learned what it is like to belong to a small, weak nation, a strange and educative experience for a citizen of a powerful country. Since most nations are small and weak, his knowledge makes him vulnerable as they are vulnerable.

Burma is the country to which I owe this figurative dual citizenship. Though I could no longer hum the tune, I think I would stand automatically and without thought if I heard the Burmese national anthem played anywhere in the United States. Yet it was Burma that fully taught me to know that I was an American. A newly independent nation has almost a fierce patriotism, a compelling nationalism. Burma taught me that these were quite respectable and even necessary emotions. Because I honored Burma's, I learned a new respect for my own and for every other nation's.

This came about just as I have described it, on a first foreign assignment for Americans who had been no farther from home than Canada. We spent two years in Burma, where my husband was on an assignment for a private foundation. We lived in a Burmese neighborhood with our headman and mentor as neighbor on one side, and a judge on the other. We traveled fairly extensively during the university vacations. We have returned twice since our assignment ended. Our communication with the country has never been completely broken, not even now.

Like most Western wives, particularly professional women detached from their own jobs, I had time on my hands. It was in Burma that I began my first exploration of the country's history and religion. From my friends, who were my most eager teachers, I started my study of its culture. I continued learning while I taught journalism and worked in an outpatient clinic.

But the learning was everywhere. One of the books I took to Burma, which I'd never had time to read at home, was Alexis de Tocqueville's *Democracy in America*. I thought to learn about my own country, but strangely it was Burma which I stopped constantly to ponder. I had never before understood with what courage an inexperienced nation acted when with almost innocent faith it set out to create a democracy.

Intimacy can seldom be complete between individuals not born to the same life pattern. There is a final barrier which even affection cannot leap. But there can be honesty, trust, and appreciation. Such appreciation for one nation increases the ability to appreciate other, equally strange nations or, at the very least, to exercise restraint of judgment in recognition of one's own ignorance of the unfamiliar life pattern.

Not every American can or wishes to spend several years in such an alien culture. Books can serve in some measure as a substitute for such residence. I hope the reader of this book will never find Burma as strange a land again, neither Burma nor other countries with cultures different from his own. Perhaps for him the world will be more nearly what it looked like from the moon, what it is in reality, a very small planet where mankind lives closer than it has usually remembered.

Knowledge of a few names and their usage provides a good entrance visa for Burma. Burman and Burmese may each be used as noun or adjective, just as American is. Burman is an ethnic term to designate the people who came to dominate Burma and are now a majority. Their language is the Burmese language.

Burma Proper is used to designate the major river-valley regions of the Union of Burma. The people living there who speak Burmese are usually called Burmese, whether or not their major blood line is Burman. Minorities from other states and districts within the country are normally called by their own ethnic names. But they are all Burmese citizens; their passports would designate them as Burmese.

Upper Burma is the northern portion of the major river valleys, the final territory of the Kingdom of Burma. Lower Burma is everything south of that, the portion of the kingdom ruled by the British after the first two British-Burma wars.

Common Burmese words are italicized when they are first used and explained. Afterwards they are set in normal type. A small glossary is included at the end of the book for reference.

BURMA

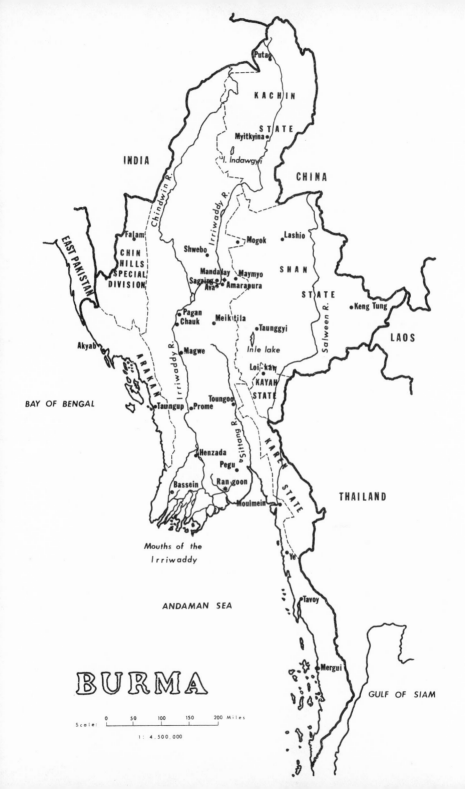

BURMA

Scale: | 0 | 50 | 100 | 150 | 200 Miles

1 : 4,500,000

1 Geography of Burma

The land mass of the Union of Burma is shaped like a kite, even to a long, thin tail. This is a cliché endlessly repeated because nothing else is quite so apt. The northern point of the kite diamond extends to the Himalayas where the Hkakabo Razi reaches up over 19,000 feet into a cold blue sky. The eastern point, jutting into the boundary between China and Laos, becomes for Burma the spot where its long border with China ends and its border with Laos begins. The western reach is to the Bay of Bengal, only a little below East Pakistan's Chittagong on the land side and a water's stretch away from Calcutta.

The many mouths of Burma's great Irrawaddy River mark the kite's southern limit. The Irrawaddy, in its birth-giving tributaries, rises somewhere above the Hkakabo Razi. After the waters have joined, it flows the entire length of the country, except for the kite tail. This thin, dangling strip of land lies alongside the Thai land mass, beginning low on the eastern slant of the kite and stretching south to within 10° of the equator. The Thai-Burmese border divides the skinny neck of land called the Isthmus of Kra, which attaches the peninsula of Malaya to the mainland of Southeast Asia.

From the Himalayas almost to the equator is a long stretch for a country slightly smaller than the state of Texas. On its 261,789 square miles live more than 26 million people. The width of the country is much less than its length. Along all boundaries except the water's edge of the south and southwest, it is sealed in by mountains.

THE FOUR LAND BELTS

Geographers divide Burma into four land belts with a common anchor point in the far north. From those 19,000-foot Himalayan peaks, two of the land belts cut down into the country like an inverted V. The Folded Mountain Belt lies to the west, while the Shan Upland is in the east. Between the two heights is the Central Belt, the heartland of the Burmese, which they call Burma Proper. Where the mountains lie wholly within Burma in the southwest, they are called the Arakan Yoma. Beyond them, along the Bay of Bengal, is the Arakan Coastal Belt.

The Shan Upland

This eastern upland thrusts up quickly, without preliminary steps, from the low Central Belt. Some of its towns, with their pleasant, temperate climate, were favorite hill stations of the colonial English, who moved there from the plains during the hot season. The rise, which averages 3,000 feet, is along a fault line where the earth's crust broke and lifted long ago; the plateau extends well beyond the Shan State of Burma into China, Laos, and northern Thailand. Robert E. Huke, an American geographer who has spent some time in Burma, says that much of it resembles the steeply rolling hills of central Pennsylvania. Some mountains rise as high as 6,000 feet, but there can be sloping grassy meadows as well, which are gently terraced for wet-rice cultivation. Some Westerners have suggested that parts of the country would make good cattleland, but most of the people are Buddhists and would not raise beef for slaughter.

As the Upland moves south through the Kayah and Karen States, the plateau breaks up into long strips of hills with narrow valleys between, and finally spends itself in the narrow Isthmus of Kra.

It is surprising how many great Asian rivers are born to the north of Burma in the Himalayas, like fingers stretching down from the same bony wrist. The Salween River drops many miles through China, traveling in an almost regimented north-south course parallel with the Mekong, the Yangtze, and the Irrawaddy. But before the Salween enters the Shan Upland, the Mekong departs southeastward on its long and mighty course to the delta of South Vietnam, and the Yangtze begins its twisting, powerful crossing of southern China all the way to Shanghai on the East China Sea. The Irrawaddy's waters, farthest west, have already entered Burma at the country's northern point to dwarf its other rivers.

The Salween pounds south through the Upland with forthright directness, pitching its way through narrow valleys of the Shan State with rapids and waterfalls, and coming out through the Karen State at Moulmein. It feeds nothing except the small alluvial delta there, for its Shan valleys are too narrow and steep for agriculture. In a world of river people and long canoes, the Salween is navigable only for its last 75 miles. Someday it might offer hydroelectric power. Today it has only beauty, and that is often hidden in the deep ravines. Yet the Salween is the Upland's main river.

The Central Belt

In quite contrary fashion, the Central Belt thrives because of its rivers. First, always first, is the Irrawaddy River, whose waters, moving broadly to the sea, are like the rib of the kite. It is impressive even as a young stream before it passes Mandalay. Standing on its high banks there, looking down, is like watching the power of the Mississippi before the Missouri joins it. The Chindwin is the Irrawaddy's Missouri; to call it a tributary is to demean it. Flowing down from the north almost in the shadow of the Folded Mountains on the west, its waters merge with the Irrawaddy well up the main valley, and only then does the Irrawaddy reach full majesty. All the major capitals of the Burmese kings were built on its banks—Pagan, Ava, and Mandalay.

There are many other streams, but two other rivers are of major value to the Central Belt. Both are short and rise in the south. The Sittang River is longer, its valley richer, but the Rangoon River, the second, has its own importance. The city of Rangoon, capital and port, is built on its banks, well up from the sea. Its waters are so swift that small boats do well to tack upstream if their goal is the bank directly opposite. Its mouth lies between the many mouths of the Irrawaddy to its west and the delta of the Sittang to its east.

It is worth noting that three major Southeast Asian ports—Rangoon, Bangkok, and Saigon—are built not on the sea but on rivers; that two cities, Rangoon and Saigon, are built on rivers which bear their name, and not on the great rivers of those countries. The many-mouthed Irrawaddy and Mekong both flow to the sea west of the port, as if the port didn't care to tangle with the shifting mouths, the swamps, the watery union of ocean and river. This is a tribute to a great river's power.

The geographic spread of the rivers through the Central Belt, their breadth even in the upper valleys, means that the distribution of their ancient alluvial soil is widespread. They nourish the people and the crops. They are roadways and fisheries. They give life to the central valleys. Scientists toy with an idea that once in ancient times—perhaps before the earth rolled over and thrust up a shoulder to make the Upland—it was the Irrawaddy which flowed in the Sittang River course, while the Chindwin flowed through the present Irrawaddy valley to the sea. It hardly matters. The soil is there, whatever name the water bore.

Sometimes in the Central Belt there are rolling hills and occasionally an isolated hill of some height like the one at Mandalay. But the only continuous break in the valleys is the mountainous stretch of uneroded rock called Pegu Yoma running northwest between the Irrawaddy and Sittang valleys, crossing the Irrawaddy in the central plain and blending in the north with the

Folded Mountains. The main road north from Rangoon toward Mandalay runs up the Sittang valley, and the traveler by car or train moves for many miles in the company of distant misty-blue walls on either side, with Pegu Yoma to the west and the Upland to the east.

The Folded Mountain Belt

The valleys of the Central Belt end on the west in rugged mountain country. The several companion ranges begin far up in the north where the system is at its broadest; though it narrows in the south, it never becomes congenial or less rugged. Like the Upland, the mountain belt reaches beyond Burma, but the portion which lies entirely within the country is named the Arakan Yoma. It has served both to wall off the central heartland from would-be invaders and to wall it in, limiting access to the region from the outer world.

Far to the north, through one of the passes, the Ledo Road permits land entry from India. This was the gate through which World War II shipments entered the country to exit into China through Bhamo by the old Burma Road. These road names are familiar to the men who fought in this wartime theater.

Much earlier, traders knew the old route between India and China, but the ways of coming and going in Burma by land have often been used only during wars or internal disturbances. So it is with the passes of the Arakan Yoma. So it has been also with the Three Pagoda Pass on the east where the boundary between Thailand and Burma divides the kite tail. Before the British came in 1825, Burmese kings frequently used this route to invade Thailand. The deadly railroad built by the Japanese during World War II went from Burma through this pass and across Thailand's Khwai Noi, a name moviegoers will remember as the River Kwai. Since the war, the jungle has reclaimed the railroad, the Ledo Road is falling into disrepair, and, except for country folk who live near the rough boundaries and ignore their difficulties, passage in and out of Burma is again limited to sea routes or by air through Rangoon.

The Arakan Coastal Belt

Most of Burma's land borders end with mountains. But on the southwest there is a narrow strip of Burmese land, above the Irrawaddy Delta and below East Pakistan, which has the Arakan Yoma at its back. The Bay of Bengal washes this long shoreline, its islands spangled on the water's surface. The mountains come close to the shore in the south; while little land can be cultivated here, the area gives Burma some of its most beautiful beaches, like Sandoway. Farther north, particularly around Akyab, the mouths of several small rivers form a common delta with rich alluvial soil.

As Burma is isolated by its mountains from its neighbors, so Arakan is isolated from the rest of the nation. East Pakistan's Chittagong, up the coast, is nearer and easier to reach than Rangoon. Modern times have brought one change: Burma's commercial airline flies regularly to Akyab and Sandoway. But there are as yet no all-weather roads between Arakan and the Central Belt. In the Union of Burma, political relationships between districts, the distribution of power among them, are largely determined by physical relationships. Nowhere is this more obvious than with Arakan. Later in this chapter, the geographic relations of these sections of the country will be reviewed.

THE CYCLE OF THE SEASONS

Generalities about the weather are difficult in a country which stretches almost as many miles from north to south as the distance from the Great Lakes to the Mississippi Delta. Burma is also set farther north than its Southeast Asian neighbors. Burma and Thailand, for example, have two major cities apiece. Each one's port and capital (Rangoon for Burma, Bangkok for Thailand) are comparatively new cities in the south. Each has an important old city in the north (Mandalay for Burma, Chiengmai for Thailand). Yet Thailand's northern city is closer to southern Rangoon than to Mandalay.

One might expect Burma to be colder than Thailand and its other Southeast Asian neighbors. But the northern mountain wall is high enough to insulate the land from the bitter winds of Central Asia. With mild exceptions like smoke-blackened chimneys at Maymyo where winter ice freezes across a water basin, Burma shares the Southeast Asian three-season cycle and a monsoon culture. The beginning and the ending of the rains are more important than temperature variations.

Burma has three seasons. The rainy season, the fulcrum of the cycle, begins about mid-May, when the parched earth thirsts for the water. The first rains are usually heavy. The monsoon wind that brings them is often an angry wind blowing from black skies, bending the mangoes, roaring through wide-bladed banana trees in the villages and in city compounds. For weeks it rains every day, but not all of each day; the sun shines in between. Downpours often come abruptly, with great density, and end as suddenly. By September they thin out until on some days there is no rain at all. By the end of October the rains have stopped entirely; the earth steams awhile and the humidity is high. But in November the cool season begins, under a high sky of clearest blue. In Rangoon it may be cool enough for a sweater in the early morning and late evening. In Mandalay some days will call for a sweater all day. But the sky is always that cloudless blue, and the sun always shines. There is no rain except for almost immeasurable sprinkles in January. These the Burmese call mango showers.

By February the weather is changing almost imperceptibly. A sweater at any hour is needed less and less frequently, and by March it can be packed away again. All through April the heat rises inexorably and with it the humidity, though there is no rain. By early May people search the sky impatiently for signs of the dark monsoon clouds. The first will come and go and bring no relief from the hot season. Then one day in mid-May the skies darken, the wind blows, the first rain pours down, and the whole cycle of the seasons sets about repeating itself.

The monsoon blows into Burma from the southwest off the Bay of Bengal, but the mountains and the Upland act as barriers and bend the entering winds to the north. This interaction of highland and monsoon winds is largely the cause of the wide variation in the amount of rain which falls in different parts of the country.

The wettest parts are in Arakan and down the kite tail, which may receive 200 inches or in some small sections even more; surprisingly, the far north, because the mountains force the clouds to drop their moisture, may also receive 200 inches. Around Rangoon rainfall averages about 100 inches a year. In the Shan Upland it drops down to 50 or 60 inches, but in the heart of the central valley of the Irrawaddy it falls to 20 to 40 inches. Mandalay averages around 30 to 35 inches.

Scant rainfall provides a sight which astonishes travelers driving north from Rangoon—the sight of cactus growing beside the road above Toungoo, its prickly masses reinforcing village fences of bamboo staves. Yet one fact must be remembered: the measured inches of annual rainfall do not in themselves make a dry belt. Kansas averages only 28 inches annually, and Iowa 30. Their plains are fruitful. Arizona, a more typical example of dry land for the United States, receives only 7 inches. But, in the United States, moisture normally falls throughout the year, most of it usable. In countries with a monsoon culture like Burma's, all the rain falls only within a few months. Some is stored, but much runs off to the rivers and the sea.

Natural Resources

A nation's first resource is its people, but the land on which the people live gives them the material resources with which to work. In a country still very short of industry, the land must provide that people's raw material for growth.

The earliest Western travelers to Burma marveled at the wealth of its kings, their gold and magnificent jewels. Ancient Indian and Chinese texts mention a "Golden Land," and so does a Greek historian of seafaring trade. That land may have been Burma, for even modern Burma still retains its share of exotic wealth though the ancient gold mines are exhausted. Far up north in the Kachin State is an ancient amber mine, and a jade mine which has been worked for many centuries, yielding a beautiful stone highly prized by the Chinese. Rubies and sapphires still come from the mine at Mogok, north of Mandalay and near the Shan Upland fault.

These are all pleasant things to have around, and a Burmese of taste is discriminating about them. Amber should be pale gold, with few air bubbles; jade should be almost translucent and dark like an emerald; the deep blue of the night is best in a sapphire; nothing surpasses a pigeon-blood ruby. But there has been a cultural change since the days of Burmese kings. For modern wealth and growth, a nation now seeks the more utilitarian yields of the earth—iron, coal, and oil. In these, Burma is not yet a golden land.

Earth oil was known even to the kings as a minor convenience, nothing more. Modern oil wells yield a modest amount, enough to keep petroleum products off Burma's import list. Some coal is scattered about, and a few years ago the Krupp firm of West Germany, working with the Burmese Mineral Development Corporation, located sizable deposits of iron ore in the Shan State. Burma mines a little of each.

Thus far, Burma has reaped more wealth from its reserves of tin, wolfram, lead, and zinc. A well-known lead and silver mine called the Bawdwin Mine is located near Namtu in the northern Shan State. (Lead and silver are frequently found together.) Burma announced the discovery of another large deposit nearby early in 1968. All of these are exported in small quantities in the form of ore or concentrates.

A more productive resource for Burma has been its magnificent forests of teak. All of Burma was probably once forest. (The word more often used here is "jungle.") In countries with a distinct dry season one species of flora usually comes to dominate the forest, and in Burma that species is usually teak, but occasionally bamboo. In the nineteenth century when the West came east to trade and to conquer, the teak was prized for boatbuilding and for dock piles. Teak resists rot and destruction by water, weather, and insects. It is also a beautiful wood which Scandinavians, among others, treasure for cabinetwork. This is one resource which the Burmese apply well to their own use. Because teak stands high on Burma's list of exports, second in value only to rice, they must be content now with the lower grades.

Burma has other beautiful hardwoods, notably padauk, which finishes like a red mahogany, and yinma, which the Burmese compare to maple. Both local use and exports of other hardwoods have been small, but, in the last decade, hardwood exports have outstripped teak in quantity.

Bamboo has always been important in Burma's culture. A man can do many things with it, from building his house to scaffolding a pagoda so gold leaf can be reapplied after the rains. Now there is the beginning of more modern uses of bamboo such as paper-making.

First on any list of resources in this agricultural land are the crops which the people plant and till, and first on that list, as it has always been in recorded history, is rice. In the days of the kings, before the development of the swampy Irrawaddy delta, the export of rice was forbidden. Now the economic health of the nation is measured by the size of its annual rice crop and particularly by the amount available for export. Rice is not only the staff of life in the people's diet. It is the resource that, more than any other, has bought the hard currency of the outside world which the nation can spend on its own imports and internal development. Thanks to rice, national famine has never been recorded in Burma, though sporadic hunger can occur through regional crop failure or floods or through faulty distribution; it must then be alleviated by relief shipments from another part of the nation to the afflicted district. There can be malnutrition, caused by lack of vitamins or protein. But Burmese are not among the world's people who go to bed hungry at night.

The other major crops are grown to satisfy Burmese personal tastes. There is tobacco, which they enjoy, and cotton, which helps to clothe them. There are the foods which they prefer to eat with their rice: sugar cane; gram, beans, and other pulses; peanuts and sesame for cooking oil; and seasonings such as chilli, onions, and garlic.

A surplus of a few of these like the pulses are exported, but others, such as cotton and peanuts for cooking oil, are deficit crops and appear on Burma's import list.

If Burma is again to become a golden land, agricultural output will need to increase to meet domestic needs. This development is theoretically possible, but no Burmese government has yet found the effective combination of incentives and goals to prod the peasant into action.

Research can supplement the farmer's efforts. Mills are being built to extract cooking oil from the small mountains of rice-bran which pile up beside every rice mill. Rice-bran cakes, the leftover after the oil is removed, have found an export market.

Any real wealth in mineral production awaits further discoveries and exploitation of larger yields of iron, coal, and oil. These may or may not exist. Once, in the 1950's, Burma considered building a larger steel mill to convert scrap metal. When the nonexpert visitor questioned the source of such metal, the nonexpert Burmese would often mention the wrecked or abandoned tanks of World War II rusting away beside such thoroughfares as the Rangoon-Mandalay road, which seemed a very temporary supply source. Wiser heads prevailed; while Burma produces some iron nails and sheeting, the mills remain modest.

The Burmese rather enjoy the idea that their country may have been that "golden land" of ancient manuscripts, but for the present they aren't tantalized by the search for such exuberant wealth. They seek instead a less fanciful goal, the sufficiency which their particular land in its particular ecological setting should make possible, with enough left over to buy the bridges and roads, schools and hospitals, and to support simple industries which their nation's health demands.

Geographic Sections

The geographic logistics of Burma have largely determined the seat of power within the country. The Central Belt holds the chief rivers, the ports of entry, the largest stretches of level land suitable for cultivation, the largest range of crops, and the most extensive areas suitable for human habitation. It has followed, naturally, that the dominant people of the land mass have lived within this Central Belt. Those people have not always been the Burmans; others preceded them historically. The Central Belt is what is now known as Burma Proper.

Today the Union of Burma is a semifederal structure uniting Burma Proper and the areas known as the Kachin State, the Shan State, the Kayah State, and the Karen State. Two other sections which lack the political definition of states must be added for a geographic discussion: the constitutionally designated Special Division of the Chins and the natural division of Arakan, which is legally but not physically a part of Burma Proper. These sections almost encircle the heartland of Burma.

A geographic area known as the *Naga Hills* lies between the Special Division of the Chins and the Kachin State. These hills are included in Burma Proper and governed directly from the seat of power, by virtue of political rather than geographic logic. The Nagas who inhabit the hills are still a primitive people. When the Union's constitution was written in 1947, the Nagas were the only fair-sized ethnic group in Burma who were not invited to participate in its preparation. The other peoples of Burma considered them uninterested in or unready for a modern form of government.

It is plain from this geographic discussion that the Union is not inhabited by a single homogeneous people. Indeed, back in the mountains and hills, there are an almost uncounted number of racial or tribal communities. All of the peoples are Burmese, citizens of the Union of Burma, including the Nagas, who may not all be aware of their citizenship. But only the people who give Burma its name and its language, the dominant people of the country, historical rulers of the Central Belt, are Burmans. This name is seldom used now in Burma itself. But there is no other way, in writing, to distinguish between all the people and this particular people. All were immigrants at one time or another, and almost all immigrations seem to have been overland from the north. All but the Kachins have been in the country at least as long as the Burmans. (See Chapter 6.)

A geographic census, pursuing a clockwise movement, begins with the Arakan Belt, where the Arakanese live, facing India across the Bay of Bengal. Indeed, the early dynasties of the old Arakan kingdom were probably Indian or Indian-related. Through early migrations the Arakanese bloodstock now is mostly Burman, even though many consider themselves to be distinct from the Burmans of the Central Belt. Isolation induced by the Arakan Yoma nurtures that feeling. Without this geographic barrier, differences might have disappeared long ago.

The Special Division of the Chins lies north of Arakan, in the Folded Mountain Belt. The Chins are a "hill people," that ubiquitous term used throughout Southeast Asia to describe minority people who either arrived late and found the plains occupied or arrived early and were pushed back into the hills by later comers. The Chins are believed to be one of those "pushed-back" peoples. They are distantly related to the Burmans, but time and isolation in the Folded Mountain Belt have made them a completely separate people with a primitive agriculture and no dreams of ancient glory like the Arakanese.

The Kachin State is set among the towering peaks at the far north. The Burmese have added two districts from Burma Proper to the state to make it more economically viable. In those more southerly districts, the population is divided between other Burmese and the Kachins. These latecomers, who didn't arrive in large numbers until around 1600, are an aggressive, vigorous people. (During the 1947 Constituent Assembly they promptly asked for a state of their own, while the Chins preferred the more sheltered status of district.) Kachins delight in highlands and are at home in the mountains.

The Shan Upland is the home of the Shans, who are not themselves hill people, though hill peoples dwell among them. Relatives of the Thais, they have lived on their plateau a long time. Two factors have probably thwarted these people—whose culture may be older than Burman culture—from greater power in Burma. Their plateau has always isolated them from the main traffic of the land, and their many rulers, called *sawbwas,* were never willing to agree on a single leader to unite the Shans into a more powerful force.

The Shan State is so large that, before the clockwise trip swings down to the next encircling state, it has reached all the way down to the Thai border. Due south of the Shan State is *the Kayah State,* no bigger than the state of Connecticut, whose people lived here long before the major Burman migration. Their land is near the end of the Upland where it breaks into narrow ridges and valleys. Most of the people live in the hills.

The Karen State, last of the encirclement, is the newest state and was the most difficult to piece together politically. The Karens are the largest minority in Burma and were among the earliest arrivals. Because many have settled through the country, the proper boundaries of a purely Karen State were hard to delineate. Few other Burmese minorities have moved about and made their homes in areas away from their kin, even though internal boundaries usually permitted relatively free movement. But many of the Karens have moved to other regions in Burma, particularly in the last few centuries. With the postindependence Karen insurrection, a Karen State became more and more bitterly necessary. It was created by an amendment to the constitution in 1951. Long and narrow, it reaches up to the southern tip of the Shan State and runs past one side of the Kayah State and down the beginning of the kite tail. The "narrow ridges, narrow valleys" configuration lies across part of the Karen State, too.

As a cultural rather than a geographic footnote, one other people must be mentioned to round out the story, perhaps the earliest arrivals of the present indigenous peoples. The Mons, now shrunken in numbers by both integration and migration, still live in the areas whose cities their kings made famous—the once mighty seats of Pegu and Thaton. But the story of their influence on Burmese culture belongs to the nation's history rather than its geography.

Here, then, is a land mass whose natural boundaries of water and highland seem to preordain it to nationhood. But within those boundaries different kinds of land invite different kinds of people to take up residence. There is no conflict over territory between the peoples. Alluvial valleys promise a life of pleasant sufficiency if not golden wealth. Those who live in the valleys have no desire to move to the highlands. Most hill people scorn the way of life which is comfortable to the people of the valleys.

The dominant people of Burma have always been residents of the valleys. No minority has ever had the strength or desire to challenge that central authority for control of the whole country. But each outlying minority can and sometimes does challenge the center for control of its own local territory. This has been a fact of life for Burma from the first historical Burman king down to the present.

The inner geography of the land must bear part of the responsibility. For just as the outer boundaries seem to preordain a nation, so the inner geographic characteristics keep the sections apart. They have slowed the spread of the dominant Burman culture into the hills. If acculturation could have taken place naturally and easily, the continual challenge of the minorities to the central power might have been blunted. Life would have then been more peaceful for all the peoples of this land.

2 The Kingdom of Burma

The people who gave the nation of Burma its name can't mark the place from which they came, the date of their arrival, or the route they traveled to reach the Irrawaddy River valley. They are kin neither to Indians nor to Chinese, though they have been touched by both these peoples between whose lands they lie. Scholars classify them as Tibeto-Mongoloid; their first home probably lay somewhere in the dry highlands between Tibet and China.

The original homeland of the Chinese was well to the east, around the Yellow River, but as they pressed to the west or south, people like the Burmans felt the pressure and moved out of the way. This happened to many others who are now indigenous to Southeast Asia—the Vietnamese who moved early because they were closest to the Chinese center of power, and the related Laotians, Thais, and Shans. The Burman migration may have begun as soon as the middle of the first millennium. These people, who probably herded sheep or goats, must have been widely scattered to reach the precious pasturage in their dry highlands.

Those on the edges, particularly vulnerable to the Chinese, probably dribbled away first under their local chieftains, driving their animals with them, walking the long and inhospitable way. In time, others would follow. All would have had to stop now and then, perhaps for a season to raise food crops so they could continue the trek, perhaps for a weary generation while the group recovered its strength and will for further movement. The first of them may have reached Burma by A.D. 500.

Western scholars, however, think the migrants entered from the northeast, perhaps along the headwaters of the Irrawaddy, the Salween, or the Mekong. Some think they first stopped for a while in the old Thai kingdom of Nanchao, near the present Chinese province of Yunnan. If so, they probably came in through what is now Bhamo, part of the old trade route between India and China. On a date presumably in the ninth century, these scholars believe, they settled first in the Kyaukse district, which already possessed a system of irrigation built by other peoples.

It is true that this district near Mandalay and the Irrawaddy would be the food basket of the Burmans under many kings and several dynasties. Inscriptions from the twelfth and thirteenth centuries also support the scholars' theory. These use old Burman place names which are classified under two headings, the "first home" and the "second home." Eleven of the place names of the "first home" are from Kyaukse. The "second home" place names all center around Pagan (pronounced Pahgáhn), some 90 miles from Kyaukse.

Yet, if the Burman people reached this new land only in the ninth century, it is hard to believe they could have settled in so snugly among strangers that in two centuries they could breed a king and kingdom strong enough to set forth and build an empire.

There is an old and persistent saying among the Burmans that the beginnings of their people were at Tagaung in northern Burma, that their name, which is pronounced Bamá, means the first inhabitants of the world and was given them by Indians. Some believe that the founder of their first dynasty of kings was an Indian prince from the same royal family into which the Buddha was born in 600 B.C. Among Burmese scholars, few defend this idea of a prehistoric dynasty founded by a descendant of the Buddha. The idea probably parallels the early Western one of the divine right of kings, with the same purpose of exalting the royal lineage.

There is a Tagaung on the Irrawaddy River, however, not much more than a hundred miles from the Indian border. There are ancient chronicles of such a kingdom. And the name of the country and the people is still Bamá. This is a phonetic translation, not an alphabetic one. The Burmese alphabet is not romanized, and when Burmese letters of the name are translated into English letters, the spelling is *Mrama*. But today, when the Burmese speak the name of their country, what they say is Bamá, with the second syllable accented and both vowels round, not flat and hard.

Perhaps both stories are true and there was a double migration, the first from the original high dry lands through northeast India and the ninth-century one through the old Thai kingdom. This would explain a good deal.

Old Buddhist pagodas and temples at Pagan, the first capital, markedly resemble those of India. While the kings needn't have seen India, parts of the community had to be intimately familiar with Indian architecture. In addition, a Hindu temple still stands at Pagan, presumably built in the middle of the tenth century. This would not be strange if some of the people had learned their Buddhism in northern India. But it stretches the mind to think that these newcomers became Buddhist under Chinese influence via the old Thai kingdom of Nanchao and so soon after their arrival in Burma built a temple to a Hindu god.

The acceptance of a double migration would also make reasonable the upsurge of Burman power. The ninth-century arrivals would not have found themselves completely among strangers. Fresh, vigorous fighting men, well trained in Nanchao, and leaders with new ideas of administration and strong government would have received a warm welcome from their kinsmen who had come first and knew the land and the people in it. Put them together and it is easier to explain not only the quick founding of a strong city-state, as Pagan was in the beginning, but of the empire itself.

However they came, on the way much must have happened to these herders to turn them into a river people, who built all their chief capitals along the Irrawaddy, into settled agriculturists who knew how to use irrigation and never seem to have tried the slash-and-burn agriculture characteristic of hill people in Southeast Asia. The evidence, thin as it is, seems to indicate that they have been a flexible people, avid learners from the other cultures through which they passed.

Some qualities no one taught them. Other migrant peoples have merged into larger, stronger groups, with only faint shadows of their differentness remaining. This the first Burmans must have resisted or they would not have moved on so indefatigably to land of their own. When they finally settled in the new land, this resistant independence, this sense of unique cultural identity were still strong in them and remain to this day.

The new land was not empty, virgin land. The most powerful people in the main river valleys were the Mons, whose origins are uncertain though they seem related to the Khmers, the present-day Cambodians. Since prehistoric times they had been a strong force in Lower Burma with scattered settlements further north. There had also been a people called the Pyus, of some power in the northern stretches of the valleys. Some must still have been around as late as the twelfth century. A Burman "Rosetta stone" of that date carries an inscription at Pagan's Myazedi Pagoda in Mon, Burmese, Pyu, and sacred Pali. But their power was already spent when the Burmans began making the history of the river.

THE BEGINNING AND THE SYNTHESIS: 1044–1287

There are legends of earlier Burman kings, but the first of them to tear away the misty curtains between legend and fact was Anawrahta, who assumed the throne at Pagan, on the banks of the Irrawaddy, in 1044, just before William the Conqueror came to power in England. Not much is known of him personally. The legends say he was a stern father figure, demanding strict obedience of his soldiers and his people, quick to punish when his orders were disobeyed. But what he did is well known and is not doubted. He made the Burmans masters of what is now Burma. There would be times when that mastery would be disputed, but the disputes, in the end, would always be settled in favor of the Burmans.

Anawrahta's people were Buddhists, but they were Mahayana Buddhists, not followers of Theravada Buddhism as the Burmese are now. The distinctions between these two great sects are marked, and, because it is Theravada Buddhism which has so deeply molded the culture of present-day Burma, they must later be examined. But for this historical moment it is enough merely to record that there are differences.

The Buddhism of Pagan in the eleventh century was an off-shoot of a particular Mahayana sect from northern India well diluted with worship of some of the ancient Hindu gods, led by Tantric monks whose erotic teachings were an affront to the somewhat puritanical Anawrahta. In Lower Burma, the Mons were also Buddhists but of the Theravada school. The story goes that Anawrahta coveted a copy of the sacred Pali scriptures from which to teach his people a purer faith. He sent a courteous note to the Mon king at Thaton, who was blessed with many such manuscripts, requesting one copy as a gift. The Mon king, Manuha, refused and a little rudely at that. So the Pagan king led his people to battle against the Mons to take with arms what had been refused as a gift.

A small pinch of skepticism about Anawrahta's motives is surely forgivable. The call for a gift of the scriptures seems to resemble very closely the requests later Burman kings would make of Thai rulers for gifts of sacred white elephants. The request is more like a challenge, a throwing down of the royal gauntlet, and from Anawrahta's viewpoint a very logical one. If he was to make his people dominant in this land, he would first have to subdue the Mons before anyone else in or out of Burma would recognize that dominance. For the Mons were more than powerful. They were rich in jewels, in gold, and in cultured artisans, as well as in copies of the sacred manuscript, the *Tipitakas*.

Yet it is significant that this first war was, at least nominally, a war for religious reasons; from this time on, all kings were considered defenders of the faith.

Anawrahta and his men were victorious. It took thirty elephants to carry north all the copies of scriptures the Burmans found in Thaton. Anawrahta built for them a special library which still stands at Pagan. But the victors carried back more than the sacred books; they brought a whole new culture. Thaton was stripped of its wealth and stripped, too, of its royal family, its artists, its builders, its craftsmen. All came to Pagan to enrich the simpler Burman culture. Burman scholars set to work to master Pali, which is to Theravada Buddhism what Latin is to the Roman Catholic Church. They mastered the Mon written language; from the Mon alphabet, they structured a Burman one.

They were more than copycats. As they had learned from all the peoples through whose lands they passed on their long trek, so they absorbed what the Mons had to teach them. The culture that flowered on the dusty plain beside the Irrawaddy was not Mon, not Indian from which the Mons had learned. It was a synthesis and it was Burman.

Anawrahta went on to defeat Arakan, the old kingdom on the Bay of Bengal divided from the Irrawaddy valley by the Arakan Yoma range. He traveled among the Shan sawbwas on the east, whose states were separated from the new power by their own Upland; these chieftains were quick to pay homage and offer gifts. There was no fighting and no conquering here, but Anawrahta built a series of forts in the hills to protect his people, as if he did not quite trust the Shans' protestations. Some other Southeast Asian records report that he went all the way over to present-day Cambodia and defeated the Khmers, that he controlled all of what is now Thailand. The accuracy of these reports is uncertain, and even if true they are unimportant. The basic victories were in the new Burman homeland, and none had a more profound, more lasting effect than the conquest of the Mons.

The first kings who succeeded to Anawrahta's throne and empire were powerful men but with a different kind of power. They still led the armies, but there was no further military expansion. No more was needed. They used military strength only when necessary to put down rebellions in the new empire. Essentially these men were a more gentle breed, the builders and synthesizers of the new nation. Typically, the public documents of their day are inscriptions in pagodas and temples.

Kyanzittha, the first of note among them, was such a builder. Of necessity, his first act was to put down a Mon rebellion. A people like the Mons was never easy to rule, and this Mon-Burman confrontation runs on for generations in Burmese history. Once the initial thrust of rebellion was subdued, the Mons were peaceful enough under Kyanzittha. He had spent some years in exile from Pagan as military governor among them and knew them well. Legend has it that he had been exiled because he fell in love with a young Mon princess sent to Pagan to become the elder Anawrahta's wife and that after his own accession to the throne she became his queen. The romantic tale would naturally appeal to the Mons, but the Burmans too were romantics where true love was concerned, and the tale did him no harm among them.

Mon was the language of his inscriptions, Mon soldiers served in his army, Mon artisans continued to be honored at the court in spite of the rebellion, and the two peoples lived together in harmony.

Kyanzittha completed the Shwezigon Pagoda, which Anawrahta had begun, and built other temples and pagodas. The most beauti-

ful and venerated of them all was, and still is, the Ananda
Temple. He began to rebuild commerce with China, sending two
trade missions to that country. It is the story of his reign which
is told in that four-language inscription at the Myazedi Pagoda,
erected by his grandson and successor, Alaungsithu.

In an elegant temple called the Shwegugyi, built near the site
of Kyanzittha's palace, there is another inscription by this same
Alaungsithu written in the sacred language, Pali, which deserves
a place in any anthology of religious poetry. These are a few
lines of this Buddhist king's prayer:

> Tamed, I would tame the willful; comforted,
> Comfort the timid; wakened, wake the sleeping.
> Cool, cool the burning; freed, set free the bound;
> Tranquil and led by the good doctrines
> I would hatred calm.

He had first been called King Sithu, but his people called him
Alaungsithu, the Future Buddha. Ironically, he was murdered
by one of his sons.

In the short period of chaos which followed the murder, a
younger brother of the Pagan line, Narapatisithu, put down the
swirl of rebellions which always came with chaos. Yet the kingdom he restored to prosperity was a kingdom with a difference.
One of his first acts was to appoint a Burman *thathanabaing* as
a primate over all monks of the kingdom. Previous primates had
all been Mons. Fine temples and pagodas were built, but the
inscriptions were now all in Burmese, not Mon. Burman customary law was spread throughout the kingdom, including the
land of the Mons.

This nationalist, proud of his Burman blood and culture, ruled
his country longer than any other king of the Pagan dynasty. It
was a good reign. The strength of the dynasty died with the great
king in 1210 even though the form of the kingdom continued to

exist until 1287. In that year, an army of Kublai Khan's from China defeated Pagan and the Burman kingdom disintegrated.

In the same year, the Magna Charta was 72 years old, the Crusades had just ended, and Edward I, the first truly English king, had been on his throne for 15 years.

INTERREGNUM: 1287–1531

Historically, the Pagan dynasty existed for only two and a half centuries. Yet in that scant time it created a lasting heritage and bequeathed it to the Burman people. The stability and self-reliance of village life and the power of Theravada Buddhism were among its greatest strengths. So was the relationship of ruler to people and people to ruler.

The ideal Buddhist monarch, comforted, would comfort his people and protect them and the faith. They, in turn, would honor him and support him with a tenth of their goods and when necessary with their arms. Ignored was the inherent ambivalence of the tranquil Buddhist and the mighty warrior in the same monarch, perhaps because most rulers made an effort to reconcile the two roles.

This ideal of a king so gripped the allegiance of the people that it created a third strength in the elements which had built and would again rebuild a nation. There might be palace coups, but the Burman people never rebelled against their king, not even a bad one.

Even the major obstructions to nation-building were already experienced at Pagan—Burman relationships to other peoples both within the kingdom and along its borders. Both strengths and obstructions have a surprisingly modern sound.

For the next 250 years, no Burman king ruled Burma. Neither did a king of any other people. In the south, Arakan was free. The Mons were free, ruled by their own kings in their city-states like those at Pegu and Thaton. The West began to move into the East in the persons of the Portuguese, not as curious travelers who would go home and write books but as traders who would carve out small beachheads for their traffic. In exchange for trade they offered cannon and Portuguese mercenaries. Both Arakanese and Mons, with ports on the sea or near river mouths, grew rich on the commerce.

On the heels of Kublai Khan's men, the Shans had burned Pagan, leaving only the masonry temples and pagodas. They had seized the ancient Kyaukse district, granary of the north. In the courts of their city-states, Burmans were welcomed much as Mons had been in Pagan.

For the Burmans, their only real legacy from this interregnum would be Ava, which one of the Shans built as his capital north and east of Pagan on the Irrawaddy. Here future Burman kings would reign. They would build half a dozen capitals in the neighborhood; Burman kings would move often for reasons of policy. But always they would "go to Ava" or "come from Ava"; in the future, for many decades the name would be a synonym for the Burmese Court in the eyes of the British, the future colonialists. But that was still a distant time.

One other event occurred in this period which would be of great moment to those future Burman kings. The Thais, ethnic cousins of the Shans and Laotians, had for centuries been drifting west from their old home south of the Yangtse River, away from the Chinese. But when Kublai Khan's men conquered the Thai kingdom of Nanchao, northwest of Burma, that migration had been accelerated. Many settled along the Chao Phraya River next door to Burma, establishing their own city-states. The strongest was Ayuthia; by 1378 that city's king was the ruler of Thailand.

The Burmans didn't disappear as their kingdom and power did, but through this interim they were inconspicuous. Most remained in their own villages; the stable, independent life went on unless fighting between the city-kings came too near. Monks continued their studies and writings at first in Pali, then toward the end of the period in polished Burmese. About this same time the spread of the *hpongyi-chaungs,* the monks' schools, was completed, and monks had assumed the responsibility of educating not only their novices but young males in general.

Some Burmans who moved farther south to the upper waters of the Sittang River, when endangered by insecurity, settled on a barren, arid spur of land they called Toungoo. In the first decade of the sixteenth century the Burman chief of Toungoo built a wall around his city. It was a symbol. He was announcing that he was now king of this small city-state. Burman nationalism was stirring again.

REVIVAL AND HOMECOMING: 1531–1752

One night in 1516 a man-child was born as heir to the city's ruler. Afterward, men swore that, even in the black night hour, the spears and swords in Toungoo's armory shone in the darkness, prescient of things to come. His father named him Tabinshwehti, "Solitary Umbrella of Gold," a mighty name in a world where only a mighty king could use a golden umbrella.

The child was born into a different world from that of the first Burman dynasty. Henry VIII sat on the throne of England; Martin Luther was about to be excommunicated for heresy. The boy's little kingdom had Portuguese and Thais for neighbors when he became its ruler at fourteen, upon his father's death.

History records Tabinshwehti as the founder of the second Burman dynasty. It was he who was crowned king with pomp and ceremony at Pagan and then crowned a second time among the Mons at Pegu, where he made his capital. The dark night's legend would seem fulfilled.

But he was not a man of strength or wisdom. The wisest act of his short life was to give his sister as wife to his constant companion and commander-in-chief whom he renamed Bayinnaung, or "King's Elder Brother." Bayinnaung thus had some legal claim on the new dynasty's throne when the young king, who had taken to alcohol, was murdered by a Mon in a bout of drunkenness.

Bayinnaung was off putting down a minor rebellion at the time. With his absence and Tabinshwehti's murder, the kingdom blossomed with new kings. Every city had one, Burman or Mon. Bayinnaung, out in the field with no city to claim, was back where he had started with Tabinshwehti a few years earlier, but this time he had an army ready to hand. He fought over the same course; first Bassein and the Delta, then city after city were conquered. The course was swifter this time, for he had a name to conjure with. By 1555, he had not only reclaimed all the cities of the south, both Mon and Burman, but he had conquered Ava and pushed deep into Shwebo district to the north, farther than Pagan kings had done. Subduing the Shan states through which he passed, he went over to take Chiengmai, ruled at the moment by a Shan prince, vassal to Laos.

It was 1558. Bayinnaung had covered much ground in seven years, taking time out only for a rich coronation at Pegu. His reach was wider even than the fabled Anawrahta, for his rule over the Shan states was more direct than that of any Burman king before him.

Twice he invaded Thailand, returning the second time in 1568 with sacred white elephants, much of Ayuthia's wealth, innumerable Thai prisoners, and the eldest son of the Thai whom he had placed on the throne as vassal. This time, Burmans would rule the Thais for fifteen years. Yet later Thai commentators looked upon the exile of their young prince in Burma as a blessing in disguise. He was trained with Burma's princes in the arts of war, and in these arts the Burmans were considered supreme, just as their military training was considered the best in Southeast Asia. The well-trained prince in time would free his people from Burman rule, after Bayinnaung's death.

The Thais called Bayinnaung "Victor in Ten Directions." For his fighting he could marshal tens of thousands of men from his empire—Mons, Burmans, and Shans—with Karens, who lived in the hills near the Mons, as bearers. His cavalry of elephants was impressive; he had Portuguese mercenaries with cannon. If those he conquered did not love him, they respected him. He was no tyrant, and, by the standards of his day, he was not inhuman in warfare.

In his own way, he attempted to play the role of the Buddhist monarch. Everywhere he went, he built pagodas. There is such a pagoda in Chiengmai, different from other Thai pagodas there because, the Thais explain, it was built by order of the Burman king. His gifts to pagodas in his own country were lavish. He forbade the Muslim slaughter of goats in celebration of the Bakr Id. Slaves could not be killed nor elephants and horses slaughtered for burial with a dead Shan sawbwa.

Bayinnaung was more than the field marshal of this empire. He had a certain gift for even-handed administration, and his country was not without prosperity, though the people had grown weary of the constant warfare. When he died in 1581, he was sixty-six years old and preparing to attack Arakan.

His death brought such an explosion of rebellion and in-fighting that for 48 years the south was in chaos. The Thais invaded and for a time held all the Burman territory of the kite tail south of the Salween's mouth. Mons fought Burmans and Burmans fought each other. The dream of a nation dissolved in the acid of personal ambition. Orchards were left untended, fields were untilled; thousands of Mons and Thai exiles fled to Thailand through the Three Pagoda Pass. Portuguese traders squirmed into kingly power at Syriam, the port on the Rangoon River south of present-day Rangoon. The final disemboweling of Pegu came with a conspiracy between the king's brother, governor of Toungoo, and the Arakanese, who divided between them the loot of the rich city.

At this point a prince named Thalun came down from the north and Burmese history underwent one of those major transformations which mark its course.

Thalun, grandson of Bayinnaung, younger brother of the last slain king, was viceroy of Ava when he marched south and seized the throne of Pegu in 1629. He has some claim to greatness, though most historians deny it; his reign was like the beautiful time which follows a stormy rainy season. To use the language of the ancient chronicles, he treated his people with kindness as if they were his own womb-children.

In the river valleys, both Mons and Burmans were tired of chaos and wanted no more war. Through Mon civil administrators, Thalun held the lower valleys of both the Irrawaddy and the Sittang. His trade policies at Pegu and the newer port of Syriam were wise; both Mons and the Western foreigners were prosperous and content.

But he took his own people back to Upper Burma away from the abrasion of living among another people, away from the temptations to military glory to which their kings seemed so prone. Though he was crowned at Pegu, he and all other kings of his dynasty reigned at Ava.

It isn't easy to penetrate the minds of the common people in this or any other early historical period. Written records are slim, except for pagoda inscriptions. History was written after the fact, sometimes long after, by the scholars of a king and for the glory of his fathers.

Yet something can be surmised, if only because the thin pictures of the past match up with surprising accuracy against the present. Kings and the boundaries of empire, capitals and dynasties might change, but much in Burman culture remained unchanged. Then as now, most people lived in villages. There never has been a network of land roads. Isolation was common.

Every stream and waterway is a road to these river people, and when all but big rivers dry up in the dry season, the soft sandy beds become land roads easy to the feet of bullocks. But it is largely district traffic, and even this ends in the rainy season. Foot trails then are slippery mud. Streams are high. Even paved roads are narrow, and their earthen shoulders, necessary for passing vehicles, are treacherous.

Change comes slowly in such a world. People like this are independent, accustomed to shifting for themselves. They have never been a meek people, any more than their kings have been meek. Aggressive to insult or imposition, they have seemed to want and support a strong ruler, up to a point. But when a king's power interfered too deeply in the traditional pattern of their own lives, they have withdrawn, uncooperative. These were the folk whom Thalun took to Ava out of the disruptive chaos of the south.

For these people, the irrigation works in the Kyaukse food basket were once more restored. Peaceful missions were exchanged with Arakan and Thailand. Regulations for traders were even-handed, no one group favored over the others, though this irked the Dutch who arrived one year after the Court went to Ava. Thalun, like any wise ruler, kept the national interest in mind in dealing with them all. If customs duties were high, Dutch, Portuguese, Indians, and Mons all made a good profit in spite of them.

Burma was a ready market for foreign textiles. In exchange, traders filled their homebound ships with ivory, gold, tin, lead, bronze, and cutch, or catechu, an extract from the heartwood of acacias used for dyeing and tanning. A twentieth-century dictionary still defines Pegu catechu as a "pure, pale form, the best commercial grade," though even in Thalun's time shipping was moving to Syriam as Pegu's harbor filled with silt. Traders could also purchase the goods of China, brought into the country from the north by Chinese merchants over the ancient trails. And word of that drew the first British traders from India with a vessel of goods in 1647.

Because there was little need for generals under Thalun, administrators and the civil service outranked the military. There had always been a *Hlutdaw,* the advisory council to the king, and that council and the primate, the chief Burman monk, had often been the only curb on the autocratic power of a king. Thalun now defined that power and, with a kind of codified constitutionality, attempted to protect his people from future kings who might seek great power and wide wars. Ironically, after Thalun's death at the end of his 20-year reign in 1648, it became obvious that only a strong king could curb the power of the traditionally conservative Hlutdaw. But Thalun's line bred no more strong kings.

In 1752 the Mons marched on Ava with arms obtained from European traders at Syriam. Burmese historians say the arms came from the French, newcomers to the Burmese picture. The capital fell with appalling ease, and the Toungoo dynasty ended with barely a whimper.

In that year twenty-year-old Major George Washington was training Virginia's militia and would shortly receive his military baptism in the French and Indian Wars, a part of the larger Seven Years' War. The Treaty of Paris, only a decade away, would not only send the French out of the American colonies and Canada; it would recognize the British Empire in India. In no very farfetched line, the battles in which Washington fought were linked to the destiny of Burma.

THE BURMANS AND THE BRITISH: 1752–1885

The Mons, confusing the weakness of a court with the weakness of a people, promptly withdrew downriver leaving only a small garrison at Ava. But almost before the riffle of their oars had died on the Irrawaddy, a man had risen to lead the Burmans.

He came of no royal lineage, this headman north of Ava. But his victories over the Mons in Upper Burma were so swift that he renamed his town Shwebo, "Home of the Golden Leader," and there proclaimed himself king with the name of Alaungpaya. Then like most strong Burman kings he set about restoring the ancient reaches of the empire. The Shans acquiesced and even China's viceroy at Yunnan recognized him as King of Burma. In the south, French help came late to Pegu and Syriam, and much of it was seized by Alaungpaya while it was still on shipboard. Over the tall mountains, Burma's natural northwestern boundary, came the Manipuri who crossed the Chindwin River to raid Burmese settlements. Alaungpaya went north and dealt with them forcefully.

He had already captured Dagon, then a little village around the Shwedagon Pagoda, and renamed it Rangoon, "End of Strife." Here, he decided, he would build a new port for the trade of his kingdom to take precedence over Syriam. By all Buddhist portents, the site was blessed. For centuries the most famous pagoda in Burma, the Shwedagon Pagoda stood on a hill, the golden shimmer of its stupa and *hti** towering high over the surrounding plain as it does today. The Mons had built it, legends said, to house sacred relics brought them by Buddhist missionaries sent by the great Indian emperor Asoka.

In Rangoon Alaungpaya first met the British. They sought trading privileges. He sought arms. He wrote a letter to King George II on gold leaf because, he said, a king could deal only with a king. He received no reply. It was the first of countless efforts by Burman kings to bypass British India and speak directly to London.

Then, his own lands in order at his back, he set out in the traditional pattern for Ayuthia. But in 1760, before the rains began, he was carried wounded across the Salween to die in his own country.

The monarch had reigned for only eight years and was in the vigor of his manhood. Except for his aberration about Ayuthia, which seemed endemic in most of these Burman leaders, he had behaved with kingly dignity and wisdom. Particularly as a northern Burman he must have known the traditional relation of the ruler to the ruled, the ideal of the Buddhist monarch. Given time, he might have taught it to his sons by precept and ex-

---

* A stupa (the word is from the Sanskrit) is a domelike mound which houses relics of the Buddha. From this base, the pagoda rises in a slender "steeple" of several parts, culminating in the *hti* (Burmese for umbrella) which is often golden, frequently jeweled.

ample. But the time was snatched from him. It is the tragedy of this dynasty and of Burma that no king reached out beyond the mighty warrior to the traditional ideal until it was too late.

The conquest of the Thais was left to Alaungpaya's son Hsinbyushin, Lord of the White Elephant. An extraordinary general, this Hsinbyushin plotted a campaign like a chess game; the campaign he planned for Ayuthia's downfall was long and complex but in April, 1767, the city fell.

The great capital of over a million people was left in ruins. The Thai king was killed. Others of the royal family together with the city's wealth and artists were borne off to Burma. Records of the past were so thoroughly destroyed that a new Thai dynasty would have to pick the memories of old survivors to learn the proper ceremonies with which to crown a king.

Long before Ayuthia fell, the moving and shaking across the land had roused the Chinese, who now attempted to cool off the expansionist drive. They invaded Burma in 1766, and for four years campaign followed campaign. But Ava was not latter-day Pagan. In every drive, the Chinese were defeated. They sued for peace in 1770. It was a battlefield peace signed by the two commanders, which infuriated the king. But the Burman commander was wiser than his monarch. Even so, trade between the two countries was interrupted for several decades.

The First British-Burma War

When an autocratic king of boundless energy rules for 38 years he sets his nation on a course which later kings find difficult to change. Such a king was Bodawpaya, fourth son of Alaungpaya, who came to the throne in 1781. A younger son, village-born, eclipsed by his older brothers and almost ignored by the Court as he grew up at Ava, he was consumed by ambition.

Seizing power by a series of blood baths which erased rivals among his own kin and wiped out the dynasty's older, experienced advisers, he was inexperienced and alone on the throne, except for that inordinate drive. He resisted appointing a tha-thanabaing, because he wanted to share his power with no one. When he found he couldn't manage without one, he quarreled with the primate he did appoint until the poor man resigned from the monkhood. Buddhists who smoked opium, drank liquor, or killed a bullock were sentenced to death before the monks managed to dissuade the king from his excessive religious zeal.

He built a new capital at Amarapura and scattered pagodas through the countryside. Thousands of men worked for seven years on a new pagoda at Mingun, north of his capital—a structure to be 500 feet high, almost 200 feet taller than the Shwedagon. The workmen, according to Burmese historians, put a whispered curse on him: "When the pagoda is finished, the great king shall die." But the pagoda was never finished.

The country almost buckled under the load of heavy taxation, forced labor, and of course warfare. Such a man as Bodawpaya was compelled to try the role of mighty warrior, and naturally he turned eastward toward Thailand.

On paper, Hsinbyushin's earlier defeat of Thailand should have tipped the power in Burma's favor. In reality he had created a kind of revolution to the east. Under a new virile dynasty, the Thais had built a new capital farther south which they called Bangkok, and the power that radiated from this new center was too great for Bodawpaya, try as he would, to penetrate. The east was now closed to Burmans.

No Burman king had ever concentrated his military power on the west. This is the point in time on which western historians' criticism of Thalun focuses. If only, they say, Thalun had not moved the throne back to the isolation of a northern inland capital, Bodawpaya and his successors would not have been ignorant of the political facts of life to the west and the history of Burma would have taken a different course. But this overlooks the man that Bodawpaya was. Even from Ava another man might have reigned peaceably within the natural boundaries and at least postponed confrontation with the new British power across the mountains. The driven Bodawpaya could not. He turned to the west.

In surprisingly similar situations, he moved on three separate states—Arakan, Manipur, and Assam—when each in turn was caught up in civil war with rival claimants to the thrones. The times were widely separated. Arakan came early in the long reign, Manipur and Assam at its end. He may only have wanted buffer states between Burma and the British. But rebels from those states kept slipping across the borders into British India.

Burmans, claiming "the right of hot pursuit" of criminals, crossed over and sometimes collided with the British. Calm would be restored only to be broken again. On these distant borders, the British could not always keep the rebels out; the Burmans didn't believe them. Finally, with increasing impatience, the British refused to surrender rebels unless Burma proved them common criminals. For Bodawpaya, the act of escape itself was criminal. Yet the king was always canny enough to stop short of ultimate arrogance, and the British were glad enough to leave it at that.

The final act was postponed for another king, but Bodawpaya's people were already a little frightened when he died in 1819. In his reign of 38 years, nothing was as momentous to his people as this confrontation.

There is something appealing and a little sad about Bagyidaw, the amiable, ineffective grandson of Bodawpaya with a strong-minded fishwife of a queen, who became the last king to reign at Ava.

There is something a little sad about Ava, too, or what is left of it today. The wooden palace is gone and its gardens are plowed into fields. The hill which rises between the palace site and the Irrawaddy is crowned with a monastery the queen built and is terraced into small gardens, half-sacred, half-secular. The whole place has about it an air of breathless flight. What were once finely carved gold-leaf chests to house *parabaiks* (folded books of bamboo paper) and palm-leaf manuscripts stand abandoned to the weather. Images of the Buddha have been removed from the monastery niches, but along a flight of steps between terraces a fine standing image of alabaster has been left behind, its carved teak shelter tumbling down around its sacred head.

Little nuns now live on the lower floor of the monastery. On the river plain below the hill stands a new, undistinguished monks' school, a hpongyi-chaung, where village children's voices rise in the traditional chant of lessons learned by rote. Today takes up where yesterday left off when it ran away. The sense of flight is probably quite real, for in 1837, when the Court left Ava for the last time, the king was mad; Tharrawaddy, his brother, was seizing power in Amarapura and threatening the lives of the queen and her family; and the British were rulers on part of Burma's soil.

The entrance of the British was provoked almost innocently. The King of Manipur sent no tribute at the time of Bagyidaw's coronation and Maha Bandoola, a powerful general of the king, went to punish him. The British blame Bandoola for what happened after that and Burma blames the British. The truth probably is that only a king like Thalun could have wrenched the nation off the course Bodawpaya had set, and poor Bagyidaw was no Thalun. The whole India-Burma border from Assam to Arakan flared up in revolt, and the Burmans crossed in pursuit of rebels all along its length. Bandoola then marched off with his army for Calcutta, seat of the British Governor-General, to settle this matter of refuge once and for all.

But the British didn't wait for him there. They embarked for Rangoon, equally determined on a settlement. The British feel fairly virtuous about this first war, and with some justification. It was never, in their eyes, an imperialist war, a plot to seize Burma, but only a necessary war to make and keep the border peace.

When it ended, in February, 1826, Bandoola was dead up north of Rangoon, where he had arrived by forced march through Arakan. An incredulous Court had been forced to sign a treaty by which the Burmans agreed to keep out of Manipur and Assam, and to cede to the British both Arakan and all the Tenasserim coast from above the mouth of the Salween straight down the thin kite tail. They agreed to accept a British resident at Ava and to pay an indemnity of 1 million pounds, a staggering sum for a country still living outside a money economy.

But the war had cost the British 13 million pounds out of the treasury of India, and some of the cost, the British felt, had to be borne by Burma. British India was always strong on balancing its books. Rangoon, however, was returned to Burma with payment of the indemnity.

The Second British-Burma War

The humiliation of defeat hastened Bagyidaw's melancholy madness and Tharrawaddy's seizure of power at Amarapura, the capital Bodawpaya had built, to which the Court moved in 1837. Today it is a silk-weaving suburb of Mandalay.

The British had exchanged border raids for a bitter king and people and a constant series of pinpricks and irritations, some quite minor, some major, but all exasperating. Tharrawaddy in his rough, rude manner was hardly settled on his throne before some of the British were demanding another war to "teach him a lesson."

Three layers of British power influenced British policy in Burma. In London there were the Foreign Office and Parliament, where awkward questions could sometimes be raised. In British India there was "the Company," shorthand for the British East India Company, born to trade and like good merchants bound to show a profit even on wars, and there was the Governor-General, who legally represented London but could hardly be unmoved by the traders' wishes. Then there were the traders and would-be traders in Burma itself.

The would-be traders were almost intoxicated with the mirage of trade which Burma offered, not in her own products but as a transit point. She lay so neatly between India and China. Until the day of Tharrawaddy, some officials had busily traveled through northern Burma marking out possible routes from the Brahmaputra River and Assam through Ava to Bahmo and China. They could see "the products of Birmingham and Sheffield" shipped up that Indian river and across Burma to China, with all the beautiful products of China making the return journey to England.

Other British officials worked out of Moulmein at the mouth of the Salween in what was now British Burma. They didn't give a fig for the Brahmaputra but they were like Raffles at Singapore in their dreams for Moulmein as transit port. They went up the Salween and Mekong Rivers, through the Kayah State and the Shan states to the Chinese border, hoping to coax Chinese caravans down with their goods. One caravan came, and complained in the next years to these trade missionaries that the road was the worst they had traveled anywhere. A young lieutenant went far enough that a Shan sawbwa delivered a letter of his into China seeking permission for his entry. But China said there was no precedent; English vessels repaired daily to Canton, and that's where he should have gone.

The Burmese considered all these men political spies trying to stir up rebellions. This was a misunderstanding, yet they were no less dangerous than spies to the territorial integrity of Burma.

Less official were the merchants who went about the reality of trading in Rangoon, seeing extortion and insult in every restraint the Burmese levied on them. All foreign traders chafed at restraints in all these Asian ports, but most were far from home and adjusted as best they could as long as there was a profit to be made. British merchants at Rangoon, in contrast, had a wailing wall right next door where they could make their complaints. That is how the Second British-Burma war came about, though no one had planned that this one should happen either.

In the summer of 1851, two British sea captains charged with murder and embezzlement at Rangoon were forced to pay the Burmese governor 1,000 rupees and claimed damages, through British India, of 1,920 pounds. Governor-General Dalhousie was a man who believed that "we can't be shown to the door anywhere in the East." The captains' claim was cut to 920 pounds, but several warships and a "combustible commodore" were sent to collect it. The man went beyond his orders, both sides felt insulted in the ensuing wrangle, and an English ultimatum, dated February 18, 1852, went up to the King, who was now Pagan Min, son of Tharrawaddy, as rough and cruel as his father.

The required compensation had jumped to 100,000 pounds, and various apologies and subserviences were also demanded. The British gave the King of Ava (now at Amarapura) until April 1 to decide. When no proper reply was received, the war began on schedule. Before the rains came, Rangoon, Bassein, and Martaban were taken, with Burmese troops melting away before the British. In the wetness, the English armies moved on to Prome on the Irrawaddy, just about midway between Rangoon and Amarapura, almost directly west from Toungoo. With all of Lower Burma in their hands, they halted, waiting. But no one surrendered, no one sued for terms.

The silence from the Court exasperated the British. In December they proclaimed the annexation in perpetuity of the province of Pegu, the territory they now occupied, and sent notification of the act to the King.

Vague rumors drifted down about some kind of trouble at the Court, some conflict between those who wanted to fight on, led by Pagan Min, who had gone mad like his father and grandfather, and those who wanted peace. Waiting around with idle hands for some response to what they'd done, the British looked upon the rich teak forests to the north of Prome and Toungoo, found them good, and moved up fifty miles to include them in their newly proclaimed province.

Negotiators came south on March 31, 1853, but they came in the name of a new king. Mindon, brother of Pagan, knew the monastery better than he knew the Court. He was a devout Buddhist, a man of peace, and totally convinced that his truncated nation's policy must be one of friendship with the British.

At the scene of negotiations the British were encouraged. When it was learned that Mindon's chief queen was exceptionally well educated and interested in astronomy, such articles as a telescope, a sextant, and celestial and terrestrial globes were sent up to Prome as presentation gifts for the happy day when a treaty would be signed.

Governor-General Dalhousie, back in India, was less optimistic. Experienced in the traumas the first treaty had produced, he didn't seriously expect any Burmese king to sign away more territory. But London couldn't understand how a war could end without a treaty and pushed for a signature on a document.

It is an open question whether Mindon would have signed any such treaty, but the question really never arose. Negotiators were faced not with the boundaries of the annexation proclamation but with those rich additional 50 miles of teak forest. The "trouble" at the capital had delayed the earlier arrival of the King's negotiators. Now that a man of peace was in power and prepared to end the war, this additional land grab seemed to his negotiators a peculiar welcome.

Negotiations broke down on May 10; the Burmese simply went home. No mention is made in the records of what happened to the Queen's gifts. But the second war was ended. Mindon sent word to the frontier guards along the border the British had set that there would be no more fighting. British citizens were free to come and go across the border, and he hoped the British would grant the same right of entry to Burmese. Dalhousie understood. Peace was as secure as any treaty could have made it, he insisted to a confused London. And so it was for the 25 years of Mindon's reign.

Mindon Min

Mindon's job wasn't an easy one. In fifty years the country had lost over half its territory and every single mile of its sea-coast. Except over the China border, all goods and travelers could enter or leave Burma only at the sufferance of the British. But the King managed to combine firmness with conciliation in unusually skillful fashion. He did sign two trade treaties with the British, though he insisted on retaining the royal monopolies on such goods as cotton, cutch, and ivory. And, when his people in Upper Burma needed rice, he sent his agents into the Irrawaddy Delta to purchase directly from the growers, not from Rangoon brokers. Both acts irked Rangoon because it cost the British establishment profits.

Mindon needed the funds for governing what was left of his kingdom. One of his first acts was to begin the building of a new royal capital, to exorcise the bitter memories of Ava and Amarapura. It, too, was, and is, on the Irrawaddy; there is even a hill as there is at Ava. But Mandalay Hill is much larger and taller than the other, though it rises alone from the plain in the same fashion. Among the many shrines and terraces of the hill, there is near the top a great golden bronze figure of the Buddha standing with one hand outstretched pointing to the land below. Legend has it that the Buddha visited here once with a disciple and, standing as the figure stands, prophesied that one day a great capital would rise there, built by a king who would do him honor.

Mindon first built the palace city in a great square surrounded by brick walls each 1¼ miles long, 10 feet thick, and 27 feet high, with graceful, many-roofed spires at each of 12 gates. A moat surrounds the wall 225 feet wide and 10 feet deep, its surface choked now by water hyacinth, a nuisance to those who still draw water from the moat, but a beautiful sight when in bloom. Nothing is left of the palace, built as tradition demanded that a Burmese king should build his palace, rich in wood carving, glittering with gold leaf smoothed over the wooden surfaces, and interset with colored glass or sometimes precious stones from the King's own mines.

The destructive fire in World War II left a few fragments of the past, like the King's own throne, which is now in Rangoon, the many Buddha figures which have been gathered into one Mandalay pagoda, a queen's palaquin, a chest-cupboard for parabaik and palm-leaf manuscripts, some of the books themselves in the National Library at Rangoon, together with a few fragments of royal clothing in a Mandalay museum. But this is all requiem.

When Mindon moved to Mandalay in 1858 with only the palace finished, there was still a hope that the independence of Upper Burma could be maintained. From the palace, he supervised the building of the outer city with streets as wide and straight as those of the new Rangoon the British had built. New docks were erected at the river, and, when the British introduced steamships on the Irrawaddy, Mindon bought some of his own for local traffic upriver. The British introduced telegraphy, and he extended it to his own realms. One son with a mind for that sort of thing was given responsibility for establishing small factories, rice mills, and textile centers.

Civilian administrators in the kingdom were given salaries, not a take from the tax collection. Mindon introduced coins to replace barter in trade, and the French built for him the royal mint. An Italian count built Mandalay's great bazaar. The choices were deliberate. Always conciliatory, Mindon still wanted to prove that an independent monarch had the right to relations with other independent nations, not just the British.

But, in Mindon's eyes, his greatest achievement must have been the Fifth Buddhist Synod, a gathering of Theravada

Buddhist scholars from all nations to read together the Tipitaka texts and agree on an authorized version of these scriptures, erasing any errors that might have crept in. Only four had been held in the life of the faith, most under the sponsorship of powerful monarchs. It was a tribute to Mindon and the purity of Burmese scholarship that the Synod was held in Mandalay.

The authorized text was afterward engraved on 729 slabs of white marble, each with a small pagoda-like shelter to protect it from the weather. The slabs, together with the great pagoda in whose courtyard they stand near the foot of Mandalay Hill, are called the Kuthodaw, the Work of Royal Merit.

To commemorate the work of the Synod and to affirm that his people were still one, he offered the gift of a new hti for the Shwedagon, a marvelous thing of gold and jewels topped by one great ruby, worth altogether 62,000 pounds. The British refused to permit him to come to Rangoon to present the gift, but they allowed the Burmese to accept it and put it in place to crown the stupa.

In 1872, Mindon, emboldened by some cordial notes from Queen Victoria, sent his chief minister of the Hlutdaw to London. The minister was presented to the Queen but by the Secretary of State for India, not the Foreign Minister. Burma, in London's eyes, was still no more than a native state of India, and the chief minister found his most enthusiastic audiences to be the chambers of commerce in various cities, which plied him with questions about trade.

After this disappointment in London came the matter of shoes in Mandalay. There are certain spots in Burma where, as a mark of respect before entering, everyone removes his shoes or sandals. Pagodas and monasteries are of course on the list, but in a traditional family so is the room of a parent or any elder. Indeed, more commonly than not, even today, all guests slip out of their sandals and leave them on the doorstep before entering any home.

Naturally, then, one removed one's shoes before entering the presence of the King. This observance had always been required of the British as it was required of everyone else. Some of the British emissaries obeyed without much thought, but to some it had always seemed a humiliation. Such a man came to Mindon's Court in 1875. When he returned to India, he complained so bitterly that authorities decided no Englishman would again be required to pay such an honor to an Asian king. This was regrettable. It meant that no Englishman could again speak directly to the King, though it was only in such direct talk that any real discussions or negotiations could take place. For the remainder of Mindon's reign, communication between the two authorities was virtually dead.

The legacy which King Mindon gave his people was incalculable. For a century their faith in themselves and their kings had been declining. With the coming of the British in Lower Burma, Christian missionaries had been allowed to move about freely without the restraints Buddhist kings had imposed. The missionaries set up new schools where the new language was taught and the new religion. Traditional Buddhist and Burmese values were downgraded in the south.

Mindon restored his people's faith in themselves and their own identity. A king of no great temporal power, he had yet been the very symbol of what their tradition told them a perfect Buddhist monarch should be. It was a psychological restoration of confidence in spite of their problems.

The Third British-Burma War

They were to need that confidence. There was trouble at the Court after Mindon's death in 1878. A minor prince came to the throne to be guided not by the Hlutdaw but by an ambitious young queen. Thibaw and Supayalat might have been vulnerable, however perfectly they reigned, for Rangoon merchants once again were dreaming of the China trade and the dream was difficult without Upper Burma. Mindon had been untouchable in the eyes of London and Parliament. These two were not.

They came to power in another blood-bath of more worthy royal princes, which roused British scorn and some demands for annexation. Though both the Rangoon Chamber of Commerce and the London Chamber of Commerce made representations to the government, London held out. But in 1885 an argument arose between Thibaw's government and the Bombay-Burma Corporation over royalties that had not been paid on what Burma called fraudulently exported teak timber. In August, the Hlutdaw levied a heavy fine on the corporation.

The British were twice angry because they believed plans were afoot to turn the forest leases over to the French. Before November ended, Mandalay was occupied, Thibaw and his queen had surrendered and were on shipboard for the journey into exile in India. All of Burma was in British hands.

3 Modern Burma

Burma was to enter the twentieth century not only as a conquered people but as a province of India, a country with which
she did not share language, culture, or history. The new British
rulers were too ignorant of Burma to grasp the incongruity when
the annexation was proclaimed on February 26, 1886.

British ignorance of Burma surfaced early. Eager for Chinese
trade, concerned about China's reaction to their seizure of a
neighbor, the British began talks with China even before the
annexation proclamation. They had no wish to disturb traditional relations between Burma and China, which they took for
granted had included Burma's payment of tribute. The Chinese
made no effort to disillusion them. The Burmese stopped this
distortion of history only by producing the proper documents
from their own files, including the battlefield treaty signed during Hsinbyushin's reign.

Then the British proposed that a new thathanabaing to head
Burma's religious hierarchy be appointed by the Chinese emperor.
They thought to flatter the emperor and satisfy the Burmese who
had already told them that the loss of such a primate, appointed
by each Burmese king, was a grave matter.

Once again, the Burmese came to their own rescue. China
wasn't a Buddhist nation, the emperor was seldom Buddhist,
and the minority of Chinese who were Buddhists were members
of the Mahayana school. It wasn't exactly the same as the Thera-

vada school, they told the British urgently. The British dropped the matter. The talks did one favor to the independent Burma which would one day rise again. Most, though not quite all, of the Chinese-Burmese border was delineated.

British judges did make an effort to learn about Burmese customary law as it applied to the people in such personal relations as marriage and divorce. Scholars translated the proper portions of the *Dhammathats* (compilations of these laws), and the judges applied those laws scrupulously, for all their enormous differences from either Indian or British law. Even here the old confusion arose. The British always inquired about Buddhist law, yet the Buddha and his laws are divorced from the temporal affairs of men. The Burmese, who speak of Burmese-Buddhist as if they were two syllables of the same noun, didn't always enlighten the British.

Few Englishmen understood the Burmese language and fewer still understood the heart of Burmese civil law, which was arbitration, resolution of conflict, not right-and-wrong absolutes. Nor did they need more than the most rudimentary knowledge of anything Burmese to do what they had come to do: keep a British peace, collect the necessary revenues, and insure conditions which would maintain and increase a lively, laissez-faire trade.

For this they had a ready-made matrix at hand. Indian troops, under British officers, finally put down the spontaneous rebellions which began in Upper Burma almost the moment Thibaw surrendered, spread to Lower Burma, and were not ended for four bloody years. Indian civil servants, both Englishmen and Indians, were available for the necessary peaceful administration afterwards. Indian dock-workers swarmed in for an expanding Rangoon port. There was little for Burmese to do but to help cut the teak timber and raise the rice which would make the whole system flourish. And Indian *chettyars* (moneylenders) were quickly on hand to aid the rice farmers.

The system did flourish. Wispy dreams of Chinese trade in quantity faded quickly, but with a greatly increased rice production which the British developed in the Irrawaddy Delta such trade was unnecessary. Rice and teak were the major exports; these together with internal revenue ranging from land taxes down to such minutiae as the taxes paid by indigenous distillers of salt enabled Burma to repay with surprising speed the costs of the third Burmese war. After 1891, the province more than paid its own way and a tidy surplus went each year to India. Mercantile interests sometimes resented the money which went to other provinces when much was needed in Burma. The chief needs, as that community saw them, were for more roads, railroads, and communications.

Once the rebellions were ended, the Burmese were rather quiet about their own needs. They learned to appreciate the stability of British rule though they didn't always understand the law which accompanied it. All self-rule, even on the village level, was more distant under the democratic British than it had ever been under the autocratic king. There were still village headmen, but only the name was the same. Now they were appointed from above. Previously they came up from the people either by hereditary rights or through election by the elders. Such men could front for their people, either by wile or wisdom, and exert some political influence over the next level of governmental authority. But the new headmen were the servants of that authority.

Some Englishmen, especially those stationed in the districts, grew fond of the Burmese, though almost to a man they considered them childlike and improvident. Men with a perceptive appreciation of Burmese cultural values were a rare handful among British administrators.

Some of the Burmese prospered. New schools, some secular, some operated by missionaries, enabled their children to learn English and become minor clerks in the establishment. A few went on to Rangoon College, which had been established as a branch of the University of Calcutta with British teachers, and some even traveled to England to study at British universities. The first received his B.A. degree in England in 1904; like many who followed him, he stayed on to complete his studies as a barrister. This British law was new but it was plain that status and power rested with the men who practiced it. The implication wasn't lost on the Burmese.

GROWTH OF NATIONALISM

The first resurgence of Burmese national identity—it would be a little strong to call it nationalism—arose with the organization of a Young Men's Buddhist Association in 1906 at Rangoon College. Soon units were springing up in all parts of Burma, but it was a low-keyed, proper group of educated gentlemen. As the Burmese jurist and author, Dr. Maung Maung, reports, the only revolution the YMBA carried out was to rewrite the prayer for the British king which opened annual meetings. Instead of "God Save the King" it became "Buddha Save the King." But it was a beginning.

In 1920, two events of moment occurred. The YMBA evolved into the General Council of Burmese Associations (GCBA), with wider contemporary interests than a religious association could hold. And the students of Rangoon College went out on strike.

Rangoon College was about to be reorganized as Rangoon University, independent of Calcutta, and the government planned a small, elite residential university, something like Oxford or Cambridge. The Burmese, thirsting for education, saw the plan as an affront to limit their resurgent sense of identity and their hopes for self-government.

Though the strike wasn't a complete success, it astounded the British, who hadn't believed the Burmese capable of such political organization. It was heady wine to the students who, camped out on the grounds of the Shwedagon Pagoda, held for a brief time the attention of the people, the monks, the newspapers, and the British. The tool would be used again.

All this time, Burma was still an Indian province—and India, promised increased self-government during World War I, had been given dyarchy* in 1920 under a new government plan. Burma, however, had been excluded from its provisions because "the desire for elective institutions has not developed in Burma." The December university boycott and the GCBA helped destroy that illusion. Dyarchy came to Burma in 1923.

The plan provided for a legislature of 103 members, 79 to be elected, to whom legislative authority was transferred for all the "nation-building" subjects, such as health, education, agriculture, forests. Several constitutional flaws weakened the success of this school in self-government, but one seems major. Finance and land revenue were among the "retained subjects," those that still lay in the hands of the British. To ask a new legislature to learn self-government without responsibility for finances is to ask newlyweds to learn housekeeping with no control over their budget.

With these limits on real power, legislative electioneering and debate was for points scored, like a university debating team. All the individualism of the Burmese came to the surface, orderly parties with party discipline were nonexistent, men were elected as passionate partisans on a major issue and changed sides immediately after election without regard for their constituents. This individualism was a habit that would continue to hamper government in Burma after independence. A new constitution separating Burma from India, operative in 1937, helped very little.

Agriculture was among the transferred subjects, yet eight years after the transfer came the Saya San rebellion of peasants, a sad and bloody business. Troops, rushed in from India, took two years to crush this array of cultivators armed with little more than stones and staves but protected against bullets, so Saya San

---

* A dual form of government in which a governor and executive council, appointed by London, controlled, retained or reserved subjects, while the governor and his ministers, chosen from an elected legislature, controlled transferred subjects.

told them, with magic amulets. The uprising was partly economic. The depression had reached Burma by 1930 and rice prices had dropped sharply. It was partly political, a deeply felt wish to drive the British into the sea. But it was also something else, an anguished desire to be rid of the present and return to the golden days of the kings. The British considered Saya San a charlatan, but older Burmese men and women who were then young student nationalists today recall their secret pride in him.

It was among those student nationalists, not in the legislative schoolroom for self-government, that the real independence leaders were rising. They called each other *Thakin,* the Burmese word for master, which was customarily used to address an Englishman, as Sahib was used in India. The first of them organized the Dobama Asi-Ayone (We Burmans) on the university campus in 1930. But those who really hit the national scene were a later student generation which in 1936 captured the elections of the Rangoon Student Union. Thakin Nu, a law student and president of the union, made a fiery speech for which he was expelled, whereupon Thakin Aung San, the union's secretary and editor of its newspaper, published a fiery article for which he was also expelled. The union called a strike in February as examinations were beginning. About 80 per cent of the university students walked out and were joined by over 20 per cent of the students from Judson College, a Christian school particularly favored by those Karens who had been converted by the early missionaries.

Like the students of the 1920's, they settled on the grounds around the Shwedagon Pagoda, the center of attention both from those who favored them and those who disapproved. Their cadres moved out into provincial high schools until the students of 32 such schools had joined the strike. Dr. Ba Maw, a politician of Mon descent who had been educated in Paris, was then education minister. Although he refused to support some of the student demands, the two expelled student leaders were readmitted to the university, thanks in large part to the pressure he put upon university officials.

In June Thakins Nu and Aung San returned to the campus and to the Student Union, both the organization itself and its headquarters, the small brick building just inside the main gates of the campus, off University Avenue. The strike was ended.

But these three would meet again, in quite different circumstances.

The student leaders left the campus soon after the strike to join the earlier thakins, including Ba Sein and Than Tun, in the Dobama Asi-Ayone, an organization which was strongly anti-British and revolutionary.

Those were exciting days for young Burmese. In the traditional English commitment to freedom of thought, all kinds of political documents came to their hands, from Nazi to Communist, and they drank from them all. The Nazi pride in "one people" had strong appeal to young men who saw the power of their land in alien hands. The Communist promise to end exploitation held equal appeal.

If they had been seeking an ideology, this combination would have been impossible. But they had their own ideology—independence for Burma. For that, they sought strength in any thought which came to hand, all the thakins but one. Than Tun was a Communist; he was a Burmese, too, and his land's independence was his goal as it was the others'. But he was a Communist then and would still be a Communist 30 years later when he died.

To complete the political roster, two younger thakins in 1939 organized a secret Burma Revolutionary Party on the university campus. Ba Swe and Kyaw Nyein were the leaders of what would become Burma's Socialist Party.

The cast of characters of an independent Burma was almost complete, except for the Thirty Comrades, and they would come soon.

THE JAPANESE PRESENCE

World War II had begun in Europe. Japanese agents were already in Burma, disguised as businessmen or newspaper correspondents. Their logical contacts were the anti-British thakins and Dr. Ba Maw. When the British arrested Ba Maw, Ba Sein, and Thakin Nu for sedition in August, 1940, Aung San escaped by sea. Early in March, 1941, he returned secretly, aboard a Japanese ship, to choose 29 young men to accompany him for military training under the Japanese on Formosa. Among them was one who took the name of Ne Win.

After six months' training, these 30 were sent to Thailand to raise young soldiers among expatriate Burmese. When the Japanese invaded Burma early in 1942, they came through Tenasserim from Thailand. The Thirty Comrades marched with them at the head of the Burma Independence Army of about a thousand hastily trained men, though the number swelled rapidly once they were inside Burma itself. Twenty-nine bore the title of *Bo*, military leader or general. They would use it proudly all their lives, even those who left military service, for this was the first independent Burmese army since the days of Thibaw. Aung San became Bogyoke Aung San, great leader.

It was a raggle-taggle army, for only the nucleus had any training at all, and some fought bravely and some did not. Some behaved with young wisdom and justice in the towns and villages they took over, and some behaved like young hellions on a spree, which they probably were—like dacoits (robbers), as the Burmese say. The Japanese, highly skilled at their military trade and single-minded about their own purpose in Burma, took few chances with the Burmese in crucial battles with the British. It is possible, also, that they did not wholly trust the Burma Independence Army. As the fighting moved north, most BIA units were left behind in the south.

Bogyoke Aung San and Bo Ne Win, however, were ordered

north with their troops, up the west side of the Irrawaddy beyond Shwebo, away from the other units. The British-Burma Army had enrolled few Burmans, but included many of Burma's minority peoples. With the British, the Karens, Kachins, and Shans were fighting their way out of Burma into India, putting up a valiant rear-guard action to protect the thousands of civilians struggling out ahead of them on the long and deadly march.

Most BIA units were scattered through the south. There were Karen villages in the south, and animosities between Karens and Burmans had ancient roots. Though explanations of the causes differ among Burmese and British writers, even the Burmese agree that some Karens suffered at the hands of some units in the BIA.

In July, the Japanese dissolved the BIA. Most historians say it was because of their indiscipline. Aung San believed it was because of the army's anti-Japanese sentiments. Army leaders had been told that Burma's independence would be declared when the troops reached Moulmein, but in July that declaration still had not been made. A new group was organized which would become the Burmese National Army, a smaller unit tightly controlled by the Japanese with Aung San still the nominal leader.

Though Ba Maw was appointed head of a provisional Burmese government in August, 1942, to most Burmese true national independence seemed far away. The Japanese were using Burma as a staging center for an effort to invade India, and nothing could take precedence over military needs. Ba Maw and the men who worked with him, including a number of thakins, were doing what they could to restore civilian life and protect the people from the Japanese military.

The Japanese habit of slapping civilian faces or boxing ears was hated throughout Southeast Asia but perhaps the Burmese male suffered more than most. In his culture, the body is honored in declining order from head to toe, and the male is more honored than the female, who would never dream of even tossing down her longyi, her skirt, on the sleeping mat where her husband's head had lain. To him the slappings and ear boxings were special indignities.

After constant pressure on the Japanese, Ba Maw with a group which included Bogyoke Aung San went to Tokyo in early 1943 to discuss "true" independence. When they returned with the promise of it, only Aung San, at the festivities which welcomed them back to Rangoon, hinted "very, very broadly," to use his later words, that this "independence" was going to be a minimal thing.

So it turned out to be. There was a new constitution. Ba Maw was to be the Adipati, a Pali word meaning leader, but there was no pretense of a legislature or any of the other trappings of democracy. Thakin Nu has related how, before the "election" for Adipati, he and two other thakins pressed Ba Maw into agreement to a "group dictatorship," an inner governing circle. Thakin Nu was Foreign Minister in the new cabinet, Aung San Minister of Defense. Ba Maw's first official act was to appoint Ne Win as Commander-in-Chief of the army.

There was, in truth, an inner circle, but not quite the kind which had been agreed on. Ba Maw had some inkling of it, but he refused to be told the details or to participate in it. He believed, and still believes, that Burma's independence had truly come in August, 1943. But in his own way he protected his young partners.

At Pegu in early August, 1944, thakins and Communists approved Aung San's draft proposal for an Anti-Fascist Organization (later to be called the Anti-Fascist People's Freedom League) and very shortly almost every group in Burma except Ba Maw's party had joined this underground. Representatives of Shans and Karens also came in. Aung San and Than Tun had long ago brought about a reconciliation between Burmans and most Karens. Certain emissaries traveled back and forth between

British India and Burma. Some arms were secretly received in late 1944 and early 1945 with the approval of Admiral Mountbatten, supreme allied commander of this theater of the war.

The tide of the struggle was turning. In late 1944, hard and difficult fighting had begun between allied troops and the Japanese in the far north of Burma. Mandalay fell to the invaders from India in mid-March. It was in this battle that Thibaw's palace was burned, though allied officers never knew whether it was from their bombings (they had tried to avoid it) or from fires set by the Japanese to burn supplies stored in it.

On March 27, 1945, Bogyoke Aung San assembled his troops in Rangoon with the consent of the Japanese to "march off and fight the enemy." Excitement was high among the Burmese who watched, but the Japanese were lacking in extrasensory perception. The troops marched out of sight and the jungle swallowed them. From there, Aung San issued the order, "We are at war."

A unified story of Burma's own efforts to free the country from the Japanese has yet to be told. Kachins in the north served the returning allies well. Karen guerrillas around Toungoo fought with incredible ferocity. From the departure of the Japanese on April 23, 1945, until the British arrived on May 3, the only authority in Rangoon was the AFPFL under the leadership of Ba Swe.

The Japanese surrendered on August 12, and two weeks later, before a Rangoon audience including a number of allied staff officers, Aung San recited the achievements of his men whom Mountbatten had officially recognized on May 30 as the Patriotic Burmese Forces. The PBF, their leader said, had killed at least 20,000 Japanese and taken a large number of prisoners. As a particular achievement, he cited action against the 54th Japanese Division, in which all important officers had been wiped out and a number of important documents captured which were turned over to Allied Forces.

Yet the story of the PBF as a fighting force is still largely omitted from historians' reports of the period, probably because no allied staff officers were with them.

STRUGGLE FOR INDEPENDENCE

Mountbatten's recognition of the PBF, which indirectly was recognition of Aung San and the AFPFL, was without approval from London. The first year of the postwar civilian reunion between British and Burmese was not a happy one. To many British, Aung San was not a great leader but a traitor, and in late 1945 London's plan for Burma was not early freedom but a return to pre-dyarchy days while the ravaged country recovered from the war.

Once again, independence had to be won by force, but it never came to the force of battle. As members of the PBF were mustered out following the Japanese surrender, many had joined the People's Volunteer Organization. This league of ex-soldiers was ready and willing to become Aung San's army again, if the need arose. Fortunately, it never did; perhaps the existence of the PVO helped to deter the need.

But there were strikes. Aung San and the AFPFL coalition could call them at will, even those of police and civil servants. The people responded with equal fervor at huge demonstrations and mass meetings which Aung San addressed. At last in September, 1946, London was convinced on both points at issue, that independence could not be long delayed, and that Aung San and the AFPFL were the real leaders of the people. Sir Hubert Rance, one of Mountbatten's men turned civilian, had arrived as governor in Burma, a move which promised to ease the transitional months. In Rance's executive council, six of the eleven members were AFPFL members. With Rance as chairman, Aung San became deputy chairman and Minister of Defense and External Affairs.

It was a tremendous victory for the young leader, but it widened a rift that had been slowly developing in the Burmese political organization. The Communists—there was a second faction now besides the one led by Thakin Than Tun—denounced Aung San for surrendering to British duplicity and called him a tool of imperialism. This was the final straw for Aung San. The Communists were expelled from the AFPFL.

In January, 1947, a delegation led by Aung San went to London and returned with an agreement that elections would be held in April for a constituent assembly to write a constitution for a free Burma, with the aim of achieving independence in January, 1948. There was also agreement that talks would begin shortly over the place of the minority peoples in a free Burma. In the meantime, the Executive Council would function as an interim government.

In April came a formal Frontier Areas Committee of Enquiry, a bi-national committee to recommend to London how the minorities felt about joining the Union of Burma. Karens were divided, but all others, the committee reported to London, were favorable. There had already been a preliminary conference in February and Aung San and Thakin Nu had spent most of the previous October and November in the upcountry areas, so that the whole idea of union was not a new one. The committee also proposed numbers for minority representatives in the Constituent Assembly.

In April also, elections were held for the assembly which would write the Constitution. Of the 182 seats in Burma Proper, the AFPFL won 171, the Communists 7. One Karen organization boycotted the elections. Sessions began in June, and included the 45 delegates of the minority groups, with Thakin Nu as the permanent president. Ironically, he had always wanted to be a writer, but of plays and novels, not political documents.

On July 19, before that task was finished, Burma suffered a tragic wound. While Aung San was presiding over a meeting of the Executive Council, gunmen hired by a Burmese right-wing politician invaded the council hall and assassinated him and eight other councillors. Today they lie buried in mausoleums of white marble on Martyrs' Hill, and in every Burmese office and shop, the thin, somber face of Bogyoke Aung San still looks down on his countrymen. The wound has never quite healed. Aung San was only 32 when he was murdered.

The people were dazed with grief and anger and the government was shattered. Not only Aung San but eight other men were dead who would have been post-independence leaders, including an outstanding Shan and Kachin. Even in purely practical terms, the loss was a major one for a people who had no leaders to spare. Yet a nation must survive the death of any man; it was good fortune that the British governor was a man like Sir Hubert Rance, trusted by the Burmese leaders and concerned with the people. He moved swiftly to appoint Thakin Nu as deputy chairman in Aung San's place. The new cabinet included not only Burmans but a Shan, a Chin, a Kachin, and a Karen.

The completed constitution was based on Aung San's proposals. The nation would be a sovereign, independent republic known as the Union of Burma with a president as titular head of state. Under a parliamentary system of government, the two houses were the Chamber of Deputies, elected by constituencies across the nation, and the Chamber of Nationalities, representing the separate segments of the population. In theory, the government was federal. But in practice, as Chan Htoon, the noted Burmese jurist, has pointed out, it was unitary, centralized, unlike the United States, Swiss, or even Indian governments.

Though the right of private property was guaranteed, the constitution had a strong socialist commitment, emphasizing the public interest over the private. The new nation would not remain in the British Commonwealth. It would include Burma Proper, the Shan State, the Kachin State, the Kayah State, and the Special Division of the Chins. A separate chapter provided that any state but the Kachin State might secede ten years after the constitution became effective.

With the constitution unanimously adopted by the assembly in late September, a treaty of independence was signed with Britain in October and ratified by the British Parliament in December. Thakin Nu dropped the title of defiance and became U Nu again. (U is the title with which Burmese address a respected male leader or elder.)

January 4, 1948, was chosen by Burmese astrologers as most auspicious for Independence Day at the hour of 4:20 a.m., that moment between the last dusk of early morning and the rising of the sun. It was chilly in Rangoon as the British flag came down and the Union of Burma flag was raised for the first time. The flag is red, like the Resistance flag during the war; the big white star of that flag is still there but now in a canton of dark blue surrounded by five smaller white stars. The large star represents the Union; the smaller stars the "Burma Proper" grouping of Mon-Burman-Arakanese, plus the Karens, the Shans, the Kachins, and the Chins.

In the early sun, the Burmese national anthem was sung for the first time. It was already familiar to most of the Burmese, for it was the old Thakin song, its fierce words tempered to be more fitting for its new use. In a conventional translation which lacks the poignancy of its melody, this is the refrain:

> As our heritage ancestral
> We love our Burma forever.
> In this world eternal
> We'll defend our Union forever
> If need be to the point of death.
> This is our sovereign society,
> This is our land of wealth—
> Our right of birth!
> Befittingly
> Let us guard our common welfare
> And in great unity our duty share
> For this, our golden earth.

Soldiers can march to its beat but its music still suggests some-thing of the wistfulness of an old folk song.

THE UNION OF BURMA—1948

On that chilly morning, U Nu, as Prime Minister, told his country that "this day of Independence dawns on a people not only free but united. . . . This is also a day for solemn thought, for, in a sense, our work has just begun."

The unity was more hope than fact, while the fact of work only· begun was not pep-talk hyperbole but more tragically prophetic than U Nu could dream. In the two decades and more which have passed, the drama of a free, united Burma remains stalled in the first act, the lines and action endlessly repeated, often by the same leading actors. Over and over the end of that beginning has seemed almost within grasp, yet it has constantly eluded the people and their leaders.

Three major problems have weighed down the reborn nation: the economic and administrative conundrums which seem ende-mic to all such newly freed peoples, Communist insurgents, and ethnic rebels.

Outbreak of Rebellion

The economy was ruined; twice in three years, armies had fought over the length of the country. Oil fields were destroyed, bridges blown up, towns and cities were in rubble. In 1939, the country had 2,059 miles of railway to unite it; in 1946, only 1,510 miles were in operation. Agricultural production, the mainstay of the country, had fallen far below prewar levels.

Nor was there a management team of political leaders and civil servants trained to move in and run the country. At first, there was friction between the political leaders, the nationalists who had been the architects of independence, and the small group of civil servants who, true to the nonpolitical character of a

British-oriented civil service, had stuck to their job of running the country no matter who was in the political saddle. The politicians, who had started their careers as students, were all young men with no experience in administration and little appreciation of its skills.

Their leader as head of the AFPFL coalition was U Nu, the prime minister who was once a schoolmaster before he returned to the university to study law, a man of some innate contradictions. No one in the country, following Aung San's death, could match his charisma. After what he said had been a boisterous youth, he was now a devout Buddhist given to seeking the monastery for meditation and capable of preaching religion to his people as earnestly as he preached a modern brand of patriotism.

Steeped in Burmese tradition and lore, he was an orator who could sway his people in the earthy speech of colloquial Burmese, yet in perfect English charm the United States Congress to complete trust with his modern stance toward nation-building. A dreamer and a writer, to use his own words, who never wanted to be a politician, he could mock, in self-deprecatory parables, his difficulties in making a decision. Yet this was the man who made the tough decisions that sustained the life of the newly born nation through a violent infancy.

In late March, 1948, Than Tun and his White Flag Communists went underground in open rebellion, charging the AFPFL with surrender to British imperialism. A few months before, U Nu and Than Tun had been touring the countryside together. But since then, an Asian Communist meeting had been held at Calcutta where Politboro orders were passed along. Burma wasn't the only nation to feel the scourge of a Communist insurgency in 1948. (Burma's Red Flag Communists, a separate faction, had gone underground in 1946.)

By June, Communist soldiers in the small Burmese army were defecting. At July's end, the leaderless PVO without Aung San split in two and one portion joined the Communists, taking along military police and two Burmese army battalions. The Karen National Defense Organization (KNDO), formed a year earlier by dissident Karens wanting a separate nation, went into armed action against the government in December and were immediately joined by mutinous Karens from military and police units. Arms were no problem. The mutinous simply took theirs with them. PVO members and Karens had both fought the Japanese, as had the Patriotic Burmese Forces, and many arms had never been surrendered when the war ended.

The Communists were the spark that set the fire. U Nu had tried to smother the first spark with his "15 points" back in May. These were a series of proposals that came innocently but perilously close to turning the country over to the Communists, yet Than Tun and his lieutenants, too confident of military victory, rejected them. Nevertheless, they began a pattern of endless negotiations in which the government has proposed to different groups of rebels that they "come into the light." Burma has never ceased for long its efforts to talk to its insurgents. Talking and fighting, talking and fighting has been almost a way of life these past twenty years and more.

By the end of 1948, they were all in the field, White Flag Communists, PVO's, and Karens. Their first victories seemed like death blows to the government. By January, 1949, the Karens had raided military stores at Mingaladon Airport and held Insein, a scant 12 miles from Rangoon. The Communists held Toungoo and all three groups joined in capturing Mandalay in March, 1949. Only Rangoon and the air itself seemed safe for the government. U Nu used the air to fly to outlying posts and keep alive the hope and confidence of the people.

But the tiny army, under General Ne Win as Deputy Prime Minister, was regrouping its loyal units (including Chins and Kachins) and beginning the counterattack. Mandalay was retaken April 3 and the tide began to turn. Much as Bayinnaung had reclaimed the country from earlier rebels, the army first retook Arakan, then the Delta, and finally the rail lines from

Rangoon up to Mandalay, including the Communist strongholds of Toungoo and Pyinmana. By November, 1949, when the Burmese army recaptured Taunggyi, in the Shan State, from the Karens, the back of the rebellion was broken.

That was not the end of it, indeed it has not yet ended. The rebels have become guerrillas now, underground in the jungle, sometimes gaining strength and sometimes losing it. They blow up a train, seize weapons from a police outpost, raid one village or punish another which has cooperated too well with the army. Like an open sore which will not heal, they continually drain the energies of the nation. But they have never again threatened its life.*

Pyidawtha

The civil government never ceased to function during the rebellion. Martial law had never been declared across the nation. But now the civil forces went about their business with increased vigor. Four times since independence, elections had been postponed and the Parliament was still the Constituent Assembly chosen in 1947 to write the Constitution. Some of its seats stood empty, their holders in the jungle. In 1951, the delayed elections were held, spread over a seven-month period so that protection could be focused on one voting constituency after another.

In the same year, a Karen State was formed in negotiations with those Karens who had remained loyal to the central government and those who had returned from the jungle.

The elections were an achievement, a visible sign of the nation's viability, yet they changed nothing politically. The AFPFL

---

* The army had another untidy job along with cleaning up behind the rebels. In 1949 when Chiang Kai-shek was losing China to the Communists, some 2,500 of his Kuomintang (KMT) troops crossed into the Shan State near Kengtung. The army has contained them but periodically the problem they create burgeons into another crisis for this beleaguered nation.

was returned to power with no minority strong enough to be called an opposition party. U Nu was again chosen as Prime Minister.

Certain international postures of the new nation took shape, chief among them its position of neutrality and nonalignment. Probably no nation in the world is more truly nonaligned than Burma. This theme runs so deep that it can hardly be called a policy, for that suggests the possibility of discussion and change. Born of high principles anchored in Buddhism and of practicality based on its geographic position, nonalignment has the common consent of people and leaders. Burma belongs to no association of states, not even regional groupings in its own part of the world, but it is a committed member of the United Nations.

The big tasks now were social and economic. The right to university education became free and universal, though the home of the thakins had been occupied by the Japanese as a military base and the Rangoon University campus was hardly ready to receive the thousands who came.

Chettyars, the Indian moneylenders who had gained control over much of the Delta land, did not return after the war, and the land control returned to the tiller. Generous agricultural loans from the government neatly thwarted any new moneylenders who might arise, but the farmers were, and still are, most nonchalant about repaying their loans. In early 1950, rice production had been less than half the prewar level and the surplus for export was only a fifth. The new land policies didn't restore the prewar production levels but, together with somewhat greater security, they did bring an increase. This was of immense importance. Hunger is seldom a Burmese problem but the government needed rice for export to support its economic goals.

U Nu, who had found time for dreaming of those goals even in the worst months of the rebellions, told his people about them in midsummer, 1952. They would lead to Pyidawtha, which literally means "sacred-pleasant-country" but has been more freely translated as Welfare State. The people, worn down by occupation`and war, deprived by the rebellions of the new life independence was to bring, were ready for dreams and hope. They responded with excitement and joy, and Pyidawtha for six years was a talisman, a sustaining promise.

It would take planning and money, more money than rice and teak exports could provide. It would also demand skilled and knowledgeable administrators.

There was assistance. The first American aid program began in 1950. The Colombo Plan helped train students abroad. A treaty with Japan in 1954 provided invaluable reparations. Private American foundations came in. The Russians offered aid, though U Nu complicated that offer by promising rice as payment. And, since most ill winds blow someone good, the Korean war forced the price of rice upward and Burma reaped a bountiful harvest in hard currency.

There was planning. U Nu chose an American team of economic and engineering consultants to survey the nation's resources and to forecast development. Briefly financed by American funds, the team's support through most of the years came from the Burmese government. Their comprehensive report was lengthy and controversial. The World Bank made their own survey and termed the scope of the country's planning unrealistic since "experienced indigenous management is almost wholly lacking." The United Nations sent missions to undertake surveys of health and social services. And every program of American aid and private foundations was preceded by surveys and planning.

The World Bank was right and Pyidawtha didn't come, but there were tangible results, nonetheless. The Rangoon docks were rebuilt; a pharmaceutical industry was begun; the bombed-out bridge at Ava across the wide Irrawaddy was replaced; schools, clinics, village wells with potable water served some of the people. The handsome Mingaladon airport was built, at great waste, but it was built. Train tracks were repaired, new rolling stock came in, and the trains ran again, though only in the daylight to avoid the insurgents who had—and still have—a penchant for blowing them up. The vast Balu Chaung hydroelectric power project was built by the Japanese. The list could go on and on. Though it still wasn't Pyidawtha, the years and the aid and the planning weren't a total waste.

Nevertheless, there were minuses on the nation-building ledger. Intermittent rebel violence had not ceased, though the army still worked at the endless task of containment. But violence seems to breed violence and the crime rate was up. Competent young administrators were appearing here and there but too rarely to make efficiency a mark of the government. Scandalous corruption is not native to Burma, but a little "tea money" to nudge the lethargy became habitual.

Garbage pick-ups were slow and piles of it collected to feed the growing packs of pariah-dogs (called pi-dogs), and the scavenging crows. The Ministry of Religion created new Buddhist councils to replace those of the old kingdom, but young saffron-robed monks were often seen in the front rows of Rangoon movie theaters.

Students swarmed into the University. When the University Senate imposed discipline or standards, they turned to U Nu, chancellor as well as Prime Minister, their elder brother, who almost invariably ruled in their favor, against the faculty. Even though the colonialists were gone, students still demonstrated on the campus, led often by "professional" students who moved to a new university division when their time was up at the old, never graduating. The people called them above-ground leftists; U Nu, remembering his student days, found it hard to be harsh to them.

The AFPFL coalition was big and unwieldy, representing many interests; each group had its favorite projects and it was difficult to rule against anyone in the top line-of-control. Editorial writers in a free press were, in a sense, the only opposition party. Still, even under one-party rule, the socialist nation remained democratic. If U Nu was not a firm administrator, he held the people's hearts and his dreams were theirs. U Ba Swe and U

Kyaw Nyein, the two socialist leaders, might be more orderly in their planning, but they were second in power to U Nu. Yet they all approached the 1956 elections with confidence.

This time there would be an opposition party, the National United Front. Built around the Burma Workers and Peasants Party, an above-ground Communist group dating from 1950, most of the NUF held the same beliefs. But not all. Some moderates joined simply because they thought the time had come to have an opposition party. Though the AFPFL won a comfortable majority in terms of seats, the national popular vote was amazingly close. Plainly something was amiss. The price of rice was down, the shine was off the Pyidawtha dream, the AFPFL had been in power too long. A little of each perhaps, enough to account for 1956.

Yet not enough to explain 1958.

Caretaker Government

In April of that year the AFPFL abruptly split apart. It was a nasty, noisy fight, like the worst family quarrel, filled with charges of private and public sins. The two Socialist leaders called their half the Stable AFPFL, U Nu named his the Clean AFPFL. Faced with a Socialist motion of no confidence in Parliament, U Nu won by only seven votes, and these came from the leftist NUF. The balance of Parliamentary power lay with the Communists.

There was no political sense to the split, nor to the vicious charges and countercharges. It resembled a divorce more than a political battle; perhaps it was, after a political marriage of convenience. Aung San had been the chosen leader; U Nu had succeeded him by default after the assassination. The people and the newspapers were both angry and alarmed. Some PVO's and Communists came running "into the light," though not Than Tun. There were rumors of private armies being organized, caches of weapons gathered, military coups being planned. The army, under General Ne Win, maintaining a scrupulous non-political stance, looked on the safety of the nation as their prime responsibility. By September, the army was stopping busses, trucks, and private cars on the streets of Rangoon, searching for arms. Military police moving to Rangoon under obscure orders were sent back by the soldiers to their posts.

In October U Nu returned from a trip upcountry to a jittery capital, and again the man who couldn't make decisions made the only one which could rescue the nation from its crisis. He proposed his own resignation and the selection of Ne Win by Parliament for the post of Prime Minister, which the general would agree to hold for six months "to restore law and order and hold free and fair elections."

It was no military coup, as much of the West believed, not even when the first six months were up and Ne Win asked Parliament for another year to complete his mandate. The country named it the "Caretaker Government" and was guardedly confident of future elections.

Not long after he came to power, a story about Ne Win circulated through Rangoon. His Ministry of Information had arranged a display of anti-Communist books and materials which they were anxious to show the General. Ne Win looked it over carefully, pronounced it good and then asked, "Now where is the display for democracy?" The story was probably apocryphal. But what it said about General Ne Win was believed.

The 17 months were a curious hiatus in the feverish political life of Burma, as if a family had exchanged a warm, compassionate, permissive parent for a stern father figure. General Ne Win never held press conferences; U Nu had practically governed the country through them. The new Prime Minister was scrupulous about reporting to the Parliament; U Nu had almost never appeared in its chambers. The new man made few public appearances; even at the 1959 Independence Day celebration, it was the President of the Union who received the salutes of the marching armed forces. The General sat somewhere in the background of the reviewing stand, invisible even to those nearby.

One of his few public appearances after he became Prime Minister was on the University of Rangoon campus as chancellor (the two posts went together). He had been a thakin on this same campus, along with Aung San and U Nu. Now he told the annual commencement convocation his ideas of students and politics:

> When a country is under alien rule as a slave, every person in that country has the duty to work for liberty and independence. Therefore, students fought in the front rank of our patriotic fighters for freedom. They were trusted and relied upon by the whole nation.

He didn't remind them that he had been one of those students. Instead, he went on,

> But once national freedom is won, the sole and single duty of a student is to acquire an education, ceasing to be mere part-time students and part-time politicians. If they fail to follow this advice, they are failing in their duty to their own country.

It was the sharpest speech the students had heard since Independence, and they were subdued throughout Ne Win's days as Prime Minister.

Though his cabinet was civilian and nonpolitical, army officers appeared in administrative posts throughout the nation. When an army faces an active enemy as this one had done continually, competence is learned in a hard school. Bad administration wastes men, not money, and men are less replaceable. An unusual number of efficient administrators turned up in colonels' uniforms.

The first surprise was that "order" as the army interpreted it also meant cleanliness, a housekeeping definition. The platform of the Shwedagon was scrubbed, alleys were cleaned of trash, the cities' drains were flushed. At first young men and women in army uniforms worked alone, but then civilians joined in, especially when government departments were assigned particular Sundays and particular projects under the "Sweat Scheme." The visual effect in Rangoon was startling.

Garbage was collected regularly. Poison was laid out at night for the pi-dogs. This last event shook the Buddhist country where all life was considered sacred, but the only really loud complaints came from owners of pet dogs. So the army moved through each neighborhood issuing warnings before laying down poison, to save the pets, and collected the dead bodies swiftly to calm sensitivities.

Beef was slaughtered and appeared in the country's bazaars in an effort to lower food costs by increasing the quantity of meat available. Again, purists among the Buddhists grumbled, but the meat sold quickly. The prices of all goods were plainly marked in all the bazaars on a scale set by the government, bargaining was forbidden, and the whole system against "economic insurgents" was reinforced when the shops of the Defense Services Institute were opened to the public. Food prices dropped.

A massive urban renewal plan in the second six months moved squatters out of Rangoon into two newly-laid-out satellite towns. With the beginning of the insurgency, people had swarmed into the relatively safe capital, crowding on any empty ground their *basha* huts of bamboo and thatching. In the emergency all this illegality had been overlooked, but the temporariness had become a permanent fact of life, accepted even by the landowners. This is where fires spread in each dry season; these were the families without sanitary facilities, even without water except for a single neighborhood standpipe. The army provided moving trucks for the grumbling squatters and their knocked-down huts. At the time it seemed a drastic act. But Okkalapa and Thaketa became thriving towns.

These were the more visible acts of the Caretaker Government.

Others were more sweeping. The contract with the American planning group was terminated, an act which pleased the ordinary Burmese who resented western salaries and the "amenities" the Burmese treasury had been providing. The group had worked hard, but whatever wisdom their plans held were for another time and other administrators. The Shan sawbwas, who were something like India's rajahs though considerably poorer, were persuaded to surrender their hereditary privileges in the Shan States.

The Russian "gift" agreement was renegotiated because, Ne Win said, the country could not afford the quid-pro-quo of rice. All future Russian projects were canceled; only the three in process were continued: the technical institute at Insein, the small hospital at Taunggyi, and the hotel on Inya Lake in Rangoon, though the papers ceased to call it "Russian Gift Hotel" and began writing of it by its present name, Inya Lake Hotel.

Work was completed in realigning the last piece of undemarcated boundary between China and Burma, and a treaty of peace and friendship signed in early 1960 which Parliament would ratify after the next elections. Even ordinary citizens sighed with relief; the overt beginnings of conflict between India and China over their undefined boundary had roused Burma's trepidation.

With both political and military power in its hands, the army moved with renewed vigor against the Communist and Karen insurgents, not even stopping during the monsoons. Now the Rangoon-Mandalay train ran straight through, with no overnight stopover at Pyinmana, though an armored car with soldiers traveled ahead of it to detonate any mines on the track. Most remarkably, Ne Win and the armed forces gained widespread cooperation from the villagers whose fear had often kept them silent. Public honors and cash awards were made to the courageous reporters of intelligence; anonymous reporters were given secret channels for information transfers and their identities protected.

On the flat plains, villagers built scraggly eagles' nests of combustibles on high poles. Fired, they could be seen for miles, signal cries for help from the nearest army outpost. Not every attack could be stopped, but the army was diligent at following bands into the jungle to rescue kidnapped males. It was scrupulous in providing aid of rice and cloth for burned-out villages. Just as violence seemed to breed violence, so order bred order. The crime rate in the country dropped markedly.

The rebels weren't defeated. They were merely pushed back farther than they had ever been before, far enough that talk started about elections. A gambling people, the Burmese began to lay at least verbal bets on whom the army would favor, the Stable AFPFL with U Ba Swe and U Kyaw Nyein, or the Clean AFPFL with U Nu. The betting leaned toward the "Stable" but the army was being persistently nonpolitical. The October Festival of Lights, always a brilliant event with Rangoon glittering in lights of red, green, blue, and yellow, demonstrated the people's puzzle. Red was the political color of the Stable AFPFL. Yellow, the Buddhist color, was U Nu's choice. To play it safe politically, the people of Rangoon in 1959 strung only green and blue lights, and the effect was cold, not gay.

In December, the Caretaker Government announced that national elections would be held in February, 1960, the winners to receive political control of the country in April.

U Nu spent several months in a monastery before the campaign began and emerged with his campaign speeches ready. Except on one point the platforms of the two parties were carbon copies of each other: neutrality, no surrender to insurgents, a socialist state, all safe, impeccable political positions in Burma. But U Nu in addition talked about a constitutional amendment which would make Buddhism the state religion. During the campaign, he also offered to grant the Arakanese and the Mons separate states, if their desire for statehood were real.

The army kept its promise; the elections were free and fair. And U Nu's party was returned by a landslide. U Ba Swe and U Kyaw Nyein did not even hold their seats in Parliament.

The Revolutionary Council

Nevertheless, the country seemed to slide downhill, and in less than two years General Ne Win and the army were back in power. It is not hard to spot the causes but it's more difficult to see why, with his tremendous mandate, U Nu could not control them.

Trouble in his party, renamed the Union Party, started almost immediately, in large measure because U Nu said he was going to resign party leadership shortly and would retire from politics altogether in 1964. Quite naturally, a political struggle for control of the party began at once. By the year's end in 1960, the Chins announced that they too wanted a separate state, and the Shans proposed that the federal-state structure in the Constitution be loosened. No one was unaware that, according to the Constitution, the time had come when the Shans, if they wished, could vote for secession.

The minorities, including the Christians, were uneasy over their position in a nation where Buddhism was the state religion. They seemed to fear religious persecution less than they feared that they would be shut out of the secular life in the nation.

The Chinese KMT's became active again in the Shan State, joining up with the Karen KNDO's and restless Shan rebels who, anxious for more state freedom, resented Burmese troops stationed around Taunggyi as "occupation troops." Burmese students rioted in front of the American Embassy against America's "complicity" in supporting Taiwan, which in turn supported the KMT, sometimes with American arms and supplies.

But the real crunch came with the Union Party struggle. It grew as vicious as the AFPFL fight had been, with U Nu maintaining a kind of Buddhist calm and distance. He had spent another 45 days in a monastery retreat in the summer of 1961; less and less did the man who had never wanted to be a politician seem willing to assume the political leadership which the nation had given him and which his party certainly demanded if it were to govern. Buddhists believe that the temporal passes, as indeed it does, that it is ephemeral and unimportant. This may be sound religious philosophy, but it is a difficult way to govern even a Buddhist country.

On March 2, 1962, in the early morning, Ne Win and the army staged a coup d'état, "owing to the greatly deteriorating conditions of the Union." In the best Buddhist tradition, it was non-violent. But it was not a rerun of the Caretaker Government and General Ne Win made that clear at once. A military Revolutionary Council would govern the country; the Parliament, the Constitution, and the State Councils were immediately abrogated, but all civil servants and the rest of the country were to go about their business as usual.

There was no genuine emotional reaction against the take-over; indeed, the people showed more relief than anything else. The university was closing for the long vacation which covers the time of intense heat and the heavy onslaught of the early monsoon rains. Thus even the students were quiet. At the end of April, the Council issued its first policy document, which it entitled *The Burmese Way to Socialism*. General Ne Win had lost faith in democracy.

The first crisis arose when the students returned to campus. As usual, the Student Union was controlled by leftists. On July 6, 1962, a demonstration against dormitory regulations got out of hand; the police, unable to quell it, called the army. With faculty families prisoners in their campus houses, there was some valid reason for uneasiness. The army was no more successful than the police and someone, either a sergeant with a nervous finger or a higher authority, gave the order to fire. Machine guns swept across the crowd. Scores were killed or wounded.

The next day, with deliberation, the army blew up the Union building, the small brick structure just inside the main university gate which had once been headquarters for Aung San and U Nu. In the two acts, the real and the symbolic, an era died.

Through most of 1963, the government carried on almost continuous negotiations with all its variety of rebels, under generous offers of amnesty. Some important Communist rebels came "into the light" and joined the Burma Socialist Program Party, though not Than Tun. After almost five months of talk, the KNDO made peace with the government. The Karen State was renamed with its traditional name of Kawthoolei as a symbol of the agreement. (Today, only Communist Karens are in the jungle.) But the demands of all the others were too extravagant and in November, the government admitted that the negotiations had failed. It had gained, however, immense good will among the people for its efforts to "relieve tensions" in proper Buddhist fashion.

In the same year, nationalization of everything from banks to small shops proceeded at a whirlwind pace. Indians, who along with the Chinese were often the merchants, were sent home to India with little more than what they wore on their backs. Some were third-generation in Burma but had not become citizens. All private technicians and foundations were sent home too. When a western ambassador asked the General why, Ne Win is reported to have said, "as long as your people stay and do for my people, they will never learn to do for themselves."

Visas became hard to get. Tourists, if they were admitted at all, were limited to 24 hours. Those few others who might be admitted for a longer period seldom left Rangoon. It was as if Ne Win was pulling a psychological Thalun withdrawal. This time the capital remained in Rangoon, but the people "went home" to their own resources, their own traditions, their own skills and talents, while they learned the hard task of running their own country alone.

It may be disputed that this was the old-time isolationism or xenophobia. Ne Win may have meant just what he was reported to have said. "My people must learn to do for themselves." It is not a poor country, this one-time Golden Land. But the results were disappointing. Prices went up, food shortages developed, it was easier to find rice "on the outside," as the Burmese called the flourishing black market, than in the People's Stores.

Most critically, peasants decreased their rice sales to the government. Even granting some bad years of drought and flood, rice for export dwindled to an abnormally small tonnage.

But in 1967 something happened which united the Burmese as strongly as if their beloved Mindon Min was still on the throne. As permanent residents in Burma, the Overseas Chinese numbered perhaps half a million, many of them in Rangoon. Not all were Maoist followers, but those who favored Taiwan kept quiet under the nation's treaty of friendship with the Communists.

A large Chinese Embassy staff was also present in Rangoon, several hundred of them technicians working under grants from an $84 million line of credit negotiated with China. Relations between Ne Win and Chinese leaders were friendly and such officials as Chou En-lai had probably been visiting Burma more often than any other nation.

The Chinese Cultural Revolution was on, now, and Maoist badges began appearing on Chinese students in Rangoon. For all students, "political" activity was illegal. Burmese teachers, ordering the buttons removed, were occasionally assaulted. Demonstrators occupied some of the schools and were fed and supported by adult Chinese outside. The Burmese exploded. Normally a mild and gentle people as befits Buddhists, they can on provocation lose their tempers with ugly violence. The Chinese Embassy was assaulted and a technician killed, a Burmese mob roamed the city streets destroying Chinese property, sometimes beating and killing resident Chinese. Martial law was declared in Rangoon.

Peking responded with fury. Ne Win was a fascist and his government must make public apologies and pay compensation. The Burmese government answered with caution, pointing out their even-handedness in dealing with both Burmese and Chinese who were responsible for the riots.

In October the Chinese threatened to stop work on the technicians' projects. Ne Win responded promptly, urging an immediate withdrawal of all Chinese technicians. They left at once. The Burmese, passionately nationalist, poured out loyalty and approval for the man the Chinese had dared call fascist. Nobody wept over the withdrawal of the Chinese technicians.

The Chinese have never quite let up on the Burmese since then. Their support of Than Tun's Communist Party became more overt. The party, however, was a weak reed, and in the fall of 1968 it was further weakened when Than Tun, in the jungle, was killed by a young cadre recently returned from China. Peking, announcing the murder, accused bloody assassins who had infiltrated the party at Ne Win's orders.

The Burmese ignored that. The important fact was that Than Tun was dead. He had been a competent administrator in earlier days and Burma had felt his loss severely when he defected. But that was far away and long ago; the only emotion now was one of relief. China still supports what is left of the party, together with the Kachin, Shan, and remaining Karen rebels. Today the Revolutionary Council worries more about the Kachins in their high mountains and deep, rugged valleys than it does about the Burmese Communist Party, though it continues its pressure on them all.

A knowledgeable westerner, in a position to know, has said that this government has accomplished more in education, public health, and public works than any previous one. Most political prisoners, high and low, have been released. But the economic situation pinches the country, from the peasant who can't find supplies in the bazaar to the government itself, which can't find the traditional exports for the hard currency it needs to finance development.

4 The Government

In 1970 it was a reasonable assumption rather than a rash prophecy that Burma would have a new constitution and a new government well before the decade ended. There were signs that after eight years the present government considered the "transitional period" of its power to be approaching an end. In Burma, such signs would be those of astrologers, and some astrologers did believe they could discern them. But they could also be seen in events within the country, and in the statements of leaders, particularly of General Ne Win.

As the decade of the 1970's began, the government of the Union of Burma was a military dictatorship led by the Revolutionary Council with General Ne Win as its chairman. After the resignation of the sole civilian, U Thi Han, as foreign minister in mid-1969, all members of the Council were officers in the armed forces. Their declared purpose was to guide the nation through the period of transition to a socialist society and a socialist democracy.

Their position papers were two. The first policy declaration, issued in April, 1962, was entitled *The Burmese Way to Socialism*. This document paid some praise to parliamentary democracy, which "came into existence with the British, American, and French revolutions against feudalism. It happens to be the best in comparison with all its preceding systems. . . . [But] the nation's socialist aims cannot be achieved with any assurance by means of the form of parliamentary democracy we have thus far experienced."

In practical translation, this came to mean that "political insurgents," i.e., politicians, were as dangerous to true democracy as "economic insurgents," i.e., capitalists. In Burma, according to the thinking of the Council, both had been exploiters of the people.

The statement bound the Council to "develop only such a form of democracy as will promote and safeguard the socialist development." An interesting parenthetical sentence stated that the "Revolutionary Council believes and hopes that there will come about democratic competitions which will promote socialist development within the framework of socialism."

Exactly what democratic competitions were in the minds of the Council back in 1962 were not publicly explained.

The second position paper, published in January, 1963, was a long, philosophical statement entitled *The System of Correlation of Man and Environment*. Based as much on Buddhist doctrine as any Marxist ideology, it attempted to express the particular Burmese quality of the Council's socialism. This paper lacks the simplicity and clarity of the first policy statement. But in mid-1964, after whispered charges from backers of the *Sangha* (the Buddhist monkhood), that the government was Communist and therefore antireligious, the Council outlined in practical terms the differences between Communism and Burma's socialism—an outline which may be considered a down-to-earth translation of the more philosophical "System."

Communism is antireligious whereas Burma's socialism guaranteed full freedom of conscience and religion to its members. In accord with the Buddhist belief in ceaseless change, Burmese socialists reject the rigidity of Communist ideology and believe that all political, social, and economic doctrines are subject to change and correction. So also the materialism of Communism is rejected because of the Buddhist belief that man is more than simply matter endowed with feeling and intelligence.

The major purpose of all this may have been to make socialism more palatable to Buddhists, but a minor and useful corollary was to make possible both a pragmatic change of course by the Revolutionary Council when that seemed necessary and a degree of self-criticism which would not be mistaken for weakness.

In neither paper was a governmental structure outlined for the transition period except the Revolutionary Council itself, leaving that body free to introduce those structures it eventually deemed useful.

COUNCIL PERSONNEL

The Council, always with General Ne Win as chairman, has functioned as both the executive branch of the government and the law-making body. Ne Win's military dictatorship, like his brand of socialism, introduced some variations from the norm. Beginning with the night of the coup, the government conducted a series of political arrests at irregular intervals. But if there were no trials of political prisoners, neither were there executions nor even underground mutterings of torture. By 1970 all the top figures and most lesser ones had been freed. The press was controlled, yet sharp criticism of the government was permitted, especially in the economic sphere, even though attacks on its socialist principles were not allowed. Ne Win, while often reported as suspicious and fearful, was confident enough to travel outside the country for several months at a time, leaving the other members of the Council to run the country. This indicated more than a meeting of minds on the Council. Plainly Ne Win had no fear of a "palace coup," which historically has been Burma's method of toppling an indigenous ruler.

This meeting of the minds did not come automatically at the beginning, nor were all the members of the Council the same officers who had efficiently operated the Caretaker Government. When that government turned the country back to civilian rule, some colonels left the army and took no part in the 1962 coup. Several were appointed ambassadors; one became a Buddhist

Near the top of Mandalay Hill, this bronze figure of Buddha stands with hand outstretched to the land below. According to legend, Buddha prophesied that one day a great capital would be built there by a king who would do him honor.

Volunteers scrub the platform of the Shwedagon Pagoda as a "sweat scheme" project of the Caretaker Government.

Monks with black lacquer begging bowls, accompanied by their pupils, who serve them, start the morning round of begging for their food. They have passed through the Sarabha Gateway at Pagan, only remnant left of the ninth-century circuit wall around the early Burman capital.

Monks and their pupils walk along a sandy Pagan road. In the background are the ruins of two pagodas and the large, carefully tended Thatbyinnyu Temple, built by King Alaungsithu in A.D. 1144. Approximately five thousand pagodas and temples were built here along the Irrawaddy River, most of them from the eleventh to the thirteenth century, when Pagan was the seat of the first Burman dynasty. Some have vanished, leaving only a bare trace; others stand in crumbling disarray; but the most precious have had respectful care, have often been renovated by Burman Kings, and are now in the charge of the archaeological department of the Union of Burma.

Near the top of Mandalay Hill, this bronze figure of Buddha stands with hand outstretched to the land below. According to legend, Buddha prophesied that one day a great capital would be built there by a king who would do him honor.

Volunteers scrub the platform of the Shwedagon Pagoda as a "sweat scheme" project of the Caretaker Government.

Monks with black lacquer begging bowls, accompanied by their pupils, who serve them, start the morning round of begging for their food. They have passed through the Sarabha Gateway at Pagan, only remnant left of the ninth-century circuit wall around the early Burman capital.

Monks and their pupils walk along a sandy Pagan road. In the background are the ruins of two pagodas and the large, carefully tended Thatbyinnyu Temple, built by King Alaungsithu in A.D. 1144. Approximately five thousand pagodas and temples were built here along the Irrawaddy River, most of them from the eleventh to the thirteenth century, when Pagan was the seat of the first Burman dynasty. Some have vanished, leaving only a bare trace; others stand in crumbling disarray; but the most precious have had respectful care, have often been renovated by Burman Kings, and are now in the charge of the archaeological department of the Union of Burma.

Medical Institute I, built with rice profits from high prices at the time of the Korean War, originally housed the School of Engineering. That school, rechristened the Rangoon Institute of Technology, has moved to a new campus built by the Soviet Union.

Typical urban buildings in downtown Rangoon have shops on the ground level and apartments above. Note the ever present black umbrellas, protection from both sun and rain.

Sule Pagoda, covered with gold leaf, is a small but old structure at the center of downtown Rangoon. Burmese believe it was built some 2,200 years ago.

Teak logs floated down the Irrawaddy River from Bahmo are pulled ashore at Mandalay by water buffalo.

This Burmese house on stilts, with walls of woven bamboo mats, its roof thatched with palm fronds, is in Naung-U, a village about four miles from Pagan proper. Beyond the house is the twelfth-century Thetkyamuni Temple.

A farmer and his daughter, with a plow drawn by two bullocks, prepare the soil for a crop of groundnuts (small peanuts), most of which will be pressed for cooking oil. Temples of Pagan are in the background.

A common sight in rural Burma is washday at Pyndia Lake, near Kalaw, a town in the hills of the Shan State.

Everywhere in the countryside of Burma are pagodas and bullock carts. At the right is a *chinthe*, a mythical lion that guards pagodas and temples.

Transplanting of rice seedlings in upper Burma is considered women's work, while preparing the main fields and caring for the seedbed is men's work.

Independence Monument rises from the middle of Maha Bandoola Square, which is always carefully landscaped, with the City Hall and Supreme Court as neighbors.

This street vendor in Rangoon sells medicinal herbs and roots, as well as cheroots. His descriptive sign is a good example of Burmese script. Such vendors have been less common in Burma's cities and towns since the Revolutionary Council took over.

This view of Sule Pagoda Road, one of Rangoon's busy downtown avenues, shows the Sule Pagoda in the background.

Young Pa-o women, with black tunics pulled down over drawn-up knees, sell produce from their household gardens at an open-air market in a small town near Taunggyi, in the Shan State.

Mintha and *minthami* are, respectively, male and female dancing and singing stars of *zats*.

This carved figure of Thagya Min, king of the major *nats,* who returns to earth at the Water Festival preceding the New Year, is covered with gold leaf and inset with colored glass "jewels."

An enormous *chinthe* guards one of the many-staired entrances to Mandalay Hill.

monk and went into the hills as a missionary. In the first year after the coup, a power struggle developed for the number two spot in the Council. Brigadier Aung Gyi, a practical-minded administrator, was second in command of the first government and, originally, of the Council. He was a gradualist, believing in the continuation of some free enterprise alongside socialism. This was a position permissible under the policy declaration, which allowed "national private enterprises which contribute to national productive forces." The more rigid ideologists, led by Brigadier Tin Pe, forced a showdown which led to Aung Gyi's resignation in early 1963. At first, the widower went with his only daughter to live in the hills. Later he returned to Rangoon and was held under arrest until 1968.

Brigadier Tin Pe's increased power strengthened the position of U Ba Nyein, General Ne Win's economic adviser. A graduate of the University of Rangoon, U Ba Nyein had gone to Australia for graduate study and returned an avowed Marxist. There is no public record that he ever visited Russia or China. Within weeks of the power struggle, the first large-scale act of nationalization occurred. All 31 banks in the nation were taken over, including those of India, Britain, and China.

SWEEP OF NATIONALISM

The Revolutionary Council did not introduce socialism into Burma. When the people were learning the ABC's of modern economics, it was Aung San himself who told them that "capitalism must face the modern music of history and transform itself into socialism." The word itself was not used in the first constitution, but phrases such as the "property of the people" and "the people's community," occurred frequently. The Union had the right to "resume possession of any land" or expropriate any property "if the people's interests required it." (To be sure, the same document guaranteed the right to private property.) Railroads, the vessels of the inland waterways, electric power, timber holdings, telephones, and telegraph had all been taken over by the Union government at independence, although some had been in private hands before the war. Most postwar politicians were socialists.

This acceptance of the idea of socialism may have had roots older than Aung San. In the days of the kings, the peasant expected the protection of the court in the possession and tilling of his own land. Otherwise most of the land belonged to the king. The ruby mines were the king's as were the forests. He controlled the export and import of goods. Small merchants and entrepreneurs were allowed to function, but larger affairs lay within the palace. Although the large world was the king's, his duties demanded that he protect his people in their smaller affairs. Fabians might not recognize this as socialism, but it bears a certain general resemblance to state-owned industries administered for the good of all the people.

Burmese who thought about socialism at all after independence tended to equate it with freedom from exploitation (that old bugaboo) in larger economic spheres, like a nonprofit, nonthreatening service agency operating the property of the people for the good of the people. Cushioned by socialism from both scarcities and impositions, the people would then be free to go about their smaller affairs as they chose. Hence, nationalization of the banks, which weren't used by most people anyhow, caused no particular furor.

Socialist-oriented economists outside of Burma were disturbed. They said banks were the wrong point of the economy at which to start socialization. Other outsiders suspected that nationalizing all banks was a way to take over the banks of China, whose funds had sometimes been lent to the Chinese community in Burma to coerce them into sending their sons to Chinese schools or giving general support to Mainland China. Given the ambivalence which must necessarily mark Burma's attitude toward its large neighbor, only such a universal act could make possible the individual one.

But in late 1963 and in 1964—a key year in several fields—nationalization whirled along at high speed. It started with commodity distribution, including import and export of goods, and moved rapidly through sawmills, rice mills, mines, cigaret manufacturing, and a wide range of other industries. The Peoples' Stores were also begun in 1964. Once again, the chief aim was to oust Indians, Pakistanis, Chinese, and other foreigners from control of the country's economic life. But it caught the Burmese as well, both as entrepreneurs and as consumers.

Off and on throughout the decade, nationalization continued, through private schools, private hospitals, movie houses, publications, and finally, to all sectors of industry. By the decade's end, although every segment of every industry had not been absorbed, the government was the dominant factor in every economic sector except agriculture. The administrative skills of the armed forces, who still had to fight insurgents on several fronts, were spread thin, and administrative efficiency was well below that of the Caretaker Government. Corruption in the Peoples' Stores and maldistribution provoked severe shortages of consumer goods and a thriving black market. The people were tasting socialism on a scale beyond their expectations.

In 1964, a Demonetizing Act was passed, declaring all K100* and K50 notes no longer legal tender. Once again, it was a measure aimed at the exploiters and the black-market operators. But of the 1.36 million who turned in their bills as ordered, over a million were Burmese citizens with K500 or less. Belatedly, three months later, the government announced that those who had deposited up to K4200 would receive refunds in full. Those who had deposited more than K4200 received an unspecified share as a refund.

Taxes, however, were a lesser burden. In 1964, the business

---

* Burmese money is based on a decimal system of coinage with 1 kyat equal to 100 pyas. It is a controlled money system, not permitted to find its value level on the international market. For many years, K4.76 have been considered equal to $1 U.S.

profit tax, the supertax, and the income tax were merged into one, with no distinction made between business and individuals. However, the tax was collected only on incomes over K4200; as nationalization proceeded and individual incomes declined, fewer and fewer paid the tax.

Because of inflation, caused partly by the shortage of goods, temporary taxes were levied in 1967, including one on the produce of state enterprises. But these failed to blot up the excess money in circulation and were repealed the following year. In 1970, the government did not look to large sums through taxation as a major source of revenue.

THE CIVIL COURTS

Since the days of the British, it has been Burma's good fortune to enjoy a series of Burmese judges of exemplary character and devotion to the concept of law, whatever their political beliefs. Such varied personalities as the conservative nationalist and devout Buddhist, U May Oung, judge of the High Court under the British, U Ba U, another judge of the High Court under the British and first Chief Justice after independence, and U Chan Htoon, adviser to the Constitutional Assembly and judge of the Supreme Court after independence, helped to establish such a tradition of quality. It has been continued in the persons of Dr. Maung Maung, Chief Justice of the Chief Court in the years of the Revolutionary Council.

All were trained as barristers in England; their respect for English law was great but fell well short of worship. Since independence, when top judges became their own men, they have attempted to blend the idea of British common law with that of Burmese customary law, which evolved from the Dhammathats and the customs of the people. U Ba U once called this "in a way, judge-made law" since it grew not out of codified laws but out of interpretation. Dr. Maung Maung has written of it as "living law," which should harmonize the statutes, living customs, and the people's notions of justice, equity, and good conscience.

Lesser judges in outlying district courts or even clerks in lower Rangoon courts might be tempted by "tea money," that small bribe, to move a case up on the docket or ease along a ruling. But men who wrote and thought like these leaders have consistently given a tone of quality to the Burmese judicial system.

Basic laws were not changed when the Revolutionary Council abrogated the 1948 Constitution. New laws, "promulgated" by the Council, were added to the code. Though socialist writers might occasionally denounce the whole system as colonial and write in glowing terms of such a judicial system as the Russian, by 1970 no such major shifts had occurred or seemed under consideration by the Council.

Two major changes did take place. The previous High Court and Supreme Court were merged into one called, in a free translation from the Burmese term, the Chief Court. It combined the duties of a final Court of Appeal with general supervision of all courts and judges in the Union. More subtle but more far-reaching was the decision of the Council that the same laws should apply to the entire nation. Previously, because of differing customs and circumstances, the states of the minorities had possessed a limited freedom to enact laws differing from common Burmese law.

Rebels and insurgents have disturbed internal security but, viewed in terms of the infractions of the usual laws of the criminal code, the nation in the 1960's was orderly and law-abiding. Penalties were severe for those active on the black market. Depending on the scope and degree of the crime, smugglers and black marketeers might be sentenced to two or three years' imprisonment plus a substantial fine, or, in flagrant cases, to life imprisonment.

Dr. Maung Maung introduced into the judicial system the concept of releasing ordinary criminal defendants on their own recognizance, without posting bail. This concept has had only experimental use in the United States. The chief justice has reported that the system works well and those charged do not leave the jurisdiction of the courts. In his opinion, it brings justice particularly to the poor of the rural areas who are almost never in a position to post a cash bond.

Justice remained even-handed to such a degree that at least once it startled the Burmese. Five Burmese youths were arrested in connection with the riots and anti-Chinese demonstrations which occurred in mid-1967. Brought to trial, they were convicted and sentenced to two-year terms. The court said it recognized that they had acted for love of country but pointed out that they had, nevertheless, broken the law. The Burmese public, who considered the young men patriots, did not wholly share the court's view. They were reconciled only by a sense of pride in the integrity of their law. Having made its point, the court in March, 1968, commuted the sentence to the time the young men had then served and released them.

Unionism

The Council's decision to make the same laws applicable throughout the Union was a fair reflection of the government's attitude toward the minority peoples. In the policy declaration of *The Burmese Way to Socialism,* the often-quoted words of Aung San were used as a text:

A nation is a collective term applied to a people, irrespective of their ethnic origin, living in close contact with one another and having common interests and sharing joys and sorrows together for such historic periods as to have acquired a sense of oneness. Though race, religion and language are important factors it is only their traditional desire and will to live in unity through weal and woe that binds a people together and makes them a nation and their spirit a patriotism.

Thirteen months after these words were spoken and less than a year before independence, Aung San and two other leaders of the AFPFL met with leaders of the minority peoples in a Shan village called Panglong to thresh out their differences and reach agreements which could lead to a united, free Burma. Where it seemed wise, as with the Kachins and Shans, Aung San promised separate states.

Though the spirit of Panglong has often been invoked by the Revolutionary Council, the federalism of Panglong became an anti-government position. Unionism replaced it. The goal was equality for all peoples, with no differences among them in responsibilities or privileges. Exceptions, such as differing laws, were ruled out. Genuine federalism, with equality between all states, had never been tried. The Burmese of Burma Proper had been always first among equals. But the brand of relationship which had been tried had not worked well; in that the Revolutionary Council was correct. The effort to raise all to the same equality seemed to its leaders the only reasonable method for maintaining the nation's unity.

In Unionism, separate states still existed, along with separate State Councils, appointed instead of elected, often with army officers as chairmen. In 1963 a new school called the Academy for the Development of National Groups was founded for selected cadres from the various minority groups. The study program of the academy continued for four years, providing the usual high school education, plus leadership training and a basic knowledge of the Burmese Way to Socialism. By living and working together, the young students also have presumably acquired a familiarity and respect for all the many ethnic cultures they represent. The size of the academy (286 students in 1969) and the length of the course precludes the idea that the government considered it a crash program. However, new schools, hospitals, and health clinics have been built in the several states to reinforce its effects. The academy represents what may be considered the flip side of the government's view of minorities—on the one hand Unionism and equality, on the other hand scrupulous respect and encouragement for cultural differences—a respect, as the Burmese of the plains were frequently reminded, that they too must offer to other peoples.

NEW MASS ORGANIZATIONS

Once it began, socialization of commerce and industry proceeded at almost precipitous speed. But the structures to support the Council's policy statement were organized much more deliberately and over a longer period. The first, both in time and in responsibility, was the Burma Socialist Program Party (BSPP) which was announced on July 4, 1962. Known in Burmese-English language publications as the *Lanzin* Party, or simply as *Lanzin,* its membership was strongest among the army and police. Technically, other parties were still allowed to exist, although political activity was frowned upon. In late March, 1964, other political parties in existence before the coup, notably the Socialist arm of the AFPFL and U Nu's Union Party, were invited to cooperate with the Council's program. When they refused, General Ne Win outlawed all other political parties and arrested those leaders not already in detention. The Lanzin Party became Burma's only political party, and membership from other sections of the population besides the armed forces was pushed. Although the Council made it plain that the Lanzin Party was being groomed to rule the country after the transitional period ended, there was no great rush to join. By the end of 1966 national membership totaled 185,000, of whom almost a third were from the armed forces or the police. Partly to remedy the situation, the party in 1966 established a Central School of Political Science where some 4,000 party cadres could be trained each year.

In that same year, however, the Council began the methodical building of two other organizations which would add some new members to the party but, even more important, would provide

ready channels through which masses of the people could theoretically be reached by party leaders. There were the Workers'
Councils and the Peasants' Councils.

In November, 1966, the first Management Training Course
was held for cadres who would lead the Workers' Councils. In
February, 1967, a similar course was held for peasant cadres.
Organizers then fanned out across the country to build local
councils. By April, 1968, enough Workers' Councils had been
organized so that the first conference of the Central Workers'
Council could be held. A colonel who was also a member of the
party's central body was elected chairman. Peasants, more numerous than workers and more widely scattered, were organized
more slowly. They did not meet to found their Central Peasants'
Council until February, 1969. Like the workers, they elected a
military officer as their chairman.

The purposes of both organizations were similar. They served
as the party's communication link with workers or peasants and
imbued their fellows with a sense of responsibility and purpose
to guard the tools of production and increase production where
the country needed it. They sent up through channels the complaints of their comrades, and received, in turn, directives for
them from central authorities. Not all workers and peasants were
members of a council in 1970, but the network was growing
steadily.

The army was still considered the "backbone of the party"
but its members were constantly exhorted to remember that
they were a people's army, that they must conduct themselves
as such, and that a sin against the people was the greatest sin
of all.

A New Constitution?

Exhortation was indeed a way of life until at times it seemed
as if the revolution might drown in a sea of words. Seminars,
lectures, short training courses were common fare, from a lecture

on the nature and behavior of the female (to a Rangoon girls' high school) to a short course in conducting a child care center for the women cigar workers in Mandalay—and both in their way were revolutionary subjects in this time and place.

But most of the words were hortatory, for this was an earnest and sober group of revolutionary missionaries, both unwilling and unable to use force to convert their people, to persuade them to stay the course through difficult times until they reached the "socialist affluent society."

This practice did not reflect the natural life style of the people. Even their religion did not expose them to constant preaching from their monks. Buddhism was an individualist's faith; the course each took was up to him alone. The Burmese are not laconic, but they are without the loquacious zeal of such a people as the Indians, who will argue pleasurably for hours over a concept or a principle about which they may care very little. The elders of a Burmese village will gather in the evening over a pot of tea to discuss the events of the day in talk laced with wit and earthy humor and in this relaxed fashion reach decisions for the village's tomorrow. But few leaders have held their attention with humorless, earnest exhortation. Aung San did. Men who heard him when they were young say that he was not really a good speaker and that he talked for long hours, while people who had come for miles sat patiently on their woven mats, their sleeping children beside them, and listened. But there was an exciting aura about that man who could be dark and moody or bright and gay as the spirit seized him, and the people would have followed wherever he led. The mantle of such a man falls automatically on no other.

Yet there were benefits to these constant lessons in participatory democracy which Council members attempted to teach their people. Peasants and ordinary workers in Burma are parochial. They travel little except to a nearby pagoda festival or a *pwe,* a secular entertainment (see Chapter 9). They have little time or money for such travel. Seminars gathered thousands together, often in Rangoon, where they met others like themselves, discovered common problems, gained a wider view of their own country. The courses were given everywhere on every subject and whether they accepted the new knowledge or not, these common people found that they were listened to when they spoke. Some even discovered a certain flair for speaking and for leadership. They could get complaints off their chests, about the weather or the quality of seed, the shortage of consumer goods or of spare parts which had stalled a factory, whether or not any action resulted from their complaints. At the least it was an event, this going somewhere and talking and listening, a change of pace in lives that held few happenings. The exhortations, which were repetitive, could always be ignored when the listener chose.

Besides, the unexpected sometimes happened. These earnest speakers could suddenly forsake ideology, turn pragmatic, and announce, as did General Ne Win while defending the coup at a Peasants' Seminar in 1966, "The armed forces took over power again against my most cherished principles. The power must be returned to the people where it rightfully belongs."

It was at another seminar that the General announced that the economy was a mess and that "if Burma were not a food-surplus country, the people would have starved." The words fed no one but people felt better for the public acknowledgment. While it might be infuriating to know that the government was no more able than the private citizen to stop the corruption which channeled legitimate goods into the black market, seldom were charges of corruption leveled against members of the Council. It happened once at the time of the Demonetizing Act when K100 and K50 bills were called in. Colonel Saw Myint, Minister of Information and Culture and secretary of the Central Organizing Committee of the BSPP, used his advance knowledge for his personal gain. He was stripped of his rank and sentenced to life imprisonment.

At one point, General Ne Win himself headed a committee

which reviewed the economy and "decontrolled" a long list of
34 basic food items, which meant that at least for a while private
retailers could deal in these commodities and not be considered
black marketeers.

Equally pragmatic and unsocialist was the one-per-cent collection fee granted in 1969 to village bank officials for collecting
delinquent agricultural loans, although the delinquents themselves may not have found it pleasant.

Even U Ba Nyein, the Council's economic architect and usually
an invisible man, spoke out in mid-1968 to a *New York Times*
reporter, saying that the corruption of the black marketeers was
"like gangrene." He said he thought, then, that the worst was
over. "After all, if it got any worse, we wouldn't survive."
Whether it could grow worse was a moot question. Whether it
improved as the months rolled on could also be argued.

Warnings against concentration of power in one clique and
"the intoxication of power" were a frequent theme of Ne Win,
along with references to the future when the people would again
hold power. But his first positive move on either subject occurred
in late 1968.

Under the title, "Union of Burma Internal Unity Advisory
Body," 33 men were called together for policy consultation. They
covered the whole spectrum of public opinion, including representatives of minorities and many political leaders who had
earlier been in detention, among them U Nu, Prime Minister
at the time of the coup. After long discussion, the group reported
to Ne Win in June, 1969. A majority approved a return to the
1948 constitution with whatever amendments were necessary for
a multi-party, democratic-socialist state. A minority opposed a
return to parliamentary democracy and called for a new constitution establishing a socialist state based on the power of the workers, with either a new single political party or a national united
front. On the matter of ethnic minorities, the majority proposed
a return to the earlier federal system, whereas a minority favored
a federal system of equal states modeled after that of the Soviet

Union, and three dissenters called for a unitary state with ethnic representatives in the cabinet.

U Nu filed an individual report. Under law he was still the legitimate head of the government, he said, and power should be restored to him. After that, he would reconvene Parliament and recommend that it elevate Ne Win to the office of President. This accomplished, U Nu would then transfer power to Ne Win legally, thus legitimizing the General's government. (There was no comment on the fact, which obviously both U Nu and the General knew, that under the 1948 Constitution, the office of the President, largely a figurehead post, was not the source of power.) *

All reports, including that of U Nu, were given coverage in Burma's newspapers. A specific response from the General was not immediate, though Council leaders intimated that all three proposals were rejected in favor of the BSPP.

In November, 1969, General Ne Win addressed the fourth annual seminar of the party, as its chairman. In the opening session, he talked at some length about the old constitution and its faults. Politicians of those days were young and inexperienced, he said, and the constitution was written and adopted in some haste.

(There was some truth in the charge of haste, but it had been necessary haste. Less than a year intervened from the time Aung San returned from London with the promise of freedom until it arrived in January, 1948. In that year, elections had to be organized and held for a Constituent Assembly, the document written, approved in London by Parliament, and preparations made for the actual Independence Day. Moreover, this process

---

* U Nu left Burma in April, 1969, ostensibly for a religious pilgrimage in India, made a trip around the world calling for support of a revolution to overthrow General Ne Win, and in 1970 was an exile in Thailand. He noted with what reluctance, as a devout Buddhist, he espoused violence, spoke with hope of uniting the ethnic dissidents in Burma against Ne Win, and declared he would accept support from anyone, including the Communists.

was violently interrupted by the assassination of Aung San in
1947. The young politicians, however, did have the guidance of
a 14-point resolution adopted at a General Convention of the
AFPFL in May, 1947, under the direction of Aung San.)

The major faults, according to General Ne Win, were the
lack of a specific pledge to socialism in the Constitution and the
lack of specific regulations to protect the people against greedy
politicians. Like the later constitutions of the Workers' Council
and Peasants' Council, the 1948 national Constitution provided
for the right of recall by citizens of all elected representatives.
It is a cumbersome process, as most democracies know. Evidently
the Council designers had found no better way.

The new constitution, General Ne Win said, must avoid these
errors and in draft form must be discussed and amended by the
people before it was passed by a Constituent Assembly. Implicitly
he seemed to be rejecting all reports of the Advisory Body.

At the closing session of the seminar, the Chairman spoke
again, this time about economic stringency, the breakdown of
commodity distribution, and the threat they posed to the building of socialism. He outlined a set of three new cooperatives
to be launched as a corrective: a network of Consumers' Cooperatives, Producers' Cooperatives, and a Cooperative Credit Society.
It had taken a year in preparation, he said, to train the needed
personnel and to work out a system which would eliminate the
present malpractices.

A new constitution and some form of new government seems
assured in Burma before the decade of the 1970's ends. There has
sometimes seemed to be even an edge of impatience to the General's words when he spoke of returning power to the people.
Presumably he has spoken for all the Council, though all may not
share his earnestness to give up power. But any public division
in the Council is improbable. When the nation is still threatened

by insurgents, the armed forces are unlikely to quarrel among themselves.

The desire of the Council is plainly for a socialist nation guided by the Lanzin Party, though perhaps with some still unspecified forms of those "democratic competitions" mentioned in the policy statement.

As General Ne Win implicitly recognized in his address to the seminar, the people judge the success or failure of the party not on the broad scope of its program but on its simple, everyday ability (or lack of it) to distribute the necessary commodities of clothing, rice, cooking oil, and medicines, and to punish the corruption which interferes with that distribution. The kind of government the people will choose when power is returned to them may rest on just such a judgment rather than the exhortations of their socialist teachers.

5 Burma's Economy

A strong push toward development in any underdeveloped country demands a large input of capital, whether the country operates under a socialist, capitalist, or mixed economy. Since capital investment needs are proportionately greater at the outset than they will be later, this developmental capital will force a postponement of investments which would be directed toward the consumer market of a more affluent society. To a degree, each developing nation exploits itself and its workers.

Since Burma equates foreign investors with exploiters, these large capital sums must come from within the nation, except for strings-free long-term loans from abroad. However, the circumstances of colonialism and the tenets of Theravada Buddhism which oppose the accumulation of wealth have made extremely rare the Burmese national with funds available for important capital investment. Hence, whatever the political ideology of the nation, such large-scale investment funds must come from the Burmese government. An informed American economist, E. E. Hagen, estimated in the 1950's that such investment funds would demand annual savings of 18 per cent of the country's gross national product.

In this period of heavy investment, the development cycle must create not only sources of production but the social and physical infrastructure to make such development possible. Basic schools must be built and staffed to create a literate population. A farmer must be able to read the pamphlets which describe new agricultural methods or the instructions on a bag of fertilizer. Technical and higher education must be widely available to produce the technicians, the administrators, and the intellectuals needed in the new society. Health facilities will need expansion, if only for the practical reason that a healthy population has the vigor to work and to produce.

A transportation network will be required, a pipeline to a refinery, secondary roads to get crops to market, trucks and/or inland water vessels for distribution of raw materials to factories and finished goods to consumers, and, in this country short of main roads, a wide-flung internal airline.

Yet the nation will find, as all such nations do, that every new school or hospital built in one year demands a share of the operating budget in the following year and makes it more difficult to keep up the large investment budget, the forced savings of the country.

The goals of all Burmese governments since independence have remained much the same, even though the means to reach them have been more elusive than the nation expected on that January morning when independence came. Stated with cheerful optimism, they run something like this: This is a pleasant land, blessed with fertile soil more than ample to feed us, with raw materials in forests and mines, with good possibilities for hydroelectric power, and with an intelligent people. For many years we were an exploited nation while a colonial power drew wealth out of our country. Now from the same resources, we can build a society where man is not exploited, where health, education, and a comfortable life are the heritage of all our people.

It was true enough, according to Britain's own records, that Burma more than paid its own way as a province of India. Hagen gives a figure of prewar savings at 16 per cent of the gross national product, most of it from large foreign enterprises. But the base from which this profit was figured provided a lower Burmese standard of living than the one which modern Burma demanded. Nor did the same facilities exist after independence. War and postwar insecurity had brought grave destruction, and various insurgent movements were still continuing. There was no shortage of intelligent personnel, but it was thwarted by lack of administrative skills and practical experience with modernization, tasks assigned largely to British and Indians in colonial days. Brisk decision-making was hampered by more than lack of skill. After all, training could be, and was, given to bright young minds. But civil servants still felt the deadening hand of tradition. Under the British, it had always been safer to pass the papers on to a higher desk and avoid the possibility of an error. Under the Burmese life style, it was customary to defer to an elder for final judgment.

Despite the fact that some progress had been made since 1948, the Revolutionary Council inherited all these old problems. Whatever the people's optimism, for council members as for earlier politicians, there was still the old necessity of finding the large sums needed for capital investments. The economy still had to be viewed in terms of what could be produced domestically to fill the people's needs, and what could be produced for sale abroad. Those exports had to provide the major portion of the nation's savings for capital development, after the necessary purchases of consumer goods not yet produced at home.

One major change, under the Revolutionary Council, was the injection of the total socialist goal. With the organization of Workers' Councils, Peasants' Councils, and the projected cooperatives, the common man, the *ludu* of Burma, was being structured and cajoled into the role of active participant. The pleasant land of plenty, under the Burmese Way to Socialism, was to be everyone's responsibility, realized not in immediate profit, but by selfless love of country and of brother.

It was an ambitious effort, not least in the psychological reformation of an independent, traditional peasantry. Yet it must succeed in agriculture or it could succeed nowhere, for agriculture was still the sector which made the economic wheels go round.

EXTRACTIVE PRODUCTION

Agriculture

Before the British came, the agricultural products of Burma were not a part of its foreign commerce. Rice in particular did not leave the country. Growing rice was the business of most able-bodied adults, but it was more than a business. It was a communion and a ceremony. Each year when the planting time came, the king with pomp and ritual plowed the first stretch of land.

All this changed when the British annexed Lower Burma in 1853. The Irrawaddy Delta, with proper ditching and drainage, yielded heavy rice harvests. The Suez Canal, opened a few years later, made shipping for export easy. The expansion of paddy acreage was rapid, from about 100,000 acres in 1850 to 8,550,000 acres in 1900 and to 12,800,000 in 1940.

The Burmese farmer could not finance this enormous expansion, even though land was available for the clearing of it. Before the end of the nineteenth century, ownership of land was falling increasingly into the hands of absentee landlords, who were often chettyars, the Indian moneylenders. The absentee landlord with large holdings and the poor landless tenant had not been the norm in Burmese history. The first Tenancy Act was not passed until 1939; by then half the land in Lower Burma was owned by absentee landlords. Rice growers were impoverished even though in the year the Tenancy Act was passed 3.3 million tons of rice were exported from Burma.

The war solved one part of the problem. The chettyars fled to India ahead of the Japanese and did not return. But when the war and the insecurity of the early postwar years drove people off the land, paddy acreage quickly reverted to a tangled snarl of jungly growth. In 1945, tilled paddy land had dropped to 6.6 million acres, little more than half the 1940 area.

In independent Burma the peasants returned neither to the ways of the kings nor to those of the British. The new life, which was to be everyone's heritage, had to be financed; rice was the most easily available coinage on the international market. Therefore, the largest responsibility for development funds was laid on the backs of the tillers. But with fresh memories of their plight in prewar days, the government passed new laws for their protection.

These laws in the 1950's set rents approximately equal to land revenue—K3.5 an acre. This alone was a discouragement to absenteeism since an absentee landlord received no more in rent than he paid in land taxes. In 1965 land rents were abolished. Tenants are assigned land in the vicinity of a village by a Village Tenancy Committee, not by the landlords. A Land Nationalization Act, permitting maximum holdings of only 50 acres, was also passed in 1953; several million acres of land under the act have been distributed to new owners by Village Land Committees. Holdings are seldom large, usually running no more than 10 acres per family.

A shortage of land is not one of Burma's present problems and may not be for some time. Authorities estimate arable land at 55 million acres. Not all this acreage is conveniently near a village, however, and the Burmese are no longer natural pioneers. They dislike leaving friends and relatives, building a new settlement, and clearing virgin soil. Until the need becomes acute or the rewards highly enticing, such new settlements are unlikely to become common.

The problem of credit was less easily solved than land. It is unclear how the farmer financed himself in the days of the kings. But since the time of the chettyars, the need to borrow in order to put in a crop has been considered a legitimate necessity and the need to provide the loans a legitimate government responsibility. Following independence, the new government cleared the books for farmers by canceling some K60 million in outstanding agricultural loans granted by the postwar interim government. Although needed agricultural credit was over K100 million annually, early post-independence governments were able to provide only about K40 million. Farmers turned to indigenous moneylenders and repaid in kind—with rice—at harvest's end. But rice in December was worth much more than it had been at planting time in May. The lender's profit was large. As compensation, the Union government between 1949 and 1960 wrote off overdue loans totaling over K100 million, 16 per cent of all government agricultural loans made in those years.

After 1962, the Revolutionary Council provided a sum closer to the annual need, though that sum has increased because of inflation. But of a total advance of K151.2 million in 1966–67, over half was not repaid. Similar deficits have been reported for later years. For the opening of the 1969 planting season, the People's Bank and Village Banks operated under new directives. Village Bank committees managed the banks, made the loans, and collected them. Each collector was to receive one per cent of the sums he collected. At this writing in early 1970, it is still too soon to tell if the new system will be successful.

The presumption in official circles is that the peasant simply has fallen into the habit of not repaying loans because of earlier write-offs. But there may be another reason. With his rice, the tiller has provided the lion's share of exports, and hence the source of most imports and development funds. He cannot bargain in selling his rice. He must accept the government's purchase price. Beyond a basic profit (i.e., the difference between tilling costs and the government's paddy price), tillers have been expected to reap most of their rewards along with the rest of the nation in the fruits of development. In terms of consumer goods, health facilities and schools, these reached the isolated farm community more slowly than the cities and district towns. Not bothering to repay government loans may have become an indirect method of claiming part of the profits farmers believed were due them.

It is true that the Revolutionary Council has shown a greater concern than earlier governments in extending education and health facilities to rural areas. Irrigation facilities have also been greatly increased. But consumer goods have either decreased in quantity or increased in price. In particular there is a scarcity of cotton textiles for clothing and of cooking oil, which, in 1969, cost almost six times the pre-1962 price. There's a vicious circle here. As rice exports drop, imports, including textiles and cooking oils, also must drop. Between high prices and poor distribution of goods, the tiller shows less alacrity to increase rice production, or to double-crop with peanuts (for oil) or with cotton—or to repay his loans.

The farmer hasn't been without his achievements. In 1969, paddy land for the first time equaled the prewar acreage of 12.8 million acres. Over 19 million acres were sown to all crops, slightly surpassing the 1940 figure. But rice exports have not reached one million tons since 1966 although through the 1950's they regularly surpassed that figure.

Planners may have to forget the huge rice exports of prewar years and rework the economy without them. Burma's population has grown from 16 million in 1941 to over 26 million in 1970. More rice is needed to feed more mouths. In addition, Burma's leading rice customers, India, Pakistan, Ceylon, Indonesia, and Japan, have either reached self-sufficiency in rice or are striving to reach it. Miracle rice and the swift Green Revolution have changed the outlook for rice exporters. To substitute other agricultural exports in the quantity of rice would be difficult, but import replacements can be grown for cotton yarn and textiles, sugar, cooking oil, and tobacco. The sources of all these finished products are already grown by Burmese farmers. The crops merely need increasing, to save millions of kyats in imports or to reduce the shortages which lack of imports brings. Farmers resist this kind of diversification and the year-round work of double-cropping with irrigation. The government hopes that the Peasants' Councils will provide the motivation.

Fishing

Not all Burmese Buddhists will catch fish, but most will eat fish. Even a higher percentage will use *ngapi*, the fish paste prized as a condiment. Fishing is not a full-time occupation for an appreciable number, nor are fish often raised as a crop, from planted fingerlings in irrigation ponds or flooded paddy fields, as in some other Southeast Asian countries. Fresh-water fish are taken from the numerous streams and rivers either by netting or with a long basket trap skillfully plopped down over the fish in a shallow stream. Being a river people, the Burmese from long habit have preferred fresh-water fish in spite of their lengthy southern coastline. During the Caretaker Government (1958–60) the army invested in a fleet of seagoing fishing vessels which brought excellent ocean fish to the Rangoon markets. In 1968–69 the total catch was 408,000 tons, an increase of 18,000 tons over the previous year; 294,000 of those tons were caught in the ocean.

Lumber

Since westerners first entered Burma for trade in the sixteenth century, the land's teak has been highly prized. Then it was used for ships. Today it is more often used for furniture and cabinetwork. Export of teak before independence averaged around 200,000 tons. In recent years exports have been pushed upward. The latest published figures, for 1968–69, reached 320,000 tons. With its drop in exports and its deficit budgeting, which began in that year, the increase in felling teak must have been welcome to the nation. Other hardwood exports totaled 981,000 tons in the same year, an increase of almost 100,000 tons.

The wealth of the forests, even the reserved forests, has always been at the mercy of slash-and-burn agriculture, and of villagers felling trees for sale as firewood. Increased cuttings may increase erosion of the land and leave Burma with a major reforestation problem like that of other countries which have stripped their trees too rapidly. In contrast, judicious management of the forests may yield a continuous wealth to justify the hopes of those who envision teak and hardwood exports replacing, for years to come, part of the drop in rice exports.

Bamboo

Bamboo is ubiquitous in Burma both in its habitat and its usage. It can be a major part of a village home, the scaffolding around a new urban building project, or piping to carry water from a spring to a hillside village. It also provides the pulp used in a paper mill which the Chinese were building before they tried to export the Cultural Revolution to Burma in 1967. The ensuing disorders resulted in the withdrawal of Chinese technicians. The completed factory has not yet brought about large-scale paper production in Burma. Some optimists add paper to the list of possible exports for a future Burmese economy. They see the whole Asian area in need of paper for which Burma could become a major supplier. But bamboo is not unique to Burma. The validity of the dream is open to question.

Rubber

Rubber has been a small but constant factor in Burmese exports for many years, though the quantity has varied erratically from season to season, presumably from lack of tappers willing to bother with harvesting the latex or from fluctuations in the world price. Sometime or other, the government will want to stand still long enough to replant the plantations with new high-yield trees and wait out the eight years necessary before tapping them can begin. Otherwise, in even small quantities, world competition will make the harvest uneconomical.

Mineral Production

Exploration for new oil wells followed rapidly and successfully on the heels of the nationalization of the British-Burma joint-venture Burma Oil Company in 1963. Since Burma's needs for both kerosene and gasoline have been rising steadily, the increased petroleum production has been a bright spot in an inadequate economy. Total consumption rose from 136 million gallons in 1963 to 220 million in 1969. In spite of this, the new wells have ended the temporary postwar dependence on imports. Burma now has two oil refineries, one near the old wells at Chauk, another at Syriam near Rangoon. They were working at 75 per cent of capacity in 1969, but full capacity was expected shortly. Since her own requirements are expected to increase steadily, Burma doesn't talk of becoming an exporter of oil again.

It is difficult not to share the nation's optimism about mining developments and their implications for the country's future. Many hills and mountains are still unexplored, many new deposits of minerals have been found by geological teams in the last few years. They range from new deposits of lead, zinc, and silver to antimony, fluorite—used for smelting iron to make steel —and beryl, a strategic metal in making rockets. Not all of these are yet available in working mines, and where older mines are being worked, Burma has no choice but to export their production as unrefined ores and concentrates. Export of these minerals dropped in the 1960's, at first because private owners feared nationalization and later because of a lack of technology and security in the mineral areas. The Director-General of the Mineral Development Corporation reported late in 1968 that costs of state enterprises were often greater than those of private enterprises, a discrepancy he hoped to correct. Coal and iron deposits await field exploitation; thus far, domestic coal has been inferior to imported coal. In the long run, however, mineral production should aid Burma not only with raw exports but in her own industrialization.

Jade, precious gems, and pearls may seem out of place along-side zinc and lead, but they also play a share in Burma's economy. Along with finds of other minerals, a new outcrop of pure jade —30 feet high and 80 feet in circumference—has been reported by the Corporation. Natural pearls are found in the far south, off the coast of Mergui. The Revolutionary Council has in-stituted an annual Burma Gems, Jade, and Pearl Emporium for foreign buyers, which in 1969 netted sales of K11,535,369. Highlight of the emporium was the sale of a single ruby for K300,000, or roughly $60,000. Sales for 1970, the first emporium after nationalization, were not yet available.

INDUSTRIAL PRODUCTION

The Revolutionary Council has enunciated a five-point indus-trial policy: Industry will (1) produce those goods needed to aid agriculture, (2) produce basic consumer goods to raise living standards, (3) use domestically produced raw materials to save foreign exchange, (4) produce goods as substitutes for imports, (5) produce goods meeting international standards for exports.

No formal plan has been announced to reach these goals, but a pattern can be discerned in what the government has done. Technical education to train workers and middle administrators has been greatly expanded (see Chapter 8). New factories have been built; these have been more widely dispersed through the country so that all do not cluster in Rangoon or its satellite towns. Examples include two fertilizer plants, two more mills for extracting oil from rice bran (making 12 in all), new textile mills, two plywood factories, a glass bottle factory whose produc-tion in part will supply the needs of the older Burma Phar-maceutical Industry, a third cement plant, a paper mill. Some have been built with long-term loans and technical assistance from Japan, West Germany, or (previous to the mid-1967 dis-turbances) from China. Only on-going nonindustrial projects have been aided with U.S. funds, except for a large, electrically operated teak sawmill under construction in 1969.

Through agreements signed in 1962 with Japanese interests, plants were set up in Burma to assemble cars, trucks, tractors, and transistor radios. The output of the first three has been rather small but is growing. Radio production rose to 31,000 in 1968–69.

In 1970 there was no shortage of hydroelectric power. Burma's resources were not generating power to full capacity, and of that generated, less than half was used for industrial needs.

To prepare for its vast capital investments, the Union government began amassing foreign exchange and gold, which broke previous records in 1965, peaked in June, 1968, and then began to decline. Plainly its capital investment plan had been a long-range one, which the government had expected to support along with necessary imports of consumer goods during the interim of development. Various factors have intervened.

Retail distributors of consumer goods were among the early businesses to be nationalized. These were replaced by neighborhood Peoples' Stores. Even with government backing, the stores could not match the intricate network of the former retail outlets which had extended through large city shops and bazaars down through the small bazaars of the villagers. Even in Rangoon, distribution broke down. Sometimes the cause was inefficiency. Sometimes it was corruption, with goods destined for the Peoples' Stores appearing on the black market. The most common goods, such as cotton longyis, condensed milk, even at intervals rice and cooking oil, have often been rationed.

With the drop in legally purchasable goods, the cultivator reduced sales of rice to the government for export. In 1967–68, exports dropped to 0.34 million tons,* an all-time low, although

---

* To match annual statistics with annual calendric events, it is useful to know that rice grown in one calendar year is exported in the following calendar year, and that Burma's fiscal (and statistical) year is not calendric but runs from September to September.

the nation's increase in rice production was reported to be a million tons over the previous year.

But along with foreign reserves, the money supply in the country also reached an all-time high, partly because of generous agricultural loans pumped into the economy to urge the tillers into greater rice production. Because repayments were low, the money was not later taken out of circulation. Inflation set in and prices climbed.

These factors forced the government to dip into its foreign reserves not only for capital investments but for the consumer goods the export receipts normally would have covered. Every government has expanded or contracted imports when necessary as a means of controlling the economy. In earlier years there was more fat, more luxury goods, to decrease. After 1967–68, the government, faced with more drastic choices, cut basic consumer imports heavily. Cooking oil, cotton textiles, condensed milk, and pharmaceuticals were sharply reduced. Basic machinery and transport equipment, necessary for the long-range development plan and by far the largest items among imports, decreased only moderately. The choice had been made in favor of the long-range development of the country.

In an effort to make the choice workable, the government decreased the size of agricultural loans, which had reached a one-year peak of K500 per tiller (for certain crops), and instituted severe penalties for black-market activities. General Ne Win announced plans to organize Consumers' Cooperatives which would in time replace most of the Peoples' Stores, both to improve commodity distribution and reduce prices.

Urban and Industrial Labor

Out of a labor force of approximately 10 million, there are roughly 3.2 million "physical and mental workers," to use the Burmese phrase, who are not employed in agriculture. Over half a million are employed in each of the fields of public administration, trade, and industry. There are over 200,000 technicians and intellectuals (teachers, journalists, etc.), and more than 300,000 in transport and communications. The balance are employed in forestry, construction, mines, electricity, and various miscellaneous classifications. These are the men and women eligible to become members of the Workers' Councils, heirs to the nation's labor legislation to which the councils trace their genealogy.

The first legislative acts were derived from late-nineteenth-century British legislation transferred to Burma and India in the early decades of the twentieth century, including the first Trades Union Act of 1926 and the Trades Disputes Act of 1929. But before independence Burmese nationals were not dominant members of the work force, outside of agriculture and a few other exceptions, notably the Chauk oil fields. It was the oil-field workers who staged Burma's first workers' strike in 1938, against the Burma Oil Company.

The strike was brief, passionate, and—if a strike is to be measured in terms of the improvement of the workers' condition—unsuccessful. But this strike, organized and led by the thakins, was basically a political demonstration (in this case against the British colonial government and "exploiters"), not the act of a group of trade unionists. It set the pattern of trade unions in Burma. Before independence, they were the willing arm of nationalist leaders. They enabled Aung San to paralyze Rangoon with strikes; they helped the AFPFL claim leadership in the interim government. It is a natural coincidence that Workers' Day was celebrated in the oil fields on May 1, 1964, where a seminar of workers approved the draft of the Burmese Socialist Program Party's law on workers' basic rights and responsibilities.

If the workers served well the cause of nationalism before independence, they did less well in serving the nation after independence, when different unions acted as the political arm of various leaders within the AFPFL, using their votes as part of the leaders' bargaining power. Geared toward political power, they never learned the trade-union principles of bargaining from the discipline of their industrial power and productivity.

Of the various pieces of labor legislation passed in the 1950's, the most important was probably the Social Securities Act of 1954, drafted with the aid of the International Labor Office. In the beginning implementation was limited, but it has grown steadily until it now covers 500,000 workers. This is still a minority of workers. Some K3.721 million were paid in workers' benefits in 1966–67, with an additional K3.8 million in medical care. All the old basic laws have also been amended at one time or another. The Trades Union Act was amended in 1959, under the Caretaker Government, withdrawing unions from politics by limiting members and officers to workers and prohibiting the establishment of political funds. It was by an amendment to the Trades Disputes Act that the Central Workers' Council was substituted for the old Industrial Court.

The rights of workers written into law cover all the basics, beginning with the right to work and ending with the right to security in old age. The government has not yet been able to provide all the advantages the laws cover. There is some unemployment. Almost 225,000 applicants registered at the Rangoon Employment Exchange in 1966–67, the last year for which figures have been published. Only 38,785 workers were placed on jobs. Nor can all university graduates find employment "commensurate with ability and skill." The minimum wage is K82 a month or K3.15 per day for casual labor. A 1959 study of income and expenditures among selected Rangoon families showed that families with a monthly income of K200 or more were able to pay their bills but that under K200, families slid into debt.

Many families contain more than one wage earner. Both in the 1948 Constitution and in basic workers' laws, women are specifically guaranteed equal rights with men, plus maternity leave. But men in general earn higher wages than women as intellectuals, agricultural workers, and industrial workers. The cheroot (cigar) industry, where women workers dominate, was paying its women workers K62 a month, according to figures published in Rangoon in June, 1969.

The major complaint of workers, as with agriculturists, has been the insufficiency of consumer goods.

Workers have often been criticized in print. In 1969, the *Working People's Daily* charged that they were more concerned with their rights than their responsibilities. The chairman of the Port Workers' Council said the "undesirable machinations of bureaucracy" had increased after 18 months of Workers' Council activities. But the *Guardian* magazine, which had been strongly rebuking workers in 1967 for not rising to their opportunity "despite their liberation from their age-old oppressions and exploitation," wrote this in October, 1969:

> Socialist consciousness is well and good, but it cannot possibly thrive on an empty stomach. The ascending cost of living has done much to demoralize workers of all sorts. Till now these arduous and well-meaning efforts [to reduce the cost of living] have not proved effective. Consumer goods are not too scarce but they clearly are not properly distributed. We are really chary of reiteration because we know that the authorities have been aware of the defects and are taking measures to correct them. Good results or even an indication of good results is hard to be seen as yet, and the people are fretful.

OVERVIEW

In the period of development, the social infrastructure of schools, hospitals, and health clinics, along with basic building of transportation facilities, may demand large quantities of investment capital, but they may often not be recognized by the individual citizen as a necessary base for increasing his personal wealth.

This is one reason that a developing agricultural nation puts as top goals the production of goods needed to aid agriculture and of basic consumer goods to raise living standards. The two fertilizer plants in Burma fall within this group; the use of fertilizer doubled in 1968–69 to 140,000 tons. This was a small quantity for almost 20 million acres of sown land, but it was improvement, even though the farmers complained about the cost of fertilizer. When the two plants are in full production early in the 1970's, the needs of the country should be met.

Many of the consumer products manufactured at the new factories filled urban needs for cement, tiles, plywood. Two kinds of factories are aimed at raising living standards of both urban and rural peoples—namely, the textile mills and the mills to extract cooking oil from rice bran. But textile mills were hampered when imports of cotton yarn had to be cut, and much of the extracted oil was of industrial, not edible, quality.

The government could point to a success, and to proof of the people's technical skills, in the new oil wells discovered, drilled, and exploited. It could suggest that patience was necessary and single out, as proof, two ventures of earlier governments, only now becoming successful. The Burma Pharmaceutical Industry as late as 1960 was still a source of irritation. Its defenders could only say at best that "it could become a useful asset." In 1970 it still did not produce all the nation's medicinal needs. But if it didn't exist physicians would be clamoring for such an industry. Burma's steel mill for scrap metal, long looked upon as no more than a sop to national pride, earned a profit for the first time in 1968.

In late 1969, an agreement was signed for a venture which possibly could remake the entire Sittang River valley, in co-operation with the United Nations Development Special Fund Project.

But all this added up to a poor track record after eight years of government by the Revolutionary Council. The people were "fretful." They still lacked those "basic consumer goods to raise living standards," whether the lack centered in the goods themselves, the prices, or the maldistribution.

A new nationwide system of distribution such as the network

of consumer cooperatives announced in late 1969 by General Ne Win cannot be built in a season. The Burmese, but particularly the Burmese women who previously operated the stalls in the country's bazaars, are not unsophisticated in the skills needed for distributing the goods the customers want. These are not the same skills needed to make a cooperative function. Until the Burmese have mastered the Workers' Councils and Peasants' Councils, another organization—one demanding decisions mutually arrived at after group examination of alternatives—may only bog down in a morass of rhetoric.

Yet a successful system of consumer goods distribution could greatly advance a solution to the problems the agricultural sector suffered in the 1960's. The first sign of improvement was visible in 1969, when peasants sold 600,000 tons of rice to the government for export. Though far short of sales in earlier years, it was the first upturn since the drop began some five years earlier. A better price for early sales plus better security conditions—and an ample supply of transistor radios available for purchase in the rural markets—were given the credit.

The farmer everywhere is a traditionalist; to urbanites he can seem recalcitrant because he changes slowly. When someone pushes him too hard, he pushes back. In Burma, the government has been disappointed because tractors imported at fair expense are underused, because new rice seeds are resisted, along with new techniques, double-cropping, and diversification of crops.

In other countries of Southeast Asia, agricultural experts unanimously defend the farmer's ability, but point out that he won't gamble with change because it means gambling with his family's livelihood. When he can see a farmer like himself succeeding with a new crop or new method on land like his own, and profiting from it, then he will change. The Burmese tiller is no different.

Each developing nation periodically reviews its developmental plans to be certain that all portions are in balance. Although, to a degree, it must exploit itself and its workers, the exploitation cannot become so burdensome that living standards drop rather than rise. Such a review could be termed the major economic responsibility of the Revolutionary Council in the transitional decade of the 1970's.

6 The Peoples

The variety of Burma's many peoples is complex and sometimes confusing. The usual ethnic, cultural, and linguistic distinctions which are presumed to be the hallmarks of a people or a tribe somehow don't always fit the actualities. All are Mongoloid, which has no more precise meaning than saying that the people of Europe are all Caucasians. Some are stockier or darker than others, and intermarriage has often blurred the types so that the job of the physical anthropologist is made difficult. But in general they are all rather short, somewhat over five feet, slight of frame, with straight black hair, high cheek bones, skin that is soft brown and fairer than that of the peoples of India, and dark eyes that lack the pronounced Mongoloid fold of the Chinese, Japanese, and Koreans. The men are often handsome, the women frequently quite beautiful.

Though some speak one of several Mon-Khmer languages and some speak a form of Tai, the languages of the majority of all these peoples fall within the Tibeto-Burman classification. But no one in Burma, nor any authority on that country, can name with assurance of accuracy the number of languages spoken here. Nor does each people remain tidily in the areas marked on the map, making itself readily available for study and counting. In the Shan State, for instance, almost half the people are not Shans.

When a census is taken (the last complete one was in 1931),

it is not enough to count as an ethnic group the individuals who live in a particular state or district. The question must always be asked, "What is the language customarily spoken in the home?" Even this may not always serve to determine who is what. Some people will change languages as casually as they change coats, while others who have moved into a new area will adopt the new language for all public purposes, yet in their home cling stubbornly and for generations to the language which they brought with them. Nor has anyone been able to figure out why some will discard the familiar language so readily and others will continue to cling to its usage within the family, at any cost, to set themselves apart, to mark their difference.

The Four Majorities

A minority is only a minority because a majority lives nearby. Minorities here seldom borrow from each other but rather from the cultures of such majorities. They are the ones who give the minorities a window on the wider world. Because of Burma's multiplicity of peoples, the easiest way to start threading through this maze is with a look at the nation's majorities, the more developed peoples.

There have been and still are four such peoples in Burma—the Burmans, the Shans, the Mons, and the Arakanese. To include the Arakanese goes against the theoretical rules because they also speak Burmese. But the realities of centuries of history leave them with a sense of separateness which defies the absence of basic ethnic or cultural differences.

Each of the four has a long history of such characteristics as a social structure which extends beyond the limits of a village or a village-cluster, an economic organization complex enough to provide the wherewithal for trade outside the basic boundaries, a common knowledge of identity held between all the parts, a common language, and a religion which is a more developed faith than animism.

Each has a written language of some antiquity. The Burman alphabet developed from that of the Mon, while the Shan script markedly resembles the Burman. This is especially interesting since the three languages represent the three major linguistic classifications of the area, Mon-Khmer, Tibeto-Burman, and Tai, and do not themselves resemble each other.

Some minorities tell legends of ancient days when they knew written languages now forgotten, but most who have alphabets and writing have possessed them only since the days of the nineteenth-century Christian missionaries who devised the alphabets and put the various spoken languages into writing.

Theravada Buddhism

One basic cultural influence is shared by these four peoples. They are all Theravada Buddhists and have been for centuries. The enormous importance of a shared religion, in terms of the eventual unity of Burma, cannot be overemphasized. These four have fought each other, ruled over each other, sometimes hated each other. Yet because they share a faith, they share values and a certain inescapable brotherhood.

Professional observers understand this. The more casual reader can find proof if he will look afresh at his own world, where basic values stem from our Judaic-Christian heritage. There, the concern for the individual is such a value and can be phrased in many ways. One of the oldest is, "But even as ye do it unto the least of these, ye do it unto me." One of the newest is, "Caution, do not spindle, bend, or mutilate. This is a human being." But the value is the same. Religious values have become social values. Arguments about what is moral or immoral are more frequently social arguments than religious.

So it is with the Buddhists in Burma. Probably among these

four peoples there are more practicing religionists than among the people of the United States. Perhaps they are no better Buddhists than we are Christians or Jews. But religious values have become social values which all four share, and the taproot runs as deep for them as it does for us.

Of the four advanced peoples in Burma, today it is the dominant Burmans from whom most minorities accept or resist culture-change; therefore the proper place to begin a discussion of Buddhism is with the Burman view of it. This will not be a philosophical discussion of a religion. (One cannot use the term "theological" because there is no God in Buddhism.) It will be an attempt, rather, to portray Buddhism as the Burman common people (the *ludu*) view it and are influenced by it culturally.

Gautama Buddha was born around 600 B.C., the son of a prince in northwest India. To keep his son content within the palace, the father gave him beauty and riches there. But when he was a young man the Buddha left the palace walls and saw the suffering of mankind. Over and over on the pagoda platforms of Burma, figures portray the sights which the Buddha saw, the old, the sick, and the dying. The last portrayal is always the same, his beautiful, young wife sleeping with their son at her breast, as the Buddha presumably saw her when he abandoned the palace for the last time to seek a way to save mankind from the pain he had seen.

First he went to sit at the feet of Hindu wise men, but he could not find the truth in their teachings. Then he went alone into the forest as an ascetic, but fasting and the neglect of his body brought him no nearer his goal. So he bathed, rested, refreshed his body with food and drink, and seated himself under a bo tree where he meditated until Enlightenment came. He was 35 then; until his death as an old man, he taught his disciples what he had learned.

What the Buddhists of Burma, Thailand, Cambodia, Laos, and Ceylon believe that the Buddha taught is contained in Theravada

Buddhism, the "teachings of the elders." The Buddhists of these lands can communicate directly with each other about their faith; they understand each other. Buddhists in China, Tibet, Japan, Nepal, and Vietnam are Mahayana Buddhists, divided into many sects of great variety whose teachings differ widely. Burmese believe, with some feeling of superiority but no antagonism, that Mahayana sects are Buddhism's deviants because some men are weak and need supernatural crutches to aid them—someone to pray to, for instance, some way besides their own difficult individual effort to reach Nirvana. Mahayanists have such "saints."

Much of what the Buddha taught can be found in Hinduism, but much that is present in Hinduism he rejected. Men are bound to the wheel of life by their own greed and desires, and until they free themselves of these desires they are doomed to be born again and again to the sufferings of life. Each rebirth is determined by Karma, the inexorable Buddhist law of cause and effect. The more a man indulges his selfhood in one life, the more pain he inherits in the next. There is a way to be free, but even for the Buddha it took many lifetimes. There must be self-discipline of the body; even more, a man must overcome the transitory illusion of selfhood until, after long lives of contemplation and meditation, he escapes through Enlightenment to Nirvana.

Nirvana is hard to explain. It is all-knowing, all-joyous, all-oneness; it is a void, it is a holy nothingness. Each man must find his own way there. For the Theravada Buddhist, there is neither god nor saint to whom he can pray for help, not even the Buddha who himself is in Nirvana now.

The key is contemplation and meditation. The physical principles of simple meditation can be taught, and even the beginnings of the strict mental discipline which is necessary, but after that each man is on his own. Laymen as well as monks may meditate, but it isn't expected that the meditation of ordinary laymen will ever reach the profound spiritual quality that a monk may achieve. Even women may meditate, though a woman is something of a second-class citizen in Buddhism. Women are among the most devout Buddhists but none can ever hope to reach Nirvana until she has first been reborn as a man. It sounds like a lonely faith. There are some in the West who call it pessimistic, though it is hard to see why. Those who practice it find it a sunny, joyous philosophy.

Each Buddhist is expected to obey five simple precepts. He is forbidden to kill anything, or take that which is not given, or lie, or commit adultery, or drink alcohol. This doesn't mean he will never do any of these things, any more than a Jew or Christian will never break any of the Ten Commandments. But like a judge, Karma will bring him suffering in his next life when he does.

The eightfold path of the monk, who has dedicated his life to meditation on the teachings of the Buddha, is far more stringent, beginning with the simple physical act of following the Buddha in the Middle Way, not abusing his body but never indulging it. There are no holy men with matted beards sitting in caves in Burma. The *hpongyis*, the monks, are chaste men who arise at daybreak, spend long hours in meditation, may not eat after noon, are expected to be in the monastery by sundown. Because the life is difficult, any monk may leave the order when he chooses.

Practically every young Buddhist boy will enter the monastery as a novice and wear the yellow robe of the monk for perhaps six months or so. Grown men may return for a few weeks, particularly during the long vacations at the Water Festival or the holidays that begin with Christmas and continue through Independence Day on January 4. When they come back to their desks, the only sign will be their shaven heads, rousing no comment. Such returns are expected now and then.

Besides obeying the five precepts, a layman of means is expected to give funds to the pagoda and provide poor boys with proper *shinbyus,* ordinations into the monkhood as novices, a solemn and important occasion. He will give gifts to the monks on appropriate days, although a monk's possessions are limited to his saffron-yellow robe, his red oiled-silk umbrella, his begging bowl, his razor, perhaps a fan with which to cover his face when he passes a woman, and the small strainer with which he lifts insects from his drinking water, not to protect himself but to save their lives. Any of these acts will gain the giver merit which will not advance him on his path to Nirvana but will aid his Karma. There is a warm and generous friendship gesture of "sharing" such merit, even with a westerner, a non-Buddhist.

Each morning, through village or city, the monks make their way with their black lacquer begging bowls, and the women of the houses will gain merit by giving them rice and condiments for the rice. The monk does not thank the woman, for by the act of begging he has given her the opportunity to give and thereby gain merit.

A monk's responsibilities to laymen are limited. He is not their priest. Indeed, there are no priests in customary terms. A monk has dedicated himself to his private goal of reaching Nirvana. His concern is not with the ephemeral, temporal world. But monks do teach in the hpongyi-chaungs, the monks' schools for boys attached to the monastery, which is the reason that Burma even in the days of the kings had a high literacy rate. A monk has no part in a wedding, but he is present at a funeral. Sometimes he may expound the Scriptures to laymen, and in a village, where he is perhaps closer to the people, an older monk may be sought out for advice on many questions of concern.

The Buddhist sabbath, which is lunar, does not fall on the same day of every week. Laymen and monks will both be at the pagoda on these duty-days, but there may be no special service as such. Indeed, a stranger might not know it was the sabbath, for people visit the pagoda at all hours of any day.

The Pagoda

In Burma, a pagoda is not a temple which one enters but a reliquary, housing some sacred relic of the Buddha. A pagoda can be of any height and may be built anywhere, for its building brings much merit. First there is a mound, like an inverted begging bowl, within which the relics have presumably been placed. From this rises a spire that grows continually smaller in diameter until the lotus bud is reached; above that is the hti, the lacy umbrella, still higher the slender vane, and then the diamond bud. There is a modern pagoda perhaps no more than six feet high on the promontory of a hill above Mandalay on the road to Maymyo. The richest and most revered is the Shwedagon in Rangoon. The whole complex reaches upward 326 feet from street level, the hill, the terraces, and the pagoda proper finally to the hti and diamond bud. The hti, gift of King Mindon, is of gold and jewels worth over 62,000 pounds sterling. When the Mons first built the pagoda, presumably in 585 B.C., to house eight hairs of the head of the Buddha, it was only 27 feet high, but later kings and queens added to its height and richness.

Some of the relics might be dismissed as myths, since no one can see them. The ancient Botataung Pagoda on the Rangoon River was always reported to contain "a hair of the Buddha and two body relics." When the Allies bombed the river wharves in World War II, they hit the pagoda and the relic chamber under the mound was revealed. A stone casket contained a second stone casket. Inside that was a beautifully made tiny pagoda of gold mounted on a silver stand and housing, of course, two body relics and a single hair. If the Buddhists ever needed proof that the pagodas house the relics they are reputed to house, they found it here.

A pagoda, built of masonry which may be either whitewashed or covered with gold leaf, stands on a platform often paved with marble. About it usually are numerous shrines with figures of the Buddha in marble, alabaster, or bronze, although these too may be covered with gold leaf. The Buddha may not be worshiped, so the philosophers say, but the people who kneel in meditation before the altars plainly kneel in love, and their meditation comes close to the prayers of other religions.

If the pagoda is very old, there may be a small museum, perhaps an ancient bell without a clapper, to be struck like a gong. Somewhere there will be a glass box to receive money offerings which will go to lay trustees for the pagoda's upkeep, since monks may not touch money.

There may be rest shelters for pilgrims, and there will be space, open space where a monk or a child may rest or a family may eat its rice. Festivals celebrated at the pagoda are happy as well as solemn. In Burma, the line can be very thin between the sacred and the secular.

Pagodas, many very simple and none as rich as the Shwedagon, dot the landscape of the entire country, most often within a compound which also contains the monastery and the monk's school. The pagodas and the saffron-robed monks are the ever-present symbols of the faith; ceremonies associated with them both are woven into the fabric of the people's lives. Burma without Buddhism would not be Burma.

Buddhism's Social Values

But, as with us, this faith begets social values that are commonly held. Their Buddhist roots are not always consciously recalled. Instead, reaction is instinctive.

The accumulation of wealth is frowned upon; its only socially accepted use is religious or semireligious. Ostentatious living gains the people's scorn. Though some Burmese may have been wealthy before nationalization, they didn't live as if they were. Instead, wisdom is respected; the wise man, the *saya*, whether he is monk or teacher or poet, ranks high in the people's esteem. Power, charisma, *hpon*, are respected. There is a generally accepted feeling that such marks of fate's favor come only from a good Karma. But wealth is not respected for itself. Thus, one never sees the extremes of luxury and poverty which are not uncommon in India.

The Middle Way is held in high esteem, coming from the

Buddha's choice of neither self-indulgence nor self-abuse. But the Middle Way carries over into the secular. All governments have tried to talk with their rebels as a matter of accepted social policy. When the Revolutionary Council made their all-out effort in 1963 and failed, they still gained the respect of the people for the effort. Only for two causes—the protection of Buddhism or the protection of the nation—is extreme behavior approved.

There are no castes in Burma, not even a priestly caste like the Brahmins of India. This has always given a kind of rude democracy to the country. Even in the days of the kings, there was no Burman hereditary nobility. In the hierarchy of the Sangha, the son of the poorest peasant could become a monk and, by holiness and wisdom, rise to the position of primate at the Court. Status is something that society, and not birth, confers on a man or woman.

When one of the five precepts forbids killing, it means killing any thing, not just another human being, for in the long aeons of rebirth, an animal's life may be one of those lives from which a man or woman may come and to which one may slip back. This is a difficult precept to live with; by necessity, socially acceptable ways have been found to get around it in certain circumstances. A westerner in Burma who used a fly swatter one morning in his office returned from lunch to find a coil of fly-paper on his desk. This is the same rationalization which some are able to use for fishing. The fish is not killed when he is taken from the water. He dies of his own accord. Walls of houses, but not the insects, are sprayed, so that the malarial mosquitoes which light on the walls will die by their own act.

These are not to be considered merely amusing sophistries. The reflex act is still there in a moment of confrontation; a driver may brake so swiftly when he comes upon a snake un-expectedly crossing the road that he endangers himself and his passengers. The violent death of a human being is not rare in Burma, but there are few murders as Anglo-Saxon law defines murder. The killings are manslaughter, unplanned outbursts of temper. Even these fall and rise with the social order or disorder in the country, as the crime rate fell when the Caretaker Government took over. The social value is held whether or not it is always scrupulously obeyed. One does not kill any living thing.

These are the standards, the values. Among the four peoples, the norm may differ. The Shans fish very little though they buy fish at the markets. But they hunt; the hills near their valleys and plateaus provide good game. The Burmans do not hunt, but they may fish, often with nets or traps. The Mons hunt a little and fish more than the others, perhaps as an inheritance of the years they lived on the sea. The Burmans prefer river fish.

The Mons and the Burmans share a belief that the soul leaves the body when a person sleeps, often in the shape of a butterfly. It is dangerous, therefore, to waken someone too suddenly. No one knows now which people held the belief first. This has nothing to do with Buddhism, of course. But there is a little superstition and animism spread through the Buddhist beliefs of all the four peoples. It's rather dangerous to make any sweeping statements about how widely or deeply these are held today. Particularly in cities and district towns, the belief in spirits, *nats* as the Burmese call them, is fading.

It is true that U Nu, as Prime Minister, annually led the ceremonies honoring the guardian nats of Rangoon who preserved the city when the insurrectionists drove dangerously near. It is equally true that, when General Ne Win was Prime Minister, he marked the same day with a ceremonial giving of gifts to the monks and rather ostentatiously ignored the nats.

Most recent anthropological studies show less belief in nats in Lower Burma, that section south of the Prome-Toungoo line, and more in Upper Burma. They are not worshiped; they are propitiated because they will otherwise cause trouble. Small nathouses, like tiny dollhouses, mounted five feet or so off the ground, can be found along secondary roads almost anywhere in Burma. Nats have been living alongside, but subservient to, Buddhism for centuries.

There are two major classifications, the *ahtet*, or upper, nats and the *auk*, or lower, nats. The ahtet nats are heavenly spirits borrowed from Hindu mythology and given a place of honor in Buddhism. Only the auk nats of a special region or of the household, the village, a particular stream, a nearby large tree are of concern to a villager.

King Anawrahta, the stern father figure who brought Theravada Buddhism to his people, tried to stamp out the nat cult and failed. So he gathered together images of the 36 major nats honored in the Pagan kingdom, placed them all in the compound of the Shwezigon Pagoda, and set over them the king of the heavenly spirits as the 37th nat. Since Thagya Min, the spirit king, already acknowledged the Buddha, this tucked the whole hierarchy into Buddhism. Even where nats are acknowledged and appeased, they do not diminish the devotion of a Buddhist, or the respect he offers its social values.

The Burmans

Among the four major peoples, the Burmans are dominant, just as they are in the nation itself. In Burma Proper, time and intermarriage have partially blurred the difference between the ethnic term, Burman, and the national term, Burmese, as the two are defined in the Introduction. Not all members of the Revolutionary Council are pure Burmans, not even General Ne Win himself.

Hence a writer must often stop to ponder which word is the correct one for a particular circumstance. In an effort at clarity, he may use Burman more often than the word is used today in the nation itself. Unionism, however, has somewhat revived its usage because unionism forces on the people of the Irrawaddy valley an awareness as fellow-Burmese of peoples with different cultures.

But it was only Burman kings who united the country, however tenuously. A distinct Burman culture, however much it borrowed from others, blossomed in those ancient capitals. Since the development of that history and culture provide the story-line for this book, it need not be discussed further here.

The Mons

The Mons would not be unduly interested in the 37 nats of the Pagan kingdom, except for Thagya Min who is common to all Theravada Buddhists. Their language is classified as Mon-Khmer rather than Tibeto-Burman. Some 350,000 still speak in that tongue, although Burmese is the lingua franca outside the home. Among these four peoples the two who have most in common are the Mons and the Burmans. How much the Pagan Burmans borrowed from the Mons, and how much the Mons in turn borrowed from the Burmans is no longer distinguishable.

This is hardly surprising. During all the generations that Mons were honored members of the Pagan court, and the many years that the Toungoo dynasty ruled the country from the Mon capital of Pegu, there had to be not only much trading of culture and habits but also probably much intermarriage. One of the more recent books on the life of a Burmese family is written by Mi Mi Khaing, a Mon, and she does not differentiate her family story from that of any other Burmese family.

This does not mean that Mons have forgotten their distinct history; some cherish it to the point of desiring a separate state. They live where they always have, in the south along the deltas of the Salween, Sittang, and Irrawaddy rivers and around Thaton and Pegu, though Pegu is now some 60 miles or more from the sea. But many other peoples are now mingled with them. To form a state for them would be a quixotic task; most Mons realize it, even those who resent the eclipse of their ancient glory by the Burmans.

The Arakanese

Far more separated are the Arakanese, who are essentially

Burman. Beyond the mountain wall of the Arakan Yoma, along the Bay of Bengal, there has been a kingdom since before the Christian era. Whether it has always been Burman or whether an early migration of Burmans crossed the mountains and seized power from earlier kings, no one knows. The people have probably been Buddhist as long as the Mons. Their most sacred image of the Buddha, the Maha Muni, is said to predate the historical Pagan kingdom by perhaps a millennium. It stands, however, at the Arakan Pagoda, in Mandalay, brought across the mountains by Bodawpaya's armies as a trophy of war. Burman they may be, but they fought the Burman kings often, beginning with Anawrahta, usually because they were attacked. They were taken over by the British after the first British-Burma War and until Independence had never been ruled as a part of Burma Proper. The Burmese in Burma Proper call the Arakanese language archaic Burmese. No census figures are given for the Arakanese; they are counted among the Burmese.

The Shans

The more than a million Shans who live in the 50,000 square miles of the Shan State occupy a unique position in Burma. Their speech is linguistically Tai; on the east the state is bordered by both Thailand and Laos (as well as China), but the Shan dialect is more closely related to the language of the Thais than to that of the Laotians, though all are classified as Tai. Only one substate among the present 33 turns its face to Thailand. Kengtung, east of the Salween, is enough separated from the others to have trade and cultural contacts with Thailand across the border. Other Shans have always faced toward Burma. This same attitude is duplicated on the Thai side. Even around Chiengmai and Chiengrai, fairly close to the Shan State, Thais consider the Shans Burmese and not Thai "cousins."

The Non-Shans Among Them: In acculturation, the Shans

have done as much giving as taking. The Burmans, of course, have influenced all peoples, including the Shans, until part of Shan culture today is merely Burman culture transported to the Shan Upland. But over many centuries the Shans were the dominant people from whom other minorities borrowed.

Perhaps this arose partly from their free-and-easy attitude toward the minorities who live among them—which may have been inspired partly by self-protection, since almost half the population of the state is non-Shan. It has always been possible for an individual from one of the hill tribes or an entire village to move down and "become Shan," if three requirements were fulfilled: they must adopt the Shan language, become Buddhist, and switch to wet-rice agriculture rather than the slash-and-burn clearings of hill people. Thus Kachins have married Shan women and literally become Shans. Even those who didn't become Shan have borrowed.

Those numerous Wa in the Shan State whom the Shans call the "tame" Wa speak the local Tai dialect, are all nominally Buddhist, practice some wet-rice cultivation, and are probably in the process of becoming Shans. Their better-known brothers, whom the Shans call the "wild" Wa, are pagan and probably still headhunters. Few go into their mountains to find out.

Wa speech is Mon-Khmer, as is that of another Shan minority who are also Buddhist, some 60,000 Palaung. But most of them seem to be maintaining their own identity in a substate with their own sawbwa while living on excellent terms with their Shan neighbors. A hill people is prosperous if it can raise a cash crop beyond its subsistence farming. Many make this crop opium, although it is illegal in Burma. The Palaung, who live less than 3,000 feet above sea level and cannot grow opium, have within this century begun to specialize quite successfully in raising tea.

A larger minority living around Taunggyi are the Pa-o or Taungthu, numbering perhaps as many as 200,000—a black-clad Karen tribe who keep to themselves. Legend has it that they fled north to the Shan State when Anawrahta first attacked the Mons at Thaton. Taungthu is Burmese for "hill people," and the Pa-o seem accurately named.

But oral history among the Pa-o relates a different story. They say "taung" also means "south" and that the Burmans first named them Taungthu when they lived to the south of the Burmans, at Thaton. They do indeed relate how they fled from the Pagan king; but in their history Thaton was a Taungthu kingdom, it was their king Manuha who was captured by the Burmans, their sacred Buddhist scriptures which were borne on the backs of elephants to Pagan. Their story makes no mention of Mons at Thaton.

The Pa-o have been Buddhists from ancient times and have an old written language, unlike other Karens. William Dunn Hackett,* who has written the most complete study of the Pa-o, relates that he has seen yellowed and worn parchment manuscripts written in archaic Pa-o in two Pa-o hpongyi-chaungs, and that the *sayadaw* (senior monk or abbot) of one of them told him that some of the manuscripts had come with them from Thaton. It is a curious puzzle.

Beside their own tongue, perhaps 25 per cent of the Pa-o men speak Burmese and most of them speak Shan, which is the lingua franca of the State between Shans and minorities, and among the minorities themselves.

Separate and Equal: For centuries the Shans, unlike any other people of Burma, have had a nobility. The sawbwas were hereditary leaders; to belong to a sawbwa family, even if not in direct line for the leadership, gave status to a man or woman. Probably the present tense should still be used. The sawbwas gave up their hereditary rights only a few years ago and status lingers. Since there were at least 15 substates under the British, probably more than 60 under the Burmese kings, and 33 now, quite a large group of men and women are of sawbwa families. They have

* Dr. Hackett's report, an unpublished doctoral thesis, is in the Cornell University Library.

always been better educated, more sophisticated than other Shans. In the days of the kings, many young men were educated at the Burmese Court. If they were partly hostages for the good behavior of their sawbwa, like young Shan women who became queens or concubines of the king, they nevertheless gained a good education for their time.

After the British came, the same kind of feudal arrangement continued with them: the same kind of tribute was paid to the British which had once been paid to the Burmese, a sum amounting to over 4 lakhs (400,000) of rupees annually. In return, many sawbwas' sons, particularly from the larger states, were educated in England.

Like Thai princes who were not in the direct line of succession to the throne, these men became the civil servants of the modern Shan State. A sophisticated group, fluent in Shan, Burmese, and English, they may wear western dress in their offices, Shan clothes in the evening—i.e., a jacket resembling the Burmese jacket with full trousers differing from the Chinese only by the trim fit through waist and hip—and Burmese clothes when they visit Rangoon. They are as much at home in the three cultures as in the clothes.

Sawbwas have differed; some have been liberal and forward-looking, others far more autocratic. They should not be confused with the wealthy maharajahs of India. They have been instead more like prosperous (sometimes very prosperous) landed gentry in an area largely nonurban. Some of them were jailed when the Revolutionary Council came to power. Most, if not all, have now been released. Even without their hereditary positions, it is difficult to see how the Shan State can fully dispense with their knowledge and services.

For all that Shan and Burman cultures share, the Shans feel themselves separate and equal. When, under U Nu, talk began of a constitutional amendment to make Buddhism the state religion, Buddhist Shans took the lead in calling a Rangoon conference on the question with minority religious leaders, both animist and

Christian. They did not want the authority of the Burmese Sangha extended over their monks.

When many Burmese soldiers who did not speak Shan were stationed near Taunggyi in 1958–60 in answer to Chinese KMT threats, many stories were told of their rude, rough behavior in issuing orders to the Shans. It is impossible to know whether these tales were exaggerated reports encouraged by the sawbwa families, the difficulties of a people who had no common language to use for order-giving, or the true arrogance they purported to reveal. The tales, whatever their source, would not have been influenced by Shan favoritism toward the KMT intruder. In spite of rebels, separatism expressed even in the constitutional right of secession, and ancient resentment of the Burmans, Shans feel no kinship with people outside Burma and resent outside interference as much as the Burmese of Burma proper.

THE CHIEF MINORITIES

Most indigenous minorities in Southeast Asia are hill tribes. (This excludes Chinese and Indians who are counted as "outsiders.") The stereotype of a hill people is of a primitive tribe whose chief's power extends no farther than a village or group of villages. They are subsistence farmers growing their grain by *swidden,* slash-and-burn agriculture. This means that every few years, fields are left to lie fallow until their fertility returns—whereupon the underbrush is once more cleared and burned and the fields are put into use again. They are superstitious and animist, fearing a hundred spirits and sacrificing to them. This is the stereotype.

The Karens

The largest minority in Burma are the Karens, who number somewhere around 1,300,000. Of four main Karen groups, those of the Kayah State and the Pa-o are the smaller.

The Kayah State is in reality the home of a small Karen tribe which long ago borrowed the Shan governmental system, though the people have remained animist and would have had difficulty in their hills switching to wet-rice cultivation. But they are separate enough from other Karens in other ways for the rule of a Kayah sawbwa to seem quite fitting to them. These are the 75,000 people previously called Karenni, Red Karens, until the time of the post-Independence rebellion of other Karens in Burma Proper. Much larger and important are the half a million Sgaw and almost that many Pwo, most of whom now live in the deltas of the Irrawaddy, Sittang, and Salween rivers, speak Burmese, are Buddhists, raise rice in flooded fields, and are generally indistinguishable from their Mon and Burman neighbors. So much for the stereotype. It's true, of course, that some still live in the hills, like the Buddhist Pa-o in the Shan State, or the animist Kayah, or some of the Sgaw who live in the Pegu Yoma range between the Irrawaddy and the Sittang.

The Karens one meets now don't fit early descriptions. It is impossible to tell whether this is because of rapid cultural change or whether the earliest travelers hit upon extremes of behavior to describe. Those early stories tell of two kinds of Karens, a very timid, shy group who fled deeper into the hills to escape outsiders, and an aggressive, warlike group who fought constantly among themselves, taking prisoners as slaves, and often selling slaves to other peoples. Some reporters even feel it necessary to record gravely that "it is not certain the Karens were ever head-hunters," a kind of reporting which must anger present-day Karens.

No one knows when the Karens came to Burma. It could be that they were contemporaries of the Mons. They were certainly around when the Burmans began their invasions of Thailand because they were often drafted as bearers by those armies. The roots of Karen-Burman enmity seem to lie in those ancient times, when the Karens themselves were treated little better than slaves. Where their languages belong, which might indicate something about whence they came, is still in doubt. They're usually placed

in a separate Karenic division in the major Sino-Tibetan classification.

Though the majority now are Buddhist, the influence of early
Christian missionaries on the Karens was enormous. The Baptist
Adoniram Judson, first Protestant missionary to come to Burma,
arrived in the Rangoon area in 1813 and found, as all Christian
missionaries have found, that Buddhists seldom become converts
to another faith. But some among the Karens listened to him.
They were animists but they also held a belief in a creator whom
they called Yawa, suggesting the Hebrew name of Jehovah.
There was a legend of woman being created from the rib of man,
and one about a lost, sacred book. Probably it is romantic fantasy
that in their ancient past they crossed paths with a group of Jews
and learned from them. But the legends are there and the Karens
listened to Judson.

Missionaries created written languages for the Sgaw and the
Pwo. They built schools and published textbooks and sacred
books in the new languages. Eventually they built Judson College
in Rangoon. An educated elite of Karens arose who were doctors,
teachers, ministers, and political leaders. Although the Christians
were a minority, they became influential beyond their numbers
among the Karen people; through them, a sense of being one
people, of what might be called nationhood, arose among the
Karens. They were close to the English and served in British
regiments after 1825.

Buddhism is normally a tolerant faith, but Judson was im-
prisoned several times. In later years, the Karens looked to the
Christian British as protectors. Some went to London to plead
for a separate nation when the British prepared to leave Burma.
Some Englishmen in Parliament spoke passionately about be-
traying the Karens by leaving them within an independent
Burma. These are all part of the bitter roots which brought on
the rebellion by a minority of Karens after Independence.

The delay in creating a separate Karen State was not mere stub-
bornness on the part of the Burmese. Where to carve out a state

for such a widely scattered people was the difficult problem. The Karen State, created in 1951, lies along the Thai border, south of the Kayah State. Townships within it have Karen majorities, but only a minority of the nation's Karens live within the State. By patience and perseverance on the part of both the Revolutionary Council and the Karens, almost all the rebelling Karens have "come into the light," to use the Burmese phrase. Those still in rebellion are only the handful of Karen Communists.

The Chins

There are some 350,000 Chins living in Burma, speaking about 44 dialects, most mutually unintelligible. Chin is the Burman name for these people. It comes from an ancient Burmese word meaning "ally" or "comrade." About 220,000 of them live in the Chin Special Division. The rest are plains Chins, living on the edges of the Division among Burmese, or in the north of Arakan.

Like the Karens, the Chins are not newcomers to Burma. There is some evidence that they were in the plains when the Burmans arrived, that they may have been well established there by the middle of the first Christian millennium. Their very name of Chin indicates some kind of relationship between them and the Burmans which predates their hill existence. For in their hills they were isolated from the Burmans, who showed a certain indifference to them, hardly befitting the name of "comrade."

Early Burman kings paid little attention to them. After re-uniting the kingdom in 1555 Bayinnaung moved into the Chin-dwin area to pacify the country, but his real concern was Manipur over the border, not the Chins. Not until 1755, when Alaungpaya, founder of the last dynasty, was also reuniting the nation, is there the first mention of Chin levies in the Burman army during an attack on Syriam in the Delta. Such levies are one of the symbols of a feudal relationship between a minority and a majority, and 1755 comes a little late in the history of Burman kings.

Yet in Chin culture there is that persistent thread of presumption of some kind of earlier intimate relationship. The Chins' own name for themselves—or names, for there are differences among the dialects—is some variant of "zo," which means backward or unsophisticated. But the term for Burman civilization is some form of "vai," a place "over there" of richer goods and greater sophistication. Certain of their words referring to the commodities of the more sophisticated world are old Burmese. Land tenure of the plains Chins in northern Arakan seems validated by old documents from Arakanese kings. Always they have seen themselves in relationship to the other culture, a world in which they should have shared and of which they were somehow deprived. All in all, the evidence suggests strongly that they've been around for some time. These attitudes seem to have prepared the Chins to accept change, when it came after Burmese Independence, with a certain easy adaptability.

The Chins have been fairly true to the stereotype of hill people. They have lived on ridges of their hills somewhere around 5,000 feet, well above the lowest level of their farmed land and below the highest level of cultivation. They consider their hill country "a beautiful land of beautiful flowers" and they sing of it lovingly. They may covet the things of Burma's plains but not the land.

They practice slash-and-burn farming, leaving fields fallow between use, with rice the chief grain crop in the south and maize and millet in the north. The fields are shifted often, but the villages only rarely. They work primitively in iron and bronze but the metals have had to be imported. Although hunting is more for sport than food, game is plentiful—leopard, Himalayan black bear, Malayan sun bear, wild boar, barking deer. Fish is important in their diet; communal fishing expeditions are social events.

In the Chin religion spirits are called *khua*, but khua is also that in which life exists here, that which has feeling or soul, according to F. K. Lehman, whose study of the Chins is most recent. A village normally has a sacrificial precinct inhabited by spirits of some power over the village life. Important sacrifices are made here, usually of the cattle known as *mithan*, a breed crossed between wild and tame beasts. Lesser house spirits protect individual households, bad spirits cause illness and misfortune. Spirits called *khuazing* may be more aptly termed gods. The conception of these gods is now blurred with the Christian conception of God.

A Feast of Merit, the most elaborate sacrificial ceremony, will continue for several days, beginning with small sacrifices of chickens and pigs and working up to the sacrifice of one or more mithan. The sacrifices are eventually eaten by the guests and the Feast may be conducted by anyone who can afford it, not by a special priest or chief class. Its aim is to claim status in the present and, by inference, in afterlife.

According to Lehman's report, the Burmese have kept their promises to the Chins fairly well. At the time of the Constituent Assembly, the Chins had asked for a special district (not a separate state), somewhat under the tutelage of the Burmese, who would provide schools, roads, communication. At that point, the Chins had progressed from a moneyless economy with little to sell to an economy with a certain amount of cash from Chins serving in the British army or as porters or road-builders, but almost nothing to buy with it. Bride prices had gone up and more elaborate Feasts of Merit were given, but to a people like the Chins, strongly oriented to acquiring the goods of the more developed culture, this was hardly satisfactory.

Now several all-weather landing strips have been built; motor roads have been pushed through the district; jeeps bring in goods to stores scattered throughout the hills—aspirin, tobacco, men's western undershorts and T-shirts, children's clothing, combs, condensed milk, cooking oil, a vast variety of goods which have been common on the plains. More importantly, the promised schools have been built. Not every village has a school, any more than every village does in Burma Proper, though compulsory education is in theory the law. But there are seven government high schools (teaching in Burmese) from which young Chins matriculate to the universities. A number of Chin women have completed nurse's training in Rangoon. Most men under 40 can read and write. Civil posts and army service are open to them.

Few have become Buddhists; perhaps with their culture's emphasis on things, on possessions, this is not to be expected, at least for the present. An increasing number are becoming Christians, though even now this is probably no more than 25 per cent.

Most interesting of Lehman's personal observations concerns the lack of strain in the social structure between the new and the old, between the educated young and the more primitive elders. This ease of change, however, does not mean any loss of pride in Chin identity. The Chins today are beginning to ask for a separate state instead of a district. In the present uncertainty of Burma, this desire is sometimes equated with the rebellions among some Shans or Kachins. It could just as well mean no more than a growing Chin confidence, a sense that their tutelage has ended.

The Nagas

Far to the north of the Chin District and to the west of the Kachin State are the Naga Hills. Much more is known about the Indian state of Nagaland, across the India–Burma border, than about Burma's Nagas, for whom not even a population figure is available. India has had trouble with its Nagas in its attempt to impose direct, systematic administration. Burma has had no trouble because no such effort has been made. But to infer Burmese Naga characteristics from the Indian group is unwise, since Nagaland has felt strong influence from India which Burma's Naga Hills have not received in equal measure.

Burmese Nagas are a primitive people. Their language bears some relation to the Chin dialects, their political organization to the Kachins. They have been headhunters. It is difficult even to hazard a guess about their number in Burma, but it is probably well under 50,000. Because dissidents of Nagaland have crossed the Naga Hills and the Kachin State to China for training and weapons, the area must be of some current concern to the Burmese government. But it has made no public statements about the people or their hills.

The Kachins

As with other minorities, once again it must be said. No one knows exactly when the Kachins entered what is now the Kachin State. But the situation is different with the Kachins than with the others. It doesn't involve trying to pin down a date in some distant past. Since the time westerners have known these people, most scholars have thought the Kachins to be the latecomers to Burma, arriving probably in the sixteenth century. The most trustworthy guess puts their numbers at 350,000. Although their own state of 33,903 square miles is not crowded, a number of Kachins live in the Shan State. The British tried to tidy up the border between the two peoples for administrative purposes, moving each back to his own area. But, since the Kachins are hill people and the Shans are valley people, they had never disputed agricultural use of land in the same area. Some of the vacant land today in the Kachin State is valley land where Shans earlier lived as serfs in a kind of feudal relationship with a Kachin chief or *duwa*. The British, terming them slaves, insisted that they be freed, though the last did not leave the Kachin valleys until 1926.

British efforts did not wholly succeed in moving each people to his own district, but they did cause some low, wet-rice land to remain fallow for several decades. Into some of these valley areas worked earlier by the Shans, Kachins have begun moving during the last decade or two, a sharp change from their hill, slash-and-burn, traditional agriculture. It is another example of the quickening momentum of change in Burma's hills since Independence. This change makes all reports of the nineteenth and early twentieth century somewhat suspect unless some reporter has been in Burma in the last decade to recheck the classic descriptions of a people. This goes for the Kachins as it does for others.

The word Kachin is used by westerners and Burmese to describe four groups who live in the Kachin State. The largest by far is the Jinghpaw; the same word is also used for their language. Three smaller groups, the Atsi, the Lashi, and Maru, who live mostly along the Burma-China border, speak quite different languages which are much closer to Burmese. Culturally and politically, the four bear marked resemblances. All, since Independence, now answer readily to the name of Kachin, all voted in the early elections of a Kachin State. But most studies available are of the Jinghpaw and only a small part of Jinghpaw territory at that.

Jinghpaws believe they are all descended from a common, remote ancestor who had five sons. Each chief or duwa can present a genealogy which leads back to one of these five. The society is divided into these chiefs and into commoners who can probably trace their ancestors back only a few generations. Inheritance is through the youngest son. A duwa's older sons who find it awkward to remain subservient to a youngest brother have often gathered a few followers and left the village to start a new settlement. They will be chiefs of the new village but not high-ranking "thigh-eating" duwas like their younger brothers, so-called because a chieftain had the right to the thigh of all animals killed or sacrificed in his village or village-cluster.

Sometimes these groups of young men became independent bands of professional soldiers, doing the fighting for one or another Kachin duwa or a Shan sawbwa. Eventually the British and, in turn, the Burmese learned the skills of Kachin soldiers in their own armies.

Kachins were never as cut off from the world around them as the Chins; they had contacts with both the Shans and the Chinese. Their resources were also greater than those of the

Chins. They came to control the jade and amber mines in what is now the Kachin State as well as certain old iron mines, though these have been mostly worked out. They also held control of the land passes along the old trading route from China through Bhamo and could levy a tax on traders passing through.

Today in the Irrawaddy River valleys around the towns of Bhamo and Myitkyina there live a fair number of Burmans. Thus from the nation's majority has come a group to live as a minority in a State belonging to a national minority. It involves a criss-cross of role-playing that can have its own complications. But it offers, too, a constant opportunity to the national minority for greater borrowings from the major culture.

Kachin villages have been known as *gumsa* or *gumlao*. The first is the aristocratic-commoner type; the second has, at least for the moment, a more democratically chosen headman. But a gumlao community can go gumsa under a strong leader who can provide himself with a properly impressive lineage, while a gumsa grouping can slide into a gumlao type under several generations of weak leaders. This is the classic pattern. It had already begun to change under the British, who imposed new duties on duwas and retained a right of veto on succession, as they did in the Shan states. It must be changing even more under the Burmese.

The duwas may be thought of as minor sawbwas; the system may have been adapted from the Shans. One of the major duties of a duwa has been the sacrificial propitiation of the ancestral spirits, either at recurring times like the first sowing of the fields or at moments of major threat or misfortune to the community. This has been an expensive proposition since it involves sacrifice not only of chickens and pigs but of cattle. Such an occasion somewhat resembles the Chins' Feast of Merit, since cattle are kept only for sacrificial purposes, not as work animals. Sacrifices at times of individual household emergencies have remained the responsibility of the household itself.

All Kachin spirits or nats seem to be ancestors; not all are benevolent. The power of the nats has probably resisted change more successfully than the power of the duwas. Few Kachins have become Buddhist, except for those who have also "become Shans"; perhaps no more than ten per cent are Christians. Hence, the nats' authority has acquired no rival in most villages.

As with the Karens, the Christians have influence beyond their numbers since they are usually better educated. The Kachins do have a written language, developed in 1895 by a Baptist missionary, but the numerous and excellent missionary schools were taught in Burmese. This training was the beginning of the Kachin swing away from viewing the Shans as the "window on the world," and of accepting instead Burmese language and literature in an educational awakening. Men with missionary education influenced the Kachins to desire entrance into the Union of Burma and have since been the State's leaders.

There is a Kachin Independence Army today, its headquarters back in the high northern hills and valleys. Its size, its goals, are not certain, perhaps even to Rangoon. Its activities could be as modern as Communist-inspired and armed guerrilla warfare with the aid of Chinese Kachins from over China's border, or as old and indigenous as a renewal of alliances between Kachin duwas and Shan sawbwas. At the time of the weak King Thibaw, there had been plottings for a rebellion to seize Kachin freedom from Mandalay and perhaps even to seize Upper Burma. Some sawbwas and a Burmese prince had been involved. But the British, without knowledge of the plot, conquered Thibaw and Upper Burma too soon for such an attempt.

Even the most ambitious Kachins surely aim at less than that today, and there is no evidence that the movement has mass support from most Kachins.

THE BURMESE LANGUAGE

This review of Burma's diverse peoples makes one fact plain. Increasingly the lingua franca of the entire country is the Burmese language. The Burmans themselves seldom speak a second indigenous language. If they have a second language, it is usually English. But the second language for all others of the country is Burmese. It spreads through schools, through civil service, through the army. Higher education is open only to those who understand it, and higher education is increasingly valued. Burmese overwhelmingly dominates the nation's publishing production.

As long ago as 1959, when the Burmese army stationed in the Shan State was reportedly cut off from the people because it didn't speak Shan, a western traveler in the Shan State, too innocent to know that Burmese wasn't supposed to be understood there, could bargain easily in halting Burmese in the State's bazaars at Taunggyi and in the villages around Kalaw and Inle Lake.

For an Asian, the Burmese language is probably not difficult to learn, particularly for those who already speak a Tibeto-Burman tongue. It is a rich, colorful, often earthy language. A westerner finds it somewhat troublesome to master because it is tonal, and he cannot always hear the three slight tonal changes of the vowels, let alone shape his own tongue and lips to duplicate them.

A few examples will make the problem clearer. It is perhaps best for the reader to try them orally with tongue and lips, not only with his eyes. In these three words, little changes except the sound of the dominant vowel.

Sâdé is the verb which means to eat. The "a" (always pronounced ah) in *sâdé* carries the slight rise and fall of the circumflex, the "e" (as in bed) an unemphasized dropping sound.

Shâdé is the verb which means to be hungry. It sounds very close to *sâdé*. The puff of breath indicated by the "h" in the transliteration marks a difference. But even more pronounced is the change in the sound of the "ah," pronounced here with the slightly dropping sound of the previous "e."

Sàdé is the verb which means to start. It differs from the "to eat" in the quick, uplilting sound of the "ah."

These are the three rhythm sounds given to a vowel, slight

but most important for meaning. All of these words as written here are, of course, only transliterations of Burmese sounds; because the Burmese alphabet is not romanized, the letters are quite different from our alphabet and the markings for sound differ greatly in meaning from those we find in our dictionaries.

There is another distinction to the language. Status and courtesy have their customary place in the culture and are reflected in the language. The syllable "ba" is frequently inserted in a verb in speaking to a superior, but also as a mark of courtesy in speaking to an equal. If there is the slightest doubt about superiority or equality, it is best to err in their favor, better to overdo courtesy to an inferior than to be rude. *Kaunde* means "it is good," or "very good," a mark of approval for food, for dress, for a particular act. But the word normally used, except to a definite inferior, is *kaumbade,* the *n* changing to *m* merely for ease of speech. A command in a transitive verb such as *eat* would simply be *sa,* but normally one says *saba.*

Questions are indicated not by the inflection of the speaker's voice, as in English, but by two suffixes to the verb, *la* if the answer expected will be a simple affirmative or negative, *le* if the reply will be a longer statement. The negative of a verb is formed by a prefix and suffix. Hence, if something isn't good, it is "makaumbu."

An interesting variation is that the sex of a pronoun is determined by the speaker, not by the person addressed. If a woman says to a man, "How are you?" she will say *"mayela shin?" Shin* is feminine. But a man speaking to a woman would always say, *"mayela khimbya?" Khimbya* is masculine.

None of these are, of course, any more tricky or difficult than the idiosyncracies of the English language. They are just different.

But this is only one Burmese language. If a Burman addresses a Buddhist monk, he will use other forms of greater honor; once there was a similar special language for use at the Court of the kings. There is still another language, more formal, more elaborate than everyday speech, which each child learns when he goes to school and learns to read and write. He will never speak in that language unless he is reading an address he has written. But he will find it in the books he reads.

Rich though the language is, it naturally lacks the words to express twentieth-century concepts of government, administration, or the sciences. For this, the Burmese frequently borrow from Pali, their sacred religious language, much as English has borrowed from Latin.

Since 1947 the Burma Translation Society has been coining such words with the aid of scholars from the University of Rangoon's Department of Translation. By 1963, over 61,000 such words were published in two volumes called a "Terms Bank." In the same year the government established the Union of Burma Literary and Translation Commission with the duty of compiling a Standard Dictionary and a Dictionary of Scientific and Technological Terms. Somewhat over a tenth of the words in the Terms Bank have now been revised by the commission and officially accepted and published as standard Burmese.

Students sitting on the steps of the university library earnestly discussing a mathematics problem in Burmese may still use the English "Pi *r* squared" dropped into the middle of their discussion as if it were only more Burmese. But increasingly there are Burmese words available for new concepts and increasingly they are used.

For those peoples to whom Burmese is a second language, it is essentially a tool, of course. Language is also a culture-carrier, and such culture-marks as the use of great courtesy, the giving but not the taking of status, these too may in time find their way into the attitudes of all speakers of Burmese. But as a tool alone, it leads them into higher education, into status of their own, into increased participation in the affairs of the nation. In both roles, a common language may, in time, increase the cultural and political unity of the Union of Burma.

7 Social Organization

Traditionally, Burma has been a nation of villages. The capital has been the single major city with an additional few ports, some for international trade, some more important to coastal commerce or transport on the inland waterways. It really has not broken with tradition today except that there are two major cities, two capitals in a sense, with Mandalay acting as counterweight to Rangoon.

Rangoon with its satellite towns has a population of around a million. It is the governmental capital and the major international port, both sea and air. Mandalay, with its own satellite towns like Amarapura and Sagaing, is only a fifth that size. But its 200,000 people feel strongly that this last seat of Burmese kings is still the capital of Burman culture. Mandalay's hpongyis—and there are an unusual concentration of them in and around the city—are believed to be holier. The language around the old capital is purer, its culture closer to the original Burman culture, or so they believe. Much of Rangoon agrees. This hardly gives Mandalay a veto-power over Rangoon. But the conservative, traditional northern city must at least be given serious consideration in Rangoon's decision-making.

The country has but one other city of more than a hundred thousand. This is Moulmein in the south at the mouth of the Salween River, that old city which early Englishmen, after the first British-Burma war, dreamed of building into a powerful port for Chinese-British trade. Only three other cities reach 50,000 or more. The largest is the ancient port of Bassein on the river of the same name, which is the most westerly of the many mouths of the Irrawaddy. Pegu, though no longer on the sea as it was in the days of the Mons, does lie on the important Rangoon-Mandalay rail lines. Akyab, once capital of Arakan, is still an important port for coastal trade. None of these cities but Akyab is outside traditional Burma Proper. All the new states, all the hill peoples are without such an urban area.

The number of smaller district towns scattered through the country added to these five are still not enough to change the old tradition. Eighty per cent of Burma's estimated population of over 26 million are villagers. Because of this numerical dominance and because most city-dwellers are only a few generations away from village living, the gentle but tenacious life pattern of the village lies across even the cities.

THE VILLAGE PATTERN

The Physical Setting

In Burma Proper, a Burmese village is set like an oasis in the middle of the flat plains of rice paddies. From the air, the concentration of sheltering trees almost hides the houses themselves. On the ground, their height of distant greenness rests the eyes of the approaching traveler. They do indeed provide the villager with welcome shade from the sun during the parched six-month dry season. But each is chosen to give something more. The flame-of-the-forest adds beauty with its brilliant, red flowers. The padauk, a good timber tree, offers its special bright yellow blossoms with their symbolic freshness for the Water Festival at the Buddhist New Year. A dozen others provide fruit, the particular kind varying with the latitude in Burma. Mangosteens from Moulmein are highly prized. Mangoes, from trees with dense, dark green foliage, are delicious but must not be eaten before the rains come. Sometime in January, in the middle of the cool season, there should be a few showers which the villagers call mango showers. Without them, they say, the rice will not grow well.

There may be a few coconut palms, perhaps some citrus fruits like the pomelo, which seems to be the grandfather of all grapefruit, cooling limes, sweet oranges which peel like our tangerines. Papaya trees grow like a palm with only a head of leaves. There may be several varieties of banana trees, which aren't trees at all but one of the largest of the world's herbaceous plants. A good husbandman will cut down the wide banana leaves at season's end, burying them in a circle around the plant for fertilizing.

If no bamboo grows naturally nearby, a village may also contain a few clumps of this king of grasses, growing higher than the houses. But the clumps spread and take up much room before they bloom, and when they bloom they die. Dead clumps are hard to dig out. So the villagers are more apt to plant the bamboo somewhere outside the village compound if nature itself doesn't do the providing.

Paddy fields are also outside the compound. Though there may be a communal grazing ground, each family owns its own fields. The present land reform act limits each individual's holdings to 20 acres; some will own less and, because the law is still not fully enforced, some may hold more, but these are apt to be absentee landlords. Even among these, there are none of the vast holdings that plague the governments of Vietnam or the Philippines. Furthermore, untilled land is still available in Burma, if the pioneer is willing to move where it is and reclaim it from the jungle. But Burmese villagers seldom care to move to a new part of the country.

Villages normally house from 20 to a hundred households. When they grow larger, they begin to take on the character of towns or market centers, and the particular village quality begins to change.

Few villages have shopkeepers or market places of their own. But some have adopted a Shan custom called "five-day bazaars." A group of five villages, not too widely separated, will each hold a market in a five-day rotating cycle. To these the village house-wife may take a few eggs, a hen, surplus produce from her kitchen garden, carrying them on a flat basket on her head, a habit which may give Burmese women their fine carriage. Before nationalization small outside merchants would also follow the five-day cycle, bringing in a few of the necessities like cooking oil, textiles, or perhaps cheroots, the cigars which all villagers, men and women, smoke, as do poorer townspeople. Tobacco, however, is something that a villager will grow for himself if his land is suitable.

There will also be food stalls for snacks, a cup of tea or coffee, and a little gossip. These five-day bazaars, where they occur, break the isolation and give the housewife a chance to buy some of her few necessities and pick up a few kyats from the sale of her own surplus. These are hardly large enterprises, for a village is surprisingly self-contained. Their greatest value may be the break in monotony, the sociability, the exchange of news. They cease, of course, during the rainy season.

Some villages are near a road or a main waterway which serves as a road in this land of rivers. But just because there were many streams and the people were so much at home on them, the British never built as many roads here as they did, for instance, in Malaya. So even in this twentieth century there are still *toywa*, jungle villages, which may be miles from real jungle but are also miles from anything else. They can be reached only by a meandering bullock cart trail or by a footpath.

In Sinzwe, which was such an isolated toywa, Communist guerrillas in 1960 tricked the villagers to gain entry, bound and executed all able-bodied men but the schoolmaster, and buried them in a common grave. The army, to impress the minds of Rangoon, flew in reporters from the city to view the carnage. Planes took them as near as they could go and then these young city men walked single-file through the jungle with the army to Sinzwe. All filed their stories of grief and trickery. But one young man, more perceptive than the others, wrote with genuine shock of the irony of such a village in the same world as Rangoon, the complete isolation, the lack of a market to sell their surplus crops if there were a surplus, the lack of any source of purchase for common consumer goods. These villages are still not rare in Burma.

Yet sometimes villagers seem to accept and even invite much greater isolation than is necessary, as if by inertia and habit. One such village near Pegu was for a year the home of an American anthropologist and his wife. About five miles away ran the main Rangoon-Mandalay Road, the most highly traveled paved road in Burma. From there, a narrow dirt road led perhaps three miles nearer the village. The rest of the way was a foot trail. Westerners visited the anthropologist, driving and then walking. But in a year's residence the anthropologist reported that no outsider but his friends came to that village and that no one from the village ever left that confined little world except the village headman, who went sometimes to Pegu by the easily accessible bus on the paved road.

Villages are often well fenced, with a gate that is closed at night. Frequently the tall fences are built of bamboo staves, carefully sharpened; in the arid region up above Toungoo, cactus may be interplanted among the bamboo, their sharp, pricking thorns reinforcing it. This preoccupation with security isn't confined to villages. Houses in towns are equally well fenced and even better guarded. Such guardedness seems to have no relation to the present insurgency. Early English observers commented on these fences, which are probably considered protection against dacoits, or thieves.

The houses within the fence, roughly laid out in patterns resembling wide walks rather than streets, are all basha huts except for a rare wooden house of teak, belonging perhaps to the headman or some family which has managed a greater prosperity than the others. Teak, which weathers well and need not be painted or stained, makes a handsome house. But a basha hut, when it is well built and kept trim and foursquare, has its own handsomeness. A man builds his own house with the aid of four or five of his neighbors. Since basha huts must be rebuilt more frequently than timber houses, he will aid each of his helpers in turn when the time comes for them to rebuild.

Bamboo can be used for the entire house, if necessary, though often nowadays the floor and perhaps some of the beams may be of wood. All village houses are built well off the ground on stilts, with a wooden ladder leading to a roofed veranda. There is frequently a second veranda at the side used for kitchen storage and perhaps food preparation. With the beams, ridgepoles, and frame in place, the floor is laid. The walls, prefabricated squares of thin strips of bamboo, dark and light woven into pleasant patterns, are then lifted and fastened against the frames.

Roofs traditionally are thatched with rice straw, palm and banana leaves, or *dahni*, from a palm that grows in the Delta. Nowadays, metal is used increasingly as a guard against fire, but thatching is both cheaper and cooler and except in the heaviest downpour is quite good protection from the rain. One of the householder's duties each year at the end of the dry season is to check and rethatch his roof against the coming monsoons. There are never glass windows. A bamboo square may be built to swing out or a wooden house may have shutters which open to provide light and air. Cooking is done at a small fireplace sunk in the floor. The danger of fire is great, especially at the end of the dry season when the whole house is like tinder. One spark from an untended fire is enough.

There is little furniture in a village home. Finely woven sleeping mats and cotton blankets are rolled up and put away during the day. There may be a low round table for eating, perhaps a few low stools for sitting. But special mats for sitting are just as common. The Burmese have a way of "hunkering" down on their heels, their knees drawn up, and they can sit like that for hours quite relaxed. Or they may sit as they do at the pagoda, slightly on one hip, knees bent and legs drawn back at one side under their longyis. This is how the king sat on his golden throne, which was a sitting platform rather than a chair. An older woman will sometimes sit comfortably with legs crossed at the ankles, knees spread wide, her longyi pulled modestly to cover even her feet. In the cities she may still sit in this fashion in a chair, feet up off the floor, in a private moment of informal relaxation. Chairs came late to Burma; their very name, *kalathain,* means, roughly, "the way foreigners sit."

Each village house has its own altar to the Buddha where rice and small bouquets of flowers are offered. A village housewife has little time to grow flowers; she takes what the land itself provides for the altar. A city family may grow flowers, even tea roses, especially in large clay pots. But the flowers go to the altar and are not arranged for household ornamentation.

Under the village house a few chickens may live, and the household pariah dog (pi-dog) who acts both as garbage scavenger and watchman; the bullocks or the water buffalo will spend the night and the bullock cart will be stored there. The animals are a necessity for plowing and threshing. It's best to have two, since a bullock cannot work a full day. Water buffalo, those dark creatures of great girth with big horns, are used, but less often. They are harder to control, they do not draw the carts, and must wallow a few hours each day in a mudhole, which may not be available everywhere in Burma.

The monastery with its hpongyi chaung is usually at a slight distance from the houses, and most villages have one even if only one monk is in residence. These structures are of teak. Even if there is no pagoda, there will be at least an altar to the Buddha here.

The ground is bare and hard except in the rainy season, for no crop is more difficult to grow than grass, with no rain for almost half the year. Around government buildings or western homes or the dwellings of the elite in Rangoon, a *mali,* a gardener, will spend long hours watering and fussing over a patch of grass. This seems somewhat absurd in a country where a tree branch thrust in the ground during the rainy season will take root and grow.

The villager has no time for such absurdities. In the dry season the tidy householder will sweep the hard ground clean with a long-handled broom of twigs. In the rainy season the family endures the mud, but the house, high on stilts, is dry.

The Planting Cycle

The cycle of the seasons dictates the cycle of the villagers' labors. Even the Buddha himself bowed to this inevitability when he decreed that, in the rainy season, hpongyis should not travel but remain in one place, intensifying their meditation and devotion. The Burmese call the season the Buddhist Lent. Nowhere in the land in this season are there shinbyus, weddings, or Buddhist festivals, not in cities or villages.

Late in the dry season, in April, the paddy fields are burned off to receive the rains. As soon as they are wet, the fields are plowed, the clods turned up to the continuing downpour. The seedbed of the rice is more carefully prepared into finer soil. All this is man's work, man and bullock. The rice is planted closely here; when the plants are about ten inches tall they are transplanted into the fields, each field surrounded by a low dike perhaps a foot high which serves as both a path and a retaining wall for the water that must flood the field through the growing season. Transplanting, a backbreaking job, is largely women's work. Sometimes bands of women, skilled and swift, work through the countryside as hired hands for the transplanting.

As the season wears on, the fields are kept flooded, mostly from natural rain in the south with a judicious use of irrigation when necessary, almost entirely from irrigation in the north where much less rain falls.

Perhaps there's something atavistic in the idea, but a field of grain seems always to have great beauty. A large wheatfield in Kansas when it ripens and the winds blow through it seems like a golden-bronze lake. The special time of beauty for the rice comes earlier. In the sunlight that intersperses the rains, the paddy fields shimmer like mirrors. The green of the plants lifted above the water is a tender, young green. There are miles and miles of this beauty, with no weeds because the water keeps them down, no people because the work is momentarily done, and only an occasional paddy bird, a kind of small, white crane, feeding on insects or small frogs.

The new strains of miracle rice ripen in about 120 days, but Burma doesn't yet use them extensively. Older strains take about 180 days, which brings harvest time there around early December. As the rains lessen and the grain begins to ripen, the water is allowed to go down in the fields. Men and women together cut the rice by hand and bind it in sheaves. The gaiety of the village, especially if the crop is good, begins to rise. There are songs for harvesting which young men and women sing at their work, a bit of mild flirtation, a touch of courtship.

The village will choose one field for the threshing and pack it down hard. The sheaves are piled in the squeaking two-wheeled bullock carts and brought there. A tethered fawn-colored bullock walks the measured circle, around and around, his hooves threshing out the grain. It is winnowed by hand from flat woven basket-trays, tossed lightly in the air so that the chaff is blown away and the rice left clean. It is then loaded into carts and taken to the rice mills. By Christmas, great hills of golden rice bran are piled outside the mills, chillies are spread out to dry like brilliant red carpets, sugar cane is being cut and going to the sugar mill. This is the harvest time. Other crops are raised, sesamum and groundnuts, even other grains—especially in the hills—but nothing has the mystique of rice. This is life.

The clean white rice from the mills is stored in great baskets, lined and waterproofed with a plaster of cow dung and clay. Enough is kept for the family to eat for a year and for seed for the next crop. The rest is sold to a government buyer or on the black market. There are no private traders as there used to be.

While the water lasts, there may be a second crop, perhaps of vegetables or of groundnuts for their oil. But these second crops are not yet important to the farmer, not nearly as important as the government has tried to persuade him that they are. Where there is irrigation water, there could even be a second rice crop, especially one of the new kinds which grow well in the sun. But the villager's goal, like that of Buddhism, puts small value on the accumulation of possessions. He must have the rice to feed his family. He needs a little surplus to buy what he does not raise, perhaps tobacco or cooking oil, certainly textiles. He will want some cash for a son's shinbyu and an offering to the monks. Beyond that, he is content.

The price offered him for his surplus is not large enough and the supplies of consumer goods are not yet varied enough to tempt him to much greater effort. And he has not yet accepted that he works for the nation's good in a socialist partnership with the city workers and the armed forces. He is passionately loyal to his country, of this there is no question. But he does not comprehend this idea of modern development, not nearly as well as he accepts Buddhist values and the seasonal cycle of hard, strenuous work alternating with the more relaxed months of minimum labor with time for festivals and gaiety.

Nor is this same cycle of living totally absent from the city, where by the end of March it grows hot and humid. Universities and schools are closed for the long vacation. Offices remain open; with their thick walls and slowly-whirring ceiling fans, they may provide more comfort to the workers than the homes. Still the work pace slows. There is a real longing for the rains. Everyone knows how interminable they are, how very wet, how much of a nuisance in the city where the principal business is not the growing of rice. But the heat is so great that somehow all the nuisance is temporarily forgotten.

Yet, as in the villages, it is a gay time because with the rains, Lent will come. Shinbyus must be held now or the boy must

wait six months. Marriages, the culmination of a season's court-
ing, must be performed now or the bride and groom must also
wait through the long rainy season. In mid-April the Water
Festival will come, prelude to the Buddhist New Year, one of
the gayest of Buddhist festivals. Besides, since it must be hot, it
is easier to forget the heat in gaiety than in work. The slow,
quiet season is just around the corner. Time enough for work
then.

Life Style

Clothing

This patterned similarity between village and city imposed by
a weather cycle is only the beginning of likenesses between the
villager and the urbanite.

All Burmese men and women continue to wear their own style
of clothing. Men who go to the west to study or travel will switch
then to western clothing and, returning to Rangoon, may very
occasionally reappear in a western suit. But even abroad, the
women prefer their own way of dressing.

Both wear a longyi, a kind of skirt. But sexual differences distinguish the type of pattern in the fabric and the manner of
wearing the longyi; these are so distinct that in time even the
western eye associates sex with them and would be as shocked
at a turn-about as a Burmese. For both men and women, a longyi
is a 2-yard length of cloth woven to a width which reaches the
ankles of the wearer. A fine, French seam joins the two cut edges
of the fabric, which may be either silk or cotton. A black cotton
band about 2 inches wide is added to the top of a woman's longyi.

Stepping into this circular garment, a Burmese woman draws
it to her right until it is snug along her left hip, holds the surplus
material straight out to her right, then with a swift gesture flips
it around and to her left where, with a twist and a tuck, she
fastens it firmly. Somehow it is around her waist and stays

there. The fold of the fabric across the front gives her walking freedom.

A man, on the other hand, stands in the center of this tubular garment, the extra fabric held out equally both left and right. With a similar assured gesture, he flips both sides to the front, twists the two top corners together and tucks them at the waist. The surplus material, like a deep box pleat at the front, accommodates his longer stride.

The pattern of a man's longyi is discreet, a herringbone weave, small checks, some kind of simple allover pattern. A woman's is more decorative, frequently with a wide woven border near the bottom and a bit of the border pattern scattered over the rest of the longyi. Distinctive regional differences occur in longyi patterns. Their weaving is almost a folk art.

Villagers wear their longyis even working in the flooded paddy fields. A man draws his up high about his thighs, pulls the surplus material forward between his legs and tucks it in at his waist. Women are more modest; they merely hike the fabric up around their waist until the bottom clears the water, falling just below their knees.

A woman's blouse is called an *eingyi.* For years the favorite fabric was nylon in a delicate pastel to blend with her longyi, and the eingyi was sleeveless. Under the somewhat strait-laced present government, more and more women have returned to the traditional long-sleeved eingyi of thin, white nainsook. Either fastens diagonally and then down, like a Chinese cheong-sam, closed by five eingyi buttons, small jeweled trinkets that can be transferred from blouse to blouse, which has loops to hold them. Sometimes, and more frequently today, the fastenings are small delicately shaped frogs or "buttons" of fabric which slip through a loop. These have always been more common in the villages, where the women indulged in fewer jewels.

Under her eingyi a woman wears a bodice of heavier cotton, with a small pocket at one side where she will carry her money, easily accessible since her eingyi does not tuck into her longyi.

Her long, black hair is combed back smoothly and knotted at the nape of her neck. A Burmese woman may wear a flower tucked into the coil of her hair with grace and insouciance, for no special occasion, simply because she passed a flower which pleased her fancy.

The man must have worn something more traditional before western imports reached the country. But today the villager wears a knitted T-shirt for an upper garment, the ordinary young townsman wears a white short-sleeved shirt over his T-shirt and the professional man wears a white shirt with a narrow stand-up collar fastened with a gold collar-button, a shirt which bears a marked resemblance to the turn-of-the-century western shirt without its stiff, separate collar. He also wears, for the office, a silk jacket, usually black, which also fastens with loops and frogs in the Chinese manner.

No one wears a hat, except the little knitted cap a small boy frequently has pulled on even in hot weather as if to emphasize the specialness of that precious male head. Both countrymen and countrywomen will wear a kind of turban, usually made now of turkish toweling, when they are at work outside. It is seldom seen in the city except among working women like those carrying up trays of brick or mortar on their heads to workmen on construction jobs. Then it is coiled high to form a kind of cushion for the burden.

But there is a special male headgear called a *gaung-baung*, a traditional symbol of status at a formal occasion. When Parliament still met, one saw M.P.'s being chauffeured to the meeting, small hatboxes on the car shelf behind them containing their gaung-baungs. Once probably they were tied on each occasion they were worn. Now they are ready-tied and shaped on a finely woven reed frame to fit the head, bulging a little in the back, probably because men once wore their hair long and it had to be coiled up. A bit of pastel silk is arranged over the frame, smooth at the top, folded around the bottom with one end fanning out free at the side by a few inches, copying the day when it had to be tied to stay on the head.

Since, except for that little pocket in the woman's eingyi, no one has a place to carry things, everyone from schoolboy on up, man or woman, carries a Shan bag, handsomely woven and about ten inches square, with a shoulder strap several inches wide. The Kachins also weave similar bags, usually of wool, often trimmed in silver, but they are luxuries. Shan bags are necessities.

Very small children today wear western clothing, a little dress for the girl, a knitted shirt for the boy. Neither will wear pants for some time because toilet training is taken casually and in due season by the Burmese, with none of the pressure western parents put on the achievement. Little boys may wear pants somewhat unwillingly for expeditions outside their own compounds.

Once the children are a little older, they wear longyis like their parents, though an active little boy may sometimes be given a belt to wear.

All, men, women, and children, in city or country, wear thonged sandals. There has been some importation of the Japanese rubber ones with which we are familiar. But most Burmese prefer the ones made in their own country, usually of leather, sometimes with the thong and upper strap of dark velvet for women. All remove them before entering a Burmese home because the altar to the Buddha is inside. Often, out of courtesy, they'll be left at the door of a western home, too.

This matter of clothing demonstrates very well the likenesses and differences between Burmese villager and townsman. All wear the same dress, except that even a headman probably doesn't wear a gaung-baung. Townspeople have more variety of fabrics available, more sophisticated silks, more jewels. Country people will wear cotton and have fewer changes of garments. But a young village girl can step out of her village along a main road, hire a passing pony cart or trishaw, drive into a nearby town, and mingle inconspicuously with the townspeople there. A young girl from a toywa might be noticeable, but as much for her timidity as for any difference in her clothes.

Adornment or Investment?

Without a doubt, good jewelry is more common among Burmese women than among British or Americans. The fact, however, must be put in context in the particular culture. Burma has a banking system, but as late as a decade ago it was impossible to pay a Mandalay hotel bill with a check drawn to the hotel on a sound, well-known Rangoon bank. Jewelry and land have been the family investment.

Besides, it is easy to buy good jewels. One need not travel to a fashionable city jeweler. Itinerant peddlers, down from the mines with a few sapphires and rubies, appear at the door. Burmese women seem to know what they're about; after careful examination of the stones they will buy with assurance from such a stranger. Of course only the wealthy can afford true pigeon-blood rubies or good star sapphires, but there are plenty of small light blue sapphires and rosy-pink rubies which cost much less. For those who can't afford these, there are the semiprecious stones, the spinels, which also come from Burma's mines. If even these are too costly, one can buy glass stones made for gems and cut, so western jewelers say, with the same care and workmanship given the real thing. Only the poorest will have their jewels set in anything but gold, and it will be 24 karat. The poor and westerners buy the silver jewelry, the latter because they admire Burmese silverwork.

Certainly more jewels are found in cities because more urban families have larger incomes. But an American who knew prewar villages said that an average Burmese village had in it more genuine gold and jewels than a midwestern town of the same size.

Perhaps all this should be written in the past tense, both because the mines have been nationalized and because cash income is less. But the black market manages to distribute all other kinds of goods and it is doubtful that the Burmese woman who wants stones cannot buy them also "on the outside."

The Burmese Diet

No one but a good Burmese cook should write about Burmese food. The outsider knows that he has never learned the whole story because he is constantly served what are to him new delicacies which he's never eaten or even heard about before. He will not find them in a restaurant because restaurant food is western, Chinese, or Indian; his own cook, if the ousider is a resident of Burma, is probably Indian. Burmese do not like accepting such posts in another's home.

What the foreigner learns, he learns from his friends. He, or she, never steps foot in a friend's house but that there is a quick command toward the kitchen, some small snack with something to drink appears on the instant, and there is the soft, gentle, but rather authoritative command from the hostess, "Saba." It may be a thin crisp cake of rice flour, twisted like a cornucopia, or a few fish chips, dried in the sun, which, when fried in deep oil quickly, puff up light and crisp. The drink may be tea or coffee or, in the city, a bottled soft drink. The hostess serves but seldom eats with her guest.

A stranger in a village is served almost as quickly, usually with coffee heavily sweetened with condensed, not evaporated, milk. A paper kyat, so it won't jingle, slipped quietly with the utmost lack of ostentation into the money box of a small-town pagoda always means that tea appears promptly from somewhere, ordered by a sharp-eyed lay trustee.

Burmese are hospitable, sociable, welcoming. They habitually show that hospitality with food or drink as they visit back and forth informally. But they give dinner parties in the western manner much less often than westerners. When they entertain with a full-course meal, it is more likely to be for a whole neigh-

borhood or a village on such a special occasion as a christening
or a wedding. In the city this food is usually catered. It won't
be up to the hostess' own standards. Lucky is the westerner who
has a few friends who entertain him at traditional, home-cooked
Burmese meals.

Usually two meals are served at home during the day, though
the Burmese also nibble between meals. In the village, during the
working months, cold rice is taken to the fields for a noontime
meal. Rice is the center of every meal. A Burmese hasn't eaten
unless he has eaten rice and eaten it in quantity. The condensed-
milk can is frequently the measure. Two such cans of raw rice
(very close to four cups) will be cooked at a meal for the physical
worker. The child at school or the office worker will need only
one can.

Hingyo, a clear soup, is usually served with leaves of green
vegetables, followed by the rice and a curry, a meat with gravy,
to serve with the rice. The meat is often fish or prawns, which
are both delicious in Burma, often chicken, occasionally mutton,
and very rarely beef. Oil is used and, for seasoning, usually fried
onions, fresh ginger, fried garlic, perhaps turmeric or coriander,
chopped dried chillies. Frying the garlic and onions is thought
to remove the strong flavor. But usually chillies are not all put
in the cooking dish and an extra amount is placed on the table
for those who wish to add their own. The curry is neither as oily
nor as dark as the usual curry, and not nearly as hot. It is a more
delicate dish.

Ngapi, a high-smelling, strongly flavored fish paste, will certainly be used as a condiment if possible. This is so prized by
Burmese that a family going abroad to live for a while will have
cases of it, packed in earthen jars, sent with their luggage. It is
one of those things which, like the strong-smelling durian fruit, a
hostess doesn't usually serve to westerners, so few have the opportunity to discover whether they like it or not.

To this basic meal many small side dishes can be added, fried
bean-sprout cakes, *mohinga* (rice noodles with their own sauce)

—the variety is endless, depending on the cook's own specialties. A leisurely meal will usually end with tea or coffee and a small condiment tray, as if hors d'oeuvres were served at the end of the meal rather than the beginning—pickled tea, very thin slices of fried garlic, small slivers of ginger, small toasted groundnuts. Sweets and fruits are to eat between meals along with small hot tidbits purchased from food vendors on the streets or at food stalls in a bazaar.

To pretend that most Burmese eat meals like this twice a day would be absurd. Most Burmese don't have enough money. But the division comes by income, not by urban or village living. That official survey of household expenditures in Rangoon, mentioned in an earlier chapter, showed that lower-income families spent 50 per cent of their income for food, mostly rice and fish. Yet all Burmese know the more lavish foods; they do eat them sometimes if only at feasts; they do enjoy food-stall snacks if only at an occasional visit to a district town; they use the same food seasonings, they all love ngapi. Differences are not in kind but in quantity.

It is important to reiterate that even Burma's poor seldom go to bed hungry. There can be a lack of vitamins, for the rice is polished, or a lack of protein. There can be floods or droughts or even at 20-year intervals the blooming of a particular kind of bamboo in the north, when the rats feed on the blossoms and multiply so greatly that their hordes destroy a crop. Then rice must be shipped in to the afflicted districts. Sometimes today, when there are tie-ups in food distribution, something like cooking oil is hard to find and must be bought either on the black market or across the border in China or Thailand. But basically, food production for the internal market is not one of Burma's problems.

THE FAMILY

The Burmese family is a nuclear family, and the country's

history would indicate that it always has been. Indeed, the Burmese word for marriage, *ein-daung-pyu*, means to set up a house. Each young couple establish their own home where they will raise their own children. But a reverence for all elders and a particular reverence for parents is a part of this culture; the independent household is not detached in love or filial duty. The family is indeed an extended family in the responsibility that each feels for all the other members, reaching through aunts and uncles and even to distant cousins.

There is a glimpse of the closeness accorded the family bond, how intimate members of it are cherished, in the curious fact that a young husband will not infrequently speak of his wife as his younger sister. To call a friend one's elder sister, one's *amagyi*, is a very special gesture of affection.

Forms of address reflect family relationships. A young boy is born to be called "Maung" and a little girl, "Ma." To my knowledge these are forms of address only and have no other meaning; they may be used throughout life. But, for instance, a young man named Hla Tun who is called Maung Hla Tun and will so call himself may be addressed as Ko Hla Tun by his friends and intimates. "Ko" means brother. Because it adds a certain stature and respect, the address may also be used by others who have a friendly respect for Hla Tun but are not really among his intimate friends.

But if Hla Tun attains a certain distinction in his society, he becomes U Hla Tun; "U" means uncle. Age and an elder's wisdom may bring the title to a man, but age isn't necessary. A young man may move in his society within a year or so from "Maung" as a college undergraduate, through "Ko" as a graduate student, to "U" on completion of his studies and appointment to a university post. But our Hla Tun will never call *himself* anything but Maung Hla Tun. Books published in English by Burmese of distinction are published with no form of title at all or with the use of "Maung." Status is given, never taken.

The occasion at which a woman moves from "Ma" to "Daw,"

which means "aunt," is not as rigidly prescribed. Marriage has nothing to do with it; the usage of the two forms does not parallel our usage of Miss and Mrs. The use of "Daw" may not carry quite as much impact on a woman's station in society as the use of "U." But it is still a mark of respect. Young adults of English-speaking Burmese families, especially if they are traditionalists, will call their families' western friends "auntie" and "uncle" as casually as any niece or nephew might. But note that all these status titles are names for family relationships.

Though families are nuclear, family closeness does sometimes produce what almost seems to be an extended family. The universities are in the cities. In this casteless society, education is what gives the individual mobility. It is taken for granted that a city family should make room for a country relative to live while he or she attends the university.

Unmarried sisters may live with a married brother, particularly if the wife is a professional woman, though the wife very definitely remains head of her own household. Poor country cousins may often come as young girls to work in the home of more prosperous city relatives, where their role will be halfway between a servant and a member of the family. But the mistress of the house has definite responsibilities under such an arrangement. It is understood that she will see that the girl has an opportunity to make an appropriate marriage, and that she will provide her with a few small bits of jewelry and fitting clothing so that she goes unashamed to her city husband. In a sense, this is another form of social mobility.

A village, while it may be in serious need of medical facilities or a school, seldom lacks what we would call the supportive structure of social welfare. A family cares for its own. If that becomes impossible, if an elderly father or mother is left alone by death, it will be assumed by the village elders that the other villagers will provide the necessities, not as charity but with due respect.

Not often but occasionally, in the city of Rangoon, urban impersonality creeps in. Rangoon is the only Burmese city I have known with an orphanage, a "home for waifs and strays," and two homes for the aged, one for Buddhists only and a Catholic one which was nonsectarian.

One of Burma's few social workers was attached to the Rangoon General Hospital, a large municipal hospital. She told once of an elderly woman patient who was ready to be dismissed but who was plainly going to be fairly immobile for the rest of her life. The patient had young married sons but they never appeared on the days set for her dismissal. Finally she sent for the social worker and asked that the young woman drive her to her home and leave her there. She particularly insisted with wry good humor that she be left, that the social worker not wait around to see what happened. Evidently she felt quite confident that in her presence, old cultural habits would be stronger than any new city ways.

With some nervousness, the social worker did as she was told and, in this later account, reported that the mother was evidently right. Her children never redelivered her to the hospital. Yet this incident of attempted abandonment was vivid in the social worker's mind because it was the only one of its kind in her several years of service.

If the village is the heart of Burma, the family is the heart of all its society, either in village or city.

Marriage and Divorce

It may be true, as many Burmese believe, that the British disrupted their traditional social culture. But when it came to the Burmese customary laws governing marriage and divorce—what the British called "Burmese Buddhist Law"—judges were scrupulous in seeking out such laws and administering all questions of marriage and divorce in accordance with them.

Actually, the laws are not tidily codified and never were, even in the days of the Burmese kings. Yet the purpose and intent have been plain in the Burmese Dhammathats. The only modern laws on the books are those intended to clarify, supplement, or strengthen the customary laws.

Rather strangely, considering the closeness of the family and the partnership quality of a Burmese Buddhist marriage, polygamy is, technically, legal under Burmese customary law. But second wives have never really been approved in Burmese society, except for kings and sawbwas. In the late 1950's, newspaper stories treated such a marriage of a university official to a young second wife as if it were downright scandalous. In spite of all his protestations of legality, social pressure forced him to resign his post.

A Burmese and his bride do not need the permission of the state in the form of a marriage license to marry. Nor does a Buddhist monk, whose interests are far removed from such secular matters, perform the wedding ceremony. Conversely, a married couple doesn't need the courts for a divorce. The only time such affairs wind up in the courts is when there are disputes which can't be settled by the families, friends, or headman.

In Buddhist Burma, there is no bride price. There are no dowries in the conventional sense, though both families will give what they can to start the young couple on their way. Nor are there, strictly speaking, arranged marriages. There never were, if by arranged marriage one means a reluctant bride and a young couple who see each other first on their wedding night. Although parents certainly have urged marriages on their offspring, no young girl could be married without her consent.

Often today there is still a go-between, but this is more a matter of arranging in advance the necessary details, such as the important comparison of the horoscopes of bride and groom to be sure that all will go well with the union, the selection of an auspicious day for the wedding, and the choice of a happily married couple to sponsor the bride and groom and lend the aura of their own happiness to the new union.

Courtship is sedate enough, but hardly as dull as it sounds.

Burmese are too gay by nature to permit falling in love to be dull. A village girl of marriageable age may sit on her veranda in the evening and young men may come calling, while she and they both know her mother is just inside. Even though the western style of dating is not usual and the family, down to the cousins, are watchful of a young girl's virtue, the Burmese girl is hardly in purdah.

In the smaller community, young people grow up knowing each other. They meet, but in groups, at the communal celebrations of a shinbyu, at pagoda festivals with their pwes. Even on more sober duty-days at the pagoda, a young man is hardly unaware of the devout miss kneeling gracefully before the altar, engrossed in her meditations. Most traditional paddy songs are part-teasing, part-flirtatious, part-courting songs.

In district towns, young people are in the same high school classes, where they begin to meet possible mates whose families are not known personally to their families. Those who go on to the universities widen even further their possible choice of mates, meet in groups at even more social events, at cinemas as well as at pwes, and always at the recurring religious festivals. They may lack the privacy of western twosome dating, but there can be privacy even in groups. Long before the time that the young man, or someone in his family, must approach the family of the young woman, the couple know their own minds and hearts.

The parents' consent is presumably a prerequisite of a marriage, in particular the bride's parents if the bride is under 20, but there is a way of circumventing parents who withhold such consent. The young Burmese girl is brought up in modesty and circumspection. Yet, thwarted by stubborn parents, the young couple may quite properly elope without marriage. After they have lived together for a week or so, the parents usually give in and accept them back into the family. A simple announcement ceremony to a few friends and to the elders gives the marriage recognition.

It is in just this way that a Burmese Buddhist wedding differs from other such ceremonies. No one pronounces the couple man and wife. The ceremony is, rather, the young couple's announcement to the public that they have decided to become man and wife and is not actually necessary for a legal marriage.

Most brides would not by choice forgo the beautiful but simple ceremony. In the cities, where the guest list is long and all must be fed following the ceremony, the festive occasion frequently takes place in the ballroom of a hotel late in the morning. The bride, who usually wears her black hair coiled smoothly at the nape of her neck, will for this occasion have it dressed in the high court style as in the days of kings. Her groom will wear a gaung-baung. Clothing of the bride and groom are the customary longyi and, for her, the eingyi, for him the jacket. But these are more sumptuous silks than everyday garb, and the bride will surely wear her family's finest jewels. They sit side by side on silk cushions with their sponsors nearby. Although the ceremony may be elaborated, basically it is a matter of binding the hands of bride and groom together with a light silk scarf, the eating of food from the same silver bowls, and a common obeisance to the Dhamma (the Law), the Sangha (the monkhood), and the Buddha.

Then all the guests, dressed in their richest finery, are served an excellent meal to much chatter and gaiety, after the solemnity and quiet of the ceremony itself.

This is an expensive affair, and a few modern young people today are merely exchanging affidavits before a legal authority of competence and intent to marry. Dr. Maung Maung writes that early in his legal practice a young couple appeared asking him to draft such a "certificate" of marriage.

"I did not know what to put in, and had to ask a clerk," he reports with a certain sympathetic amusement; "I did not know how much fee to charge and, as a small fee might make their great venture look small, charged 500 kyats ($100), stamped the documents with the largest seal I had, tied them up in ribbons of gold and red. The young couple went away happy, and, as far as my knowledge goes, remain so with their growing family."

Headmen are supposed to keep a register of marriages. One of the life patterns of the village which has crept into the city are these very headmen, though somewhere else they might be called ward or precinct leaders. Thus marriages are normally registered even though the ceremony itself is neither a religious nor a civil one, but a personal "consensual contract."

Such a contract can also be ended by the same mutual consent, though, again, it is expected that the headman be notified of the divorce. He and the couple's families and friends can be expected to try to dissuade them. If that is unsuccessful, the wife will take with her what property she brought to the marriage and so will the husband. What has been accumulated during the marriage is divided between them, including the children. Yet there are few such visits to headmen, very few divorces in Burma.

The Status of Women

There are strong hints of the equality of Burmese women in these customary laws, and these hints are not misleading. This is what the British found early in the nineteenth century when they arrived from India, where the position of women was far different. Although British judges administered the laws scrupulously, many Englishmen reacted somewhat irritably to the position of Burmese women. They called the men henpecked. They talked about a matriarchy, and said the women were domineering. After all, their own wives had no such rights, though this they never mentioned.

Burmese women mention it with some pride. They point out that they have always had rights which western women gained only in the twentieth century. They keep their own names after marriage; there are no surnames in Burma except among a few families who have adopted the western custom. They have had a "community property" law before the west ever heard of such a marriage right, but they call it a partnership. A husband cannot sell or mortgage or encumber in any way the property of the marriage unless his wife also signs the documents. This is the legal acknowledgment of the fact that husband and wife are expected to talk over privately such family decisions and come to a common conclusion.

A Burmese Buddhist cannot make a will under customary law. On the death of husband or wife, the survivor inherits. Only on the death of the surviving parent do the children inherit. All the details concerning the children get fairly complex. But this is the gist of it: The widow inherits her husband's share of the joint property, just as her husband would inherit hers. She does not become dependent on her children by a division of the property among them.

There were headwomen as far back as Pagan, businesswomen, and women with enough property of their own to make gifts to pagodas, gifts large enough to be noted with appropriate inscriptions. Most bazaar stalls and many of the small shops have until recent times been run by women. The professions are open to them and, since the country has need of trained minds, most women continue to practice their professions after marriage. They have been admitted to the universities since those were founded, and no Burmese male thought of denying them the vote when rules about the electorate were made in the first degree of independence under the British.

The husband, of course, has one advantage over his wife if they are Buddhists, and most are. His very maleness gives him precedence over her in Buddhism because only a man may reach Nirvana. When the next Buddha comes to earth, it will of course be as a man. This husband of hers has probably been a hpongyi, at least for a while; he could be one again. All of this is denied her, unless in another life she is reborn as a man. It makes a difference.

She offers him a certain deference for this. Perhaps that is why she leaves the larger affairs of the nation to him, why women have not occupied in the Union of Burma the important posts that some have held in India. Perhaps, though she herself is a devout Buddhist, her role makes her more secular-minded, more practical, and more shrewd in business dealings because this is the way that is open to her in this life.

With all this, there is a very nice balance in the partnership between a Burmese husband and wife—discriminating, tactful, subtle on both sides. He is not henpecked. She is not dominated. They both know their own role and the role of the other. Whatever happens in private joint decision-making about the children or the family's affairs, in public the man is the head of the house. And the woman still retains her independence.

Child-Rearing

The boys and girls of these marriages are brought up in ways that fit the roles they will play. Children of both sexes are loved and wanted, and life for all of them is relaxed and easy-going the first few years. They are weaned late, often not until the next child comes along, but they are started on solid food when they are quite young—soft rice, of course.

Until about the age of six, little boys in villages usually have only one responsibility, that of tending the animals, especially the long-horned water buffalo, while they're grazing. But it doesn't look very exhausting. They spend much of the time stretched out lazily on the backs of the animals, as much at ease as they might be on a sleeping mat at home. A little girl, before six, is introduced to her mother's duties, which are somewhat more strenuous. She will also baby-sit a younger sibling, carrying the child straddled on her hip as her mother does, or rocking it in the cradle.

Traditionally, a boy's discipline really began when he entered the hpongyi-chaung around the age of six, for the monks accepted little nonsense from their young pupils. The impression is that today all the children go to secular schools, but that isn't entirely accurate. From the heart of Rangoon to the quiet shores of the Irrawaddy below Ava, there can still be heard the shouted rhythmic chant of young voices in unison which means that a monks' school is nearby.

By six, the young boy probably already knows that in another six years or so he will be appearing at the monastery for his shinbyu, wide-eyed, riding a white pony, dressed in the gilt and tinsel of a pretend-prince, to renounce temporarily the world and put on the saffron-yellow robe of a novice monk. The special quality of his maleness is something he is already learning.

His young sister is learning her role, too. Today little girls also go to school—not all, but many, and more and more each year as the nation becomes able to provide more schools and teachers. But a little girl learns also from her mother, and not only her household duties. She will watch her mother shopping at the bazaar, the shrewd examination of the goods, the sharp bargaining. She will absorb her rights and her responsibilities.

Both of them will grow up with the proper respect for their elders, making the graceful shadow of a *shikko*, bending down a little, when they pass between two older adults. Unless the little boy decides to remain in the monastery as a monk, both in time will go on to marry and assume the same roles their parents have played in a warm, outreaching family structure. Burma isn't a bad place to be a little child, except for the appalling mortality statistics.

HEALTH

Burma's health problems are severe. Life expectancy in recent times has been under 30 years, but a look at the available statistics shows plainly that it is young children's deaths that pull down the figure. If a child can survive his early years, he has a reasonable chance to live to a decent maturity.

Total detah rates in Burma are 18 per thousand annually. In

the United States, they run somewhat under 10 per thousand. But infant death rates in Burma are still running around 100 per thousand, compared to the 22 in the United States, which itself has far from the best record among western nations.

Of what do these children die? Here, Burmese statistics are weak. Eighty per cent of the people of the nation have no access to any medical service at all, and of that large group more live in villages than in towns or cities. It is the duty of the headman to record deaths and their causes, but he seldom can pretend to any medical knowledge and usually has no one to help him. So the records often show that children die of "childhood diseases," younger adults of "complications," and the elderly of "old age." Observation would seem to indicate that more babies die of some form of dysentery or of bronchial illness in the damp raw days of the monsoons, with the first leading the second.

There's some irony in this, for Burmese are immaculately clean about their persons and their clothing. They bathe often, at the well, in the river, in a washing room to which water is carried from the well, at a standpipe in the city, or in a modern indoor bathroom. Their frequent lack of privacy does not conflict with their innate modesty. The women draw their longyis up over their breasts in sarong style, the men bathe with their shirts removed. They bathe over their longyis in running or poured water; when they finish, they deftly drop a fresh dry longyi over their heads as they release the wet one. The running water is important. They do not understand the western custom of bathing in a tub of water that naturally becomes unclean during the ablutions.

But they do not boil their drinking water, they do not wash their hands habitually before handling food, their sanitary facilities are either absent or odorous (except in middle-class homes), so that relieving themselves in the fresh out-of-doors seems cleaner than going to the privies even when they're available. And so the streams and wells are further tainted in a nation where the dysenteries are endemic.

Other major illnesses in the population as a whole include malaria, tuberculosis, some cholera and plague, venereal diseases, leprosy, filariasis, the liver illnesses which are the aftermath of chronic amoebic dysentery, and what seem to a westerner an abnormally high number of undiagnosed "fevers" which defy even well-trained doctors.

The brighter side of this picture is the real effort which the present government is investing in health programs. Health expenditures have virtually doubled between 1965 and 1970. Control of malaria is pushed strongly, and in some districts the disease has been virtually eradicated. Smallpox vaccinations have been stepped up and deaths from it have dropped sharply. Cholera inoculations are on the increase. More and more the people understand that rats carry the plague. Less and less often do they flee at the first sign rather than standing their ground and fighting the rats, in spite of their Buddhism.

Despite the dismissal of foreign doctors and the fact that there's only one doctor for each 10,000 people, the figure of 1,500 doctors in 1962 has grown to more than 2,500. The high proportion in private practice as against public, governmental employment is almost reversed. Today doctors, on graduation, must accept government posts for several years, usually as township or district health officers, before they are permitted to enter private practice.

There's always been a Red Cross in Burma, tuned to disaster relief. But today Red Cross societies are being organized in the villages—there are 6,000 now—active not only in disaster relief but in health education. With Dr. Maung Maung, Chief Justice of the Chief Court, as the national president, the organization should be something more than a paper chart in a Rangoon office.

In spite of the nation's efforts to improve its people's health, the distance to travel is still long.

When death does come, the people's attitude reflects their belief in Buddhism and rebirth. There is natural grief, but the family does not enter a long period of mourning. The body may be either buried or cremated. The cremation of a wise and elderly hpongyi is like a festival, a time of rejoicing, because surely such a good man has died with a good Karma, and may even have reached Nirvana.

The tombs and burial grounds are not usually tended carefully or visited frequently, for there lies only the body of one who will live many more lives. But on Martyrs' Hill where Bogyoke Aung San and the men who were assassinated with him lie in their white marble tombs, visitors come almost every day, not celebrities but the common people, the ludu, who honor him and leave small bouquets of flowers. Even the tomb of Queen Supayalat, near the Shwedagon Pagoda, is whitewashed each year after the rains. This last queen of Burma, who was allowed to return from exile in India after King Thibaw's death, was certainly not the best-loved of Burma's queens. Still, now and then, flowers are left at her tomb.

RANGOON AND MANDALAY

The contrast between the two states of mind of Rangoon and Mandalay is well epitomized by two buildings. Each city has a new Institute for Advanced Buddhistic Studies. Rangoon's was built first, a handsome, modern building of advanced architecture embodying all the old precious symbols, such as the lotus bud. Mandalay's, erected a few years later, is a big, square teak building, architecturally resembling a nineteenth-century American city public school but for its roof. This is many-tiered in the traditional Asian manner, which must originally have been for ventilation. But this one, touched with the red and gold of all the ancient palaces and wooden monasteries, is evocative, standing there as cover for that conventional building.

It is easy to become bemused in Mandalay where the great wall of the palace compound still stands, the wide moat around

it covered with water hyacinth, the main gateways in the brick
wall covered with that same tiered roof line. There stands the
Kuthodaw, the work of royal merit, with its scriptures on stone.
There is the Shwe Nandaw Monastery, once the royal apart-
ment where King Mindon died. The structure was moved outside the palace walls by his successor to become a monastery.
Probably the most beautiful example of old wood carving left in
Burma, it is now slowly deteriorating. In the sunset and the dusk,
ghosts of the past move about the city, and Mandalay's citizens
feel them. It's a rude shock to remember, then, that the city
wasn't begun until 1857, that even by New World standards it
isn't old, and that Mindon, who built it, was Burma's most
modern king.

Rangoon is older. Its wide central streets, laid out by the British, were copied by Mindon for Mandalay. In Rangoon, many of
the street signs are still in English letters, though the old English
names may be replaced by Burmese ones. Rangoon has grown a
little shabby (and much cleaner) in the last few years. In its once-
crowded streets, the traffic has thinned with a ban on import of
cars or even spare parts for private use. Many Burmese who
built angular stucco houses to rent to westerners, houses their
tenants dubbed "Rangoon modern," are forced to live in the
structures themselves now. Their own dwellings are more usually
of teak or a soft, pinkish native brick.

Even though it has grown more quiet, Rangoon is still a
metropolis, capital of a sovereign nation, with some of the pomp
that goes along with a capital, the embassies, the foreign flags on
ambassadors' cars, the old government buildings the British built
in the same lovely brick, the handsome City Hall, its brick
painted gray, dwarfing most other buildings in the city except
the Shwedagon itself.

The British had a gift for building important structures so
that they mirrored the country. Just as Kuala Lumpur's railway
station evokes that Muslim city, so Rangoon's City Hall could
belong only in Burma. Its tiered roofline, its wide courtyard, the

outer galleries or verandas on each floor which substitute for inner hallways and let the air sweep into all rooms, its noble traditional peacock seal high over the entrance, painted in gold and bright colors—these are all fitting for Burma.

The City Hall stands opposite Independence Park, with its tall obelisk the symbol of that independence; on the other side is the American Embassy and nearby the golden Sule Pagoda, small compared to the Shwedagon but of some antiquity. The pagoda's charm lies in the small oasis of quiet it brings to the heart of the city's life.

Once Independence Park was no more than a playing field, but now it is a true, landscaped park with flowers and bright foliage plants. The present government has landscaped this and many smaller spots, such as the turn-arounds on the wide avenues where traffic splits and moves around the grassy circle.

Flowers are more prevalent now, but Rangoon has always been a city of trees, shading both the wide avenues and the narrower, winding residential streets. Most of them are blooming trees whose flowers redeem the parched, dry season. Several varieties of acacia drip their long, wisteria-like sprays in yellow and pink. Fragrant frangipani with their waxy-white blossoms are common. Along the road around the Royal Lake, giant royal palms tower over the cars and pedestrians. Indeed, Rangoon has many small lakes besides the larger Royal Lake and Inya Lake next to the university where student boat races are held.

This is the city which experiments with the new while preserving the old, in contrast to Mandalay which preserves the old and admits the new grudgingly. Yet Rangoon is older than Mandalay.

Such dichotomies recur again and again in Burma. Villagers don't like to move about, they say. A while back, the government moved several entire villages south to good land from their poor village sites in the north. Within a few years all the villagers went home. Yet if that urge to immobility were absolute, Rangoon would be an empty city today. Most of its families have come from villages, perhaps via district towns, within this century. Bogyoke Aung San, leader of Burmese independence, himself was a village boy.

It is said that the people don't want to get involved. They remember an old Burmese proverb about the five great evils, one of which was government, so they prefer the isolation of their villages to the outer world. Yet between 1964 and 1967, primary-school pupils increased from 1.8 million to 2.8 million. Education is the way to become unisolated, mobile, and schools are filled as fast as the government can build them and train teachers.

Both sides of all the dichotomies are true, though no one really knows how equally balanced they are. But a scale can find its balance not just by two equal masses but by the tension of a spring. The tension exists in Burma between the new and the old. It keeps the one from moving too fast, prevents the other from not moving at all. Yet the balance is true. Whatever changes come, all want Burmese life and this Burmese social structure to remain Burmese, not to be a copy of any other world.

8 Education

THE EARLY BURMESE PATTERN

The degree of literacy in the whole of Burma astonished the colonial British. The country held an enormous lead over all other provinces of India. "The number of literates among the men is, indeed, almost as high as the number in Ireland, and higher than the proportion in Italy," wrote Sir J. G. Scott early in the new century.

In 1901, even counting the illiterate immigrants from India in Lower Burma and part of the hill people, one of every five persons living in Burma could read and write. But in a count of the ethnic Burmans alone, then numerically strongest in Upper Burma, the figures were much more impressive. Among every 1,000, 490 males and 55 females—close to 55 per cent—were literate.

The obvious explanation lay in the hpongyi-chaungs, the monks' schools, which most Burman Buddhist boys in village or town were expected to attend even before they became novice-monks. But it must also lie in some element of Burman culture. Mons and Shans were Buddhists; their hpongyis also taught in their chaungs. Yet the literacy figure for both was considerably lower than for the Burmans. One can only surmise that the difference rose out of the classless society of the Burman people and the respect for learning ingrained in all of them. Though few aspired to become sayas, most boys learned to read, write, and work simple arithmetic problems, in addition to acquiring the principles of their Buddhist faith.

If the number of Burman women literates seems small, it was still far greater than for any other ethnic female group. The late U Kaung, Independent Burma's first Director of Education, traced the explanation to lay schools. He found their early history obscure and could put no date on their beginnings. Yet long before the British came they did exist in towns, though their numbers were far below those of the hpongyi-chaungs.

Their purpose was to educate young girls and little boys still too small to go to the chaungs. Laymen and women ran the schools, seemingly as an act of merit, charging no fees. There seems to have been no inherent discrimination against education of women as such. Rather, their womanhood and its position in Buddhism kept them out of the inner circle of the monasteries and therefore out of the chaungs. Wealthier families and those at the Court engaged tutors for their daughters.

Only novice-monks advanced in their education to what might be termed middle-school standards. Only the monks themselves normally became scholars, with certain outstanding exceptions among gifted men at the Court.

This traditional pattern of education had served Burmese Buddhists well, giving them cultural cohesion and a standard of literacy well beyond their neighbors. Burmans in particular had thrived on it. But Shans, Mons, Arakanese, and other small pockets of Buddhists had also shared its benefits.

THE BRITISH PATTERN

The British effort to build a system of education for Burma combined the old Burmese pattern with the system then in force in England itself. Both were, in fact, elitist systems. The masses received a basic education; only a minority advanced beyond it.

But there was a major difference in the two. The English system was based on class. In Burma a gifted novice-monk, even if he were the son of a peasant, would find it possible to continue his learning as a permanent member of the Sangha.

No Englishmen originally proposed setting up primary schools in the villages; all recognized that these would seem to be in opposition to the monastery schools and therefore doomed to failure.

A bold scheme was outlined as early as 1864 by A. P. Phayre, Chief Commissioner of British Burma, by which books on secular subjects would be given to the monks and their contents added to the curriculum of the monks' schools. Phayre recognized that the effort would require "very great tact, judgment and discretion," because such teaching would also have to meet certain British standards and undergo regular inspection.

The Government of India approved Phayre's plan for a one-year trial period and appointed a Director of Education. American missionaries, the only people then capable of translating from English to Burmese, made Burmese copies of the selected text-books, though such translators must hardly have endeared the texts to Buddhist monks.

Statistically, the plan was a success. Educationally, it was a failure, both in the first year and in those that followed. The reasons aren't far to seek.

The sayadaw, the senior monk, would have accepted the books and the plan out of courtesy and a sense of *arnarde,* that emotion which makes a Burmese almost physically incapable of embarrassing or putting down a fellow human being.

A monastery education then and now is not basically secular. Reading and writing are needed for the lessons of the Tipitaka. A little arithmetic only seems secular. Should the boy become a monk he would need this in his later studies, if only in calculations to determine the days on which special lunar festivals fall.

Besides, a hpongyi has never been a full-time teacher, which

Phayre didn't seem to know. His daily life also includes hours of meditation and his own studies of the Tipitaka. He hadn't time to do all that Phayre's plan asked of him.

Fortunately for the new scheme, the second director in 1867 discovered the existence of the lay schools. Teachers here were more amenable to the discipline and supervision of the Department of Education in return for grants-in-aid. The monks couldn't accept such grants anyhow, since they weren't permitted to handle money.

Monasteries remained in the program, at least nominally, until well into the 1920's. But their number declined and the number of lay schools rose. Together they provided the primary vernacular schools, giving the first four years of education, often the children's only education, to the mass of students. It was not easy for a villager to pass from a vernacular, i.e., Burmese, school to a town Anglo-vernacular middle school.

Grants-in-aid also remained as a key part of the total educational program. It was some years before the government or municipalities provided schools of their own. Instead, they made payments not only to the lay schools but to all mission schools —Anglican, Catholic, Baptist, and Methodist. These provided Burma's middle and high schools.

Not all the Chief Commissioners of Burma approved such arrangements. The Hon. Ashley Eden, Phayre's successor, wrote sharply that he "hardly thought it right" that Burmese "must send their children to missionary schools or to no school at all." The Burmese often complained that their sons were educated to be mere clerks in the government; Eden, however, saw such education, outside mission schools, as their right, to "qualify them for appointments which they now see in the hands of aliens."

It was a biting report but had little immediate result. Grants continued until World War II, though in time some government institutions were established. A handful of the mission schools provided the best secondary education in Burma. All their teaching was in English. Graduation led almost automatically to matriculation at the University of Rangoon, then considered the best university in Asia. This by 1920 was the goal of most able Burmese students.

But travel on this road to successful participation in the new life the British had brought the nation had to begin early, in a good primary school. The schedules of these schools, available only in towns and cities, no longer allowed a young boy time for his years as a monastery student. Indeed, he could afford no more than the three-month school vacation for his traditional service as a novice monk. Villagers usually continued in the traditional fashion at the hpongyi-chaungs, imbibing the traditional Burmese culture-pattern that town boys were losing.

It was a troubling split. If Burma and Burmese culture were to survive in this new world, some Burmese had to be educated in the English fashion to meet the British on equal terms, and that is precisely what happened. Independence leaders came largely from the university. Yet, to reach the university, most young people had to pay a cultural price.

They learned western knowledge from western teachers in a language that was not their own and in a religious atmosphere not their own. British law forbade overt proselytizing, which might give parents the idea the British government was interfering with their religion. But the religious air of a mission school was pervasive. The children, especially the girls, were often given English names because teachers found it too difficult to learn the Burmese ones. Many students came through unscathed; some still bear scars from this subtle putdown of everything Burmese.

In 1938 the country had 110 high schools, of which 54 were mission-centered and 33 were operated by governmental institutions. The other 23 were "national schools" which Burmese themselves had founded in the wave of nationalism in the 1920's and for which they had then claimed grants on equal footing with missionary education.

By then, besides the University of Rangoon, the government

was also managing ten other special schools, ranging from agricultural and intermediate colleges in Mandalay to a medical school in Rangoon, a lacquerware school at Pagan, and a weaving institute at Amarapura.

Then came World War II. During the Japanese years, education virtually ceased because of national disruption. Only the hpongyi-chaungs were able to keep going in somewhat normal fashion. Other schools were often occupied for military purposes. In Rangoon the Japanese took over the entire University Estate; indeed, the formal Japanese surrender in the city was staged outside the University's Convocation Hall.

Peace didn't automatically bring an educational revival. Until Bogyoke Aung San and the AFPFL were recognized by the British, students were busier demonstrating than studying. Only afterward did revival begin. By the eve of Independence in 1948, 120 new high schools had been established, and some 4,327 primary schools had an enrollment of almost half a million pupils.

EDUCATION AFTER INDEPENDENCE

The First Decade, 1952–1962

But this bedeviled nation had one more river to cross. Coinciding with Independence the insurgency began; something like three-quarters of all school buildings were destroyed or looted by the rebels. It seems a hallmark of these guerrilla "wars for liberation" that schools, and often schoolmasters, are high-priority targets. The building of Burma's present system of education could not begin until 1952.

The goal was free education (except for textbook purchases) for all young citizens of the Union. Primary schools, for students 6–10, would carry through the fourth standard or grade; middle schools, for children 10–13, through the seventh standard; high schools, for those 13–15, through the ninth standard.

Besides these planned State institutions, there still remained certain "recognized" schools, those of the missions and a number of private Indian and Chinese schools. Although State control over them was not strong, they were required to register with the Ministry of Education, were liable to inspection, and followed certain directives of the Ministry.

This led to an occasional interesting phenomenon. When Pope Pius XII died, the Ministry ordered all schools closed to honor "a great hpongyi." This included Christian, Hindu, and (Communist) Chinese schools; it must have been the only place in the world where such institutions closed to honor a Catholic Pope.

Government educational goals spanned the spectrum from literacy to higher education. At the top, all students capable of passing the matriculation examinations would receive a free university education. At the base, mass illiteracy was to be eradicated.

The drive for literacy was pushed on two counts. Through most of the decade from the entrance of the Japanese in 1942 to the time the back of the insurgency was broken in 1952, many children of school age had known no formal education. In addition, there was now a Union of Burma; to talk about literacy in terms of Burma Proper was not enough. The goal included literacy for all the minorities as well.

These were all brave goals. But they demanded enormous effort merely for the sheer numbers of buildings and teachers required. Even in a calm, orderly nation, the job would have been difficult. Burma had been ravaged twice by war; the insurgency had added to the destruction and was not yet ended; tilled agricultural land was far below prewar levels. The people had little to work with but faith.

Burma has 30,000 village tracts. The plans called for a village primary school in each tract plus those additional ones needed for Rangoon and other cities and towns. Middle schools were to be built in each township headquarters and every market center of more than 2,000 population. High schools were scheduled for each district, plus those in cities and certain specialized high schools. Coeducation was built into the system.

At the end of the first developmental decade in 1962, there were 11,935 primary schools and almost 1,400,000 pupils. A village school often meant no more than a basha hut with a single schoolmaster who mended the thatched roofing himself before the monsoons. In many a village tract, pupils still attended the hpongyi-chaungs, if they went to school at all. For lack of buildings and teachers, compulsory education even in primary standards couldn't be required nation-wide. Only in a few places, like certain Rangoon areas and Syriam, was it now enforced.

Over 700 middle schools taught 235,000 students. A strong effort had been put behind the building of State high schools. In 1962 they numbered 681, including the "recognized" institutions, with something over 300,000 students. A few special high schools had also been built, such as the excellent technical one in Rangoon.

At the start, quality had been sacrificed for numbers. Primary teachers sometimes had little more education than their pupils. But in this same decade teacher-training institutes were also being pushed. Inevitably teaching quality showed some improvement.

Without manpower and resources, the drive for mass literacy accomplished little. For every adult taught to read and write, groups of young people arriving at maturity out of the reach of schools stepped up to take his place.

As for the university, the result of free education there was overwhelming, quite literally. In 1950–51, 3,620 students were enrolled at the University of Rangoon, where several new faculties had been added to the original College of Arts and Sciences. The old Judson College had been absorbed into this college. By 1954–55 on a University Estate built for a small elite number of students, enrollment had tripled and continued to climb.

There was a shortage of all facilities, both buildings and teachers. Classes were crowded. Standards fell, standards for matriculation and graduation as well as standards of discipline. Not all student-activists were interested chiefly in education. The disruptive results, described in Chapter 3, were inevitable.

Other events in these years in higher education included the building of a new Engineering College on a separate campus in Rangoon, the founding of several intermediate colleges for younger students, and the growth of Mandalay College into a separate university in 1958. That was the last year its graduates received their degrees from the University of Rangoon, which they might not have seen before, at the December commencement. (Though commencement comes eight months after students have completed their work, the time is chosen because it is dry and cool.)

Since 1962

The first decade in education had been under a parliamentary government. The Revolutionary Council, assuming power in March, 1962, abrogated the Constitution just as the school year was ending.

Its first major crisis developed with a demonstration of Rangoon University students in July, 1962, culminating in the shootings related earlier and the blowing up of the Rangoon Student Union Center. For months afterwards, students kept the University's main vehicular gate locked and draped solidly with signs of mourning.

The Council did not interfere. Instead it quietly made new plans for higher education. Today, the goal of all education is to make the student a useful member of a socialist society, concerned with the interests of that society, not his own personal ambitions. The new system equates education with livelihood and the development of moral character. Basic education is to be brought within reach of all, but only the talented can now aspire to higher education.

In line with such a goal, the Union of Burma Education Act of 1964 reorganized the whole structure of higher education. The large universities with their crowded classrooms are gone. In their place are smaller independent institutions, some of them new, some of them parts of the previous whole. Entrance standards have been raised, as were the standards required to remain in any institution. The result is a more sober, hard-working student body and a more fragmented one, less able to act as a unit.

A high degree of coordination between the institutions is assured on the administrative side, however, under a new directorate in the Ministry of Education. Although each has its own rector and governing body, all operate within the framework of the Administrative Council of Universities, which sets general policy. Most rectors of the 18 institutions are members of this central council.

The Rangoon Arts and Sciences University has returned to its original unit. Its twin in Upper Burma is the Mandalay Arts and Sciences University. Three intermediate colleges, at Magwe some 80 miles south of Pagan, at Taunggyi in the Shan State, and at Myitkyina in the Kachin State, feed into the Mandalay University. A fourth at Bassein in the Delta feeds into Rangoon. A fifth at Moulmein, in the south at the mouth of the Salween River, is in the process of becoming a third four-year university. Thus, today basic institutions for advanced education are well scattered through the country.

Burma now has three medical schools, or institutes. Medical Institute I, formerly in crowded quarters across from the Rangoon General Hospital, is housed in newer, more spacious buildings previously occupied by the School of Engineering. Medical Institute II, outside Rangoon at Mingaladon, is affiliated with the Ministry of Defense. Most of its graduates are absorbed by the Army Medical Corps. The third is the Mandalay Medical Institute.

The Rangoon Institute of Technology, formerly the School of Engineering, has a new campus near Rangoon at Insein with buildings erected by the U.S.S.R. The Economics Institute, fashioned from Rangoon's Faculty of Social Sciences, late in 1969 moved to new quarters constructed with United States AID funds, under a 1960 grant.

The other schools of higher education are the Institute of Education, Mandalay Institute of Agriculture, Institute of Veterinary Science and Animal Husbandry, Institute of Dental Medicine, Paramedical Institute (for medical technicians), and Workers' College. Altogether the 18 institutions in 1968–69 had a total enrollment of about 40,000.

One difficult problem remains. All instruction is now in Burmese, although previously it was in both English and Burmese. Most library books are in English, since few Burmese books in such major subjects as science and economics yet exist. Librarians report that university students read the English books "for comprehension" to supplement their teachers' Burmese lectures. But proficiency in English declines both because it is taught less well in lower schools and because it is little used; comprehension must be declining also.

A sympathetic observer can appreciate the desire of a nation to teach and learn in its own tongue and still wonder how in the present circumstances the universities can maintain standards, let alone raise them to the prewar level. To translate into Burmese even one text for every subject is a mammoth undertaking and far from completed. Yet a single text is not enough for a university student in such a subject as economics. In this field, and many others, he should be reading a variety of books. The problem must occupy the minds of many faculty members.

Under the Council, the greatest educational changes are those that have occurred in higher education. But in 1967 an eighth standard was introduced into the middle schools. High schools now cover the ninth and tenth standards, with an eleventh standard proposed. This wisely advances college entrance to students of 17 or 18 years. Fifteen or 16 had always seemed a little young for a student to begin grappling with a college education.

In 1967, after the Chinese difficulties, control of all private schools was completed. Only the hpongyi-chaungs remained outside direct State control, though a national seminar had helped to bring monastic schools more closely into current trends. For many children monastic schools remained the only ones available. Still, by 1968 the latest figures reported 2.8 million students in primary schools, a growth of almost a million in six years. Another half million were in middle schools, double the 1952 enrollment. The number of high schools had dropped, perhaps because some "recognized schools" no longer existed. In spite of this, enrollment had risen steadily and now touched half a million.

With the push in technical education, a second technical high school in Rangoon plus one in Taunggyi and another in Myitkyina were all opened late in 1968 with the help of the Colombo Plan. These join Rangoon's first technical high school, another at Mandalay, and the agricultural school at Pyinmana to provide specialized training for middle-school graduates who will not attend institutions of higher education.

Outstanding students, called *luyechuns,* are honored with vacations at the State's expense; the whole emphasis on scholastic achievement is strong. Few students, except the youngest, enjoy a long vacation of leisure. Many work in mills and factories, on public works, or with villagers.

Thousands have joined since 1966 in an impressive literacy campaign, along with missionary monks especially trained to teach children through the primary years. If the statistics are correct, the drive is showing remarkable success. The *Guardian* magazine reported in January, 1969, that the literacy rate for all of Burma was 57 per cent, a higher figure than the one for Burmans alone at the beginning of the century which the British had found so amazing.

This new educational program is stringent, disciplined, practical. Students applying for admission to higher education name three institutions of their choice and are assigned to one, determined as much by the State's needs as by the student's desires. In 1968–69 alone, 11,000 were accepted for admission in these institutions. The previous year's entering classes had totaled only 3,000. This rapid growth gives rise to some concern for teaching quality.

A humanist would wish for more intellectual fare and more privacy of choice. Yet, although some of the newer institutions may need fleshing out, for the first time Burma seems to have the skeletal structure of a higher educational system sufficient to its needs. Special high schools will give wider livelihood choices to students who terminate their education there. Whether by percentage or in total numbers, more young people are attending school today in Burma than ever before, an achievement of some magnitude.

9 Burma's Culture

Burma's art, like the rest of the nation, is in a state of transition. Historically, the kings were the patrons of the arts. The most talented dancers, singers, and musicians appeared at the Court. The finest woodcarvers served the king. Their work graced his palace and the monasteries, temples, and pagodas which he built, often glittering with gold leaf and artificial jewels, or sometimes real rubies and sapphires. Poets occupied places of honor at the capital. Some were members of the Court itself, even the king's ministers, for this was a literate people. The only sculptors were those who created the statues of the Buddha. These artists were never known by name, for it was the act and not the creator that was honored. He gained merit but not fame. Nor was there room for an innovative artist when each figure must be done as it had always been done traditionally, whether the Buddha was standing, reclining, or sitting.

When a silversmith's craft was recognized by the king, when his great bowls, often as large as punchbowls, were purchased for use at the palace, the artisan became artist. He could receive no greater honor. Nor may it be coincidence that the best lacquerware in Burma comes from a village near the old capital of Pagan.

There were no painters, although there are wall paintings in some of the oldest temples at Pagan. Indeed, early in 1969 an archeological expedition photographed other "wall paintings" in

caves in the southern Shan State. The caves, in the spur of foot-
hills below the Shan Plateau, had been discovered by a Burmese
geologist only in 1960. The painted animals, in red ochre, closely
resemble such prehistoric art as that found in the caves of
southern France. But far earlier hands than Burmese artists
executed them and neither Pagan nor the Padah-lin Caves left
any immediate heritage for later Burmese painters.

After Hsinbyushin conquered Ayuthia in 1767, he brought to
the Burmese Court many Thai artists and members of the royal
family. The Thais, accustomed to performing in their own court
a Thai version of the Ramayana, the Indian epic concerning
Rama and Sita, introduced this dramatic performance to the
Burmese Court. In typical fashion, the Burmese reshaped the
story to fit their own culture and pleasure. The demon king
changed to a comic figure, the epic became a love story, for the
Burmese relish humor and are a romantic people. Room was
made for Burmese singers and dancers, the whole was given a
Burmese name, *zat*, and Burmese drama was born.

Today, zat means a drama based on history or legends, sometimes one of the Jataka stories, tales of the earlier lives of the
Buddha before he became the Buddha, familiar to every Buddhist
Burmese. Indeed, zat comes from Jataka because originally the
Burmese mistook the Ramayana epic for one of the Jataka tales.
There is also the *pya-zat,* a similar drama based on contemporary
themes, and the *anyein pwe*, more familiarly the pwe, a show or
entertainment combining humor, dancing, and singing but without a story.

Long before the disappearance of the kings, the zats and pwes
escaped the confines of the royal Court to become the delight of
people everywhere. The best artists still appeared on command
at the Court, then went among the people boasting that they
were the choice of the king.

Though even the common people were literate, most were
without books. The people's literature was an oral literature, and,
with the birth of the zats, that oral literature was given visual

color, excitement, love, sorrow—all the elements of good drama. Actors were also singers and dancers; some were also clowns.

Thus, the zats and pwes suffered less with the disappearance of the royal courts and their patronage. Scholars have mourned the passing of the dramatists; they say the zats have "fallen into the hands of the actors." The star performer of a zat came to matter much more than the drama in which he appeared. But at least they survived handily; when later they did run into difficulty, it was of a different kind.

The artists who worked in such media as wood, lacquerware, and silver weren't as lucky. Many a woodcarver today will mourn that he is not the master his grandfather was. The skill to create the intricate carvings of a king's throne, a wooden shrine to cover a figure of the Buddha, or a delicate screen for a monastery seem to have disappeared. The skill might have been turned to the creation of carved furniture in one of Burma's many fine woods, but Burmese homes are largely without adornment. Furniture, even in urban homes, is of simple design. Today's artists are forced endlessly to carve figures of elephants, or *chinthes*, the mythical Burmese lion, with perhaps a rare order for a set of Burmese chessmen.

Traditional Burmese lacquerware is unique, very light in weight, on a woven bamboo base covered with a fine paste. The background is a soft orange. The surface is infinitely detailed in patterns or in pictures, usually of the Court, with natural dyes of black, dark green, yellow, and the same soft orange. Plates, cups, trays, and betel boxes were made of lacquerware. A fine, handleless cup was so flexible that it could be pressed between forefinger and thumb until the two sides met and it would not crack. Since neither porcelain nor china, only village pottery, is native to Burma, well-to-do families used lacquerware at the table.

Such excellent work grows more difficult to find. Its patterns may still be the traditional ones, but today's lacquerware is often made on a wood base; since the wood is not kiln-dried, it may crack. Much of it is now executed in gold and black—small trays or boxes in the shape of the *hinthe*, mythical bird of Lower Burma, or the owl, a good luck symbol. But the gold and black is derivative of other people's art and lacks the unique quality of the detailed traditional Burmese work.

Lacquerware is often given as gifts and most homes will have a piece or two. But china and enamelware, which are common now, do not demand the care in use which lacquerware does. The original utilitarian purpose is gone.

Silversmiths have managed somewhat better in a modern day. Centered in Rangoon or Sagaing, near Mandalay, they still make their bowls, the whole surface pounded out in bas relief with the simplest of tools. But the figures of the frieze have changed from Court symbols to such ornamentations as a passenger bullock cart, working elephants, a Burmese sampan, a cultivator plowing with his bullocks. Bowls have traditionally been an honored gift to an honored guest, and there must still be occasional orders even for the largest ones, if only as governmental gifts to visiting heads of state. Smaller ones are made for individuals, with the same quality of workmanship. An artisan will occasionally make a tea service on special order, and some have added silver bracelets, cigaret-lighter cases, and cigaret boxes for less wealthy customers. All have the same distinctive raised frieze.

A new medium has come into use in modern Burma. The distant sons of the wall painters of Pagan have taken to oils and water colors. Itinerant artists sell their small water colors, mostly of village scenes, from door to door. The more ambitious save their work for the annual exhibition, where the works exhibited are also on sale. Oils must be imported at some expense, so that an oil painting is usually beyond the pocketbook of any but an embassy or a government ministry. The water colors are more popular purchases.

There are no abstracts in Burma. Many paintings are scenes from nature, a padauk tree in bloom, a favored pagoda with perhaps a pwe in the foreground, or any well-loved spot. A Burmese dancer is often a popular subject. Occasionally there have been excellent portraits of famous Burmese men. In the 1969 annual exhibit, some sculpture was also on display. Paw Oo Thet, one of the country's leading artists and more innovative than many, has recently illustrated a book of Burmese folk tales for children published in the United States. Without being imitative, the fluid drawings capture the feel of old lacquerware detail, yet are plainly the work of a modern artist.

LITERATURE

Printing came to Burma, too. Books were not new but they had been written as parabaiks or palm-leaf manuscripts. Parabaiks were of soft but sturdy bamboo paper, rubbed over with a mixture of charcoal and rice water, each page folded in accordion fashion. A steatite pencil was used for writing on the darkened surface. Of the two, this was the more familiar: schoolboys used it for learning their writing in the monastery; merchants kept their records on it.

More highly valued was the palm-leaf manuscript. Leaves of the palmyra were cut into strips, boiled in water, then repeatedly moistened and pressed until they became flat, smooth writing surfaces, ready for a stylus. Each leaf, or page, was pierced at either end and cords were strung through the series of holes and through boards of the same size which became the book's cover. Pages were oiled for preservation; boards were beautifully decorated.

A work of any length demanded much laborious writing, and neither kind was as long-lived as, say, a parchment manuscript. Books had remained largely the treasures of kings and monasteries, carefully locked up.

Now printing came. The first book printed in Burmese was not published in Asia but at the Propaganda Press in Rome in 1776 for the use of Catholic missionaries in Burma. Its circulation in Burma was small. Early in the nineteenth century, American missionaries also had books published in Burmese for devotional purposes and for use in their schools. But the printing of Burmese literature did not begin generally until early in the twentieth century.

Traditionally, prose had been the scholar's medium; scholars were usually monks, and their works were usually thoughtful dissertations on religious subjects. A venturesome Burmese, James Hla Gyaw, turned to prose in 1904 and published what has come to be known as the first Burmese novel, an adaptation with Burmese characters in a Burmese setting of *The Count of Monte Cristo,* done with considerable ability. Novels and short stories have continued to be published since then. Few of either have been translated from the Burmese.

On the other hand, poetry has always been the natural creative medium of the Burmese, whether in poems to be read, songs to be sung, or the blank verse of the zats. Even among the monks' writings, the people themselves prize most highly the epic poems which relate the stories of the ten major lives of the Buddha and are said to reach a high literary standard. Like the modern paintings, poems and songs have celebrated nostalgically the special beauty of a season or a particular spot in Burma. Like the zats, they often tell of love, both its joys and its sorrows.

Unfortunately, much is lost in translating Burmese poetry into English or any other language. All poetry loses in translation, but Burmese poems may lose more than most, for two reasons. The original, classical poetical form was the *ratu,* four syllables to the line. (Burmese is basically a monosyllabic language with longer words created by combining single-syllable words.) The rhyme scheme was elaborate, both at the end of lines and within lines. In such a scant line length, the translator has little room to maneuver toward even approximation of the rhyme scheme. Such complex rhyme schemes are important in most Burmese poetry.

The poet delights his readers with puns and plays on words, yet what other language but Burmese provides a word which can mean three things with only the stroke of a tonal mark?

Even if translators attempt the rhymes, they give up on the puns, and that part of the pleasure is lost to one who must read in translation.

The Burmese also have a sharp ear for metaphor which appears even in brief proverbs. These two, translated by U Hla Pe, have lost their Burmese rhymes but not their imagery, as they warn a husband against neglecting his wife. "Stay away from a harp three months, you forget how to play it." "The wax hardens when it's away from the fire."

As nationalism rose, particularly after the student strike of 1926, all these lyrical qualities rose almost in a flood. Poets were born everywhere, particularly among the students and young university graduates. They sang Burma's praises as older poets had, in a loving evocation of her beauty and her festivals which in itself was a form of nationalism. But the Burmese, skilled at reading between the lines, could often find more explicit cries for unity and freedom in such poems as those of U Thein Han, writing under the name of Zawgyi (Magician) in the 1930's and '40's. One particular favorite was an ode to the Water Festival, at which good Buddhists, to gain merit, set free birds or beasts or fish. U Thein Han wrote in Burmese of a bullock freed for this purpose:

> Its head smeared with unguent,
> Its horns bedecked with padauk blossoms,
> Could I but enter into its spirit—
> How jolly!
> We love to set things free.
> Would that our race can be
> Similarly free!

So numerous were the poets that it was natural one should be among the martyrs assassinated with Aung San. U Ba Choe, as Minister of Information, was at that fateful cabinet meeting.

In the early 1950's came the poetry of "N.N.," U Myo Sein, which may fail somewhat as lyric poetry. But, even for a foreigner, his passion warms the words he writes of Aung San, like those in "The Martyrs":

> Burma is one and Burma has won
> But at what a price!
> Dear Bogyoke,
> Alas, what a price!
> They led us to the Dawn and left us
> After the forced march through the Asia night.

U Myo Sein was also the translator of the national anthem appearing in Chapter 4. Among younger poets writing in English, U Win Pe for more than a decade has commanded attention and shown continual growth.

At the moment, while there is no lull in quantity, there has been something of a lull in quality, as least in that work published in English, whether written so or in translation. Many would-be poets are writing verses either with a didactic, political voice, or merely to relate in rhyme some old legend or folk tale.

Nonfiction has shown an interesting growth. Researchers are going back to early sources to recover their past under Burmese kings as Burmese eyes saw it. Men who shared more recent events, such as the years under the Japanese, are getting their memories on paper. These are not definitive works but rather the necessary building-blocks from which future historians can tell in Burmese a story of the Burmese past. Until now, much of this history has been written by foreign writers or in a foreign language.

The Burma Research Society, founded by J. S. Furnivall, a British civil servant with respect for and knowledge of Burmese culture, and by U May Oung, an honored Burman jurist and the society's first president, in 1910 had begun this task of exploring Burma's culture. The files of its journal are now invaluable source material for younger writers; members also continue publication of their own writings in current issues.

Another supportive influence on modern writers has been Sarpay Beikman, a quasi-public, government-underwritten organization, founded shortly after Independence. It is usually known in English as the Burma Translation Society, familiarly called the BTS, although its name translates literally from Burmese as the Palace of Literature. Its responsibilities were many, but a number of them have now been assumed by the Ministry of Culture.

Equipped with printing and binding machinery, including monotype machines, the first adaptation of the monotype process to Burmese script, the BTS has the best printing resources in Burma. These were the gift of a private American foundation. Some solid translations of texts for the universities were published, and millions of cheaper texts for grade-school. Work was begun on a Burmese encyclopedia.

In addition to its printing and publishing, Sarpay Beikman established annual awards for Burmese writers in many classifications. Although awards for novels were not always presented (U Nu complained in 1954 that the authors ignored nature, life, and character and wrote only of love and love-making), the recipients were always highly honored by the reading public. The Ministry continues these awards.

Sarpay Beikman also has maintained one of Burma's best public libraries. Its books freely circulate, and its reading rooms have been well used. Outdoors, in the dry season, the society sponsored presentations of the best of the traditional zats, including the Rama story. Sarpay Beikman was the original sponsor of the annual art exhibit to encourage the new generation of artists, which also continues under the Ministry's sponsorship.

Private publishers still exist in this socialist society, at least into 1969, with the Government keeping watch only on the political and religious books. The number of books published declined by 25 per cent from almost 2,000 in 1966 to around 1,500 in 1968, with no more than 3,000 copies of any single book. The cause of the decline isn't wholly clear. Certainly one major reason is the necessity to import practically all newsprint.

The English-language *Guardian* magazine, in March, 1969, complained editorially of the malpractices of such "capitalistic" publishers. A major example was a flood of James Bond novels which followed on the heels of James Bond films in Rangoon's cinemas. The editor was careful to explain that he did not object to James Bond novels as such but to the hurried, slipshod translations for the sole purpose of making money quickly.

With so few copies published of any single book, it seems plain that books, even James Bond books, don't reach beyond the city-dwellers. Only the songs to be sung, the poems to be learned and repeated, must reach the villagers, as a modern version of the people's oral literature.

NEWSPAPERS AND RADIO

Nor can newspapers take up the slack, either for entertainment or for creating a widely based, informed public opinion. In a country of more than 26 million, 12 daily newspapers have a total circulation of only 231,000.

Before the Revolutionary Council came to power, the country had 32 newspapers and a number of independent-minded editors. The dean of them all was U Law Yone, editor of the English-language *Nation,* recipient of the Magsaysay Award,* sometimes called the father of modern Burmese journalism. Outspoken, quick-witted, he wrote what he thought. It was he who began a 1959 editorial on the eve of a visit from Khrushchev,

* To honor the late president of the Philippines, Ramon Magsaysay, the Magsaysay Award Foundation was established in 1957 by the Rockefeller Brothers Fund to make awards "in recognition of greatness of spirit shown in service to the people." Selection is made by a Philippine Board of Trustees, including a brother of Magsaysay.

"Lock up the girls and hide the silver. Khrushchev is coming to town."

It was also U Law Yone who made a collector's item of his own front page in reporting a speech by U Nu. The speech was delivered in Burmese. The copy reached the newspaper office without an English translation and was translated there. There is in Burmese a perfectly respectable, modest word which is usually translated into English as passing wind. U Nu had used that word. U Law Yone, as fluent in English as U Nu himself, translated it into an English word which is not customary in polite society and used the word in his headline. He wasn't feuding with U Nu at the moment; the act seemed merely one of high-spirited mischief which he could not resist.

But in the days of the AFPFL, when the only opposition party seemed to be the free press, he could speak up as impressively on grave subjects. Other editors might not be as free-spoken but they were free and they spoke. It was almost inevitable that U Law Yone be jailed within the first year of the Council's rule.

The *Nation* is now the *Working People's Daily* and is published by the Ministry of Information. The *Guardian*, the second English-language daily, is also nationalized, though it survived longer in independence. Yet these and other nationalized Burmese-language newspapers are not total carbon copies of each other. Some leeway is allowed each editor. There are no official newspaper censors in Burma; a previous policy direction board was dissolved early in 1967. Criticism is muted but some is permissible both in editorials and letters to the editor. When General Ne Win himself declared that "the economy is a mess," it was an invitation to editors to add their own comment. Direct criticism of General Ne Win or the basic premise of the Burmese Way to Socialism is not acceptable, however.

Even in the days of a completely free press, the public opinion it helped to form, for all its importance, was limited to the cities, particularly Rangoon and Mandalay. The nationalized press does not command a larger audience.

Perhaps the radio does. The country has fewer than 400,000 radio sets, which averages out to one for about 65 people. Concentration is heavier in the cities, but in villages surely some headmen's homes own radios. The broadcast fare is not rich or plentiful. Burmese transmission has covered seven hours a day, broken into morning, midday, and evening segments. The evening hours also include brief broadcasts in Karen, Kayah, Chin, Shan, and Kachin. News goes on the air in each segment; there is some educational programming and considerable recorded music. The English transmission is only three hours a day, mostly news and recorded music. But evening broadcasting on the two transmissions is consecutive so that a Burmese can switch at 9 p.m. to the music on the English transmission.

Radio's greatest value may be in times of crises. In the mid-June, 1967, riots, Rangoon Burmese rose against the Chinese in the city because Chinese students were wearing Mao buttons and otherwise attempting to import China's Cultural Revolution, with some aid from the Chinese Embassy. For several days, the situation was critical. Martial law was declared in Rangoon. In those touchy days, radio must have served the people well over much of the country, for listeners would have spread such important news orally to nonlisteners. It must also serve the government well, enabling it to reach a larger audience than it could otherwise at the moment of any important announcement. But normal listening can reach only a minority of the people.

Drama

If the vigor of the zats had endured, they might have both mirrored and created public opinion, for topics of the day were frequently introduced into the standard script. Even the naming of a crown prince was influenced by a zat performed before the king, according to U Htin Aung. In Lower Burma, the British learned from a zat how extreme the people felt a new building code to be. A clown appeared on-stage as a tree nat, weeping.

When his companions asked him why he wept he cried out, "The government says I must put a zinc roof on my banyan tree!"

U Htin Aung, former rector of the University of Rangoon, student of the old dramas, believes they died because of the entry of novels into Burma. This seems improbable. Htin Aung considers only the pure prose drama, but others with song and dance were being performed at the same time as these, back in the nineteenth century, and they survived healthily until after the entry of the Japanese.

One typical drama called *The Silver Hill*, translated into English in 1870, is a story of a crown prince who falls in love with a fairy princess, daughter of the fairy king of the Silver Hill, loses her, and wins her back after much travail.

San Dun was one of a troupe who performed the play before Thibaw and Supayalat in 1879 on the three nights when other young princes and princesses were being put to death, to secure the throne for this new king. The music of the festival drowned out any untoward cries, except for one moment of a quiet song which began:

> Do come, my darling,
> Though your pretty feet are tender,
> Please do not tire so soon.
> Do come along, my darling.

San Dun was the father of a son who took the name Po Sein and became the most important figure in the Burmese theater in the twentieth century. No novels injured him or his career either in Rangoon or throughout the countryside. He was decorated by the British and was beloved by his own people everywhere. When he died after Independence he was past 70. The streets about his home were so thronged with people that even Prime Minister U Nu could not reach the funeral service. On the day of his death Kenneth Sein, his son and successor, was performing at a pagoda festival in Pegu, singing those same words: "Do come, my darling, though your pretty feet are tender."

Kenneth Sein, while he may not have matched his father, has been the best *mintha*, male zat performer, in Burma. He has performed in the United States, Russia, and China. In spite of him, the zat began to lose its hold on the people.

Partly it must have been the insecurity of the early postwar years when travel for both troupe and audience through the countryside was difficult and dangerous. Partly it may have been the cinemas which began to spring up thickly in Rangoon and even in Mandalay, and were scattered throughout the district towns.

The Burmese love the cinema. Only the producers know for sure, but outside evidence would indicate that the most popular motion picture ever to appear in Burma was *The Ten Commandments*. A giant figure of Yul Brynner as tall as the marquee grew weathered and drab while the crowds thronged the theater for almost three months. The film then went up to Mandalay for over a month, and returned for a final showing in Rangoon of several more weeks. It was an epic, a love story, and a touch of morality, the same qualities the Burmese had always loved best in the zats.

The Burmese are developing their own motion picture industry, although the product cannot yet compete at the Cannes Festival. Even the Burmese have preferred western movies. However, the cinema houses were nationalized in late 1968. No drastic changes occurred immediately, but control over imports is tightening and more Burmese movies are in production.

The zat, however, may be in for a revival. Since Independence, the government has maintained a school in Mandalay for singers, dancers, and musicians, and young artists are growing up. Two zat troupes performed in Rangoon on Independence Day in 1969, and the large tent was crowded for all performances of both zats and pya-zats, the old and the new.

SPORTS AND GAMES

Probably a villager does not subscribe to the *Working People's Daily*. His wife may not arrange her offerings of flowers for the altar of the Buddha in a silver bowl. But the villager still shares certain common pleasures with his urban brother.

One is a joy in male physical fitness, in the body's agility and strength. Burmese boxing is ancient, resembling the Thai sport which permits kicking and all other attacks but hair-pulling and biting. But in Burma the boxers are merely local heroes; the organization of the sport doesn't wind up with a national championship, as it does in Thailand.

Chinlon, the most common game, produces no winner, except in the eye of the beholder. Though it isn't a contest, it is played everywhere. A chinlon ball is woven of reed, with open interspaces in the weaving. The aim of the game, to keep the ball in the air without using the hands, demands discipline, skill, and long practice, for the player must maintain remarkable control of the ball. A good player can catch it in the hollow of his shoulder, allow it to roll down the back of his arm to the elbow, catch it on his knee, then like a flash switch his stance and strike it into the air from the back with the sole of the opposite foot.

When he completes his virtuoso performance, he sends the ball up high, steps back, and another player catches it on shoulder or knee to continue the game. One player can amuse himself with chinlon, but it is usually played by a circle of young performers, with bare feet and bare torsos, longyis drawn high and tucked at the waist, much like a paddy cultivator's.

Golf and tennis are played in the cities but they are somewhat elite sports. On the other hand field hockey and soccer teams can be found everywhere from the armed forces and universities to the cinema workers and district schools. It is a soccer team that carries Burma's colors to the Southeast Asian Peninsula games; these carefully selected SEAP footballers are heroes, win or lose.

Racing is universally popular, bullock-racing, boat-racing, and horse-racing. General Ne Win was a regular visitor at the Rangoon race track and knowledgeable about its thoroughbreds until he closed the track down. Not only were its workers unproductive in a socialist state, but the gambling that accompanied it was a waste of a family's funds.

That hasn't stopped all gambling because the Burman is a gambling man, perhaps not as inveterate as the Shan, but still by tradition a believer in the luck of chance. Bullocks are still trained for racing. Villagers will join in challenging another village to a boat-race, as they have since the days of the kings when boats were raced for the pleasure of the Court. University students stage an annual boat-race on their neighboring lake. There is no pari-mutuel board but who is to know if an alumnus places a wager on his favorite crew?

As late as 1963 when trishawmen in lieu of taxis waited at night for passengers outside the Strand Hotel, morning light showed chess or checker boards scratched in charcoal on the sidewalk. Whichever game that tough breed had been playing, it seems a safe bet that they weren't playing just for the fun of it. Perhaps of most significance, Burma's state lottery continued under all post-Independence governments with top prizes of 100,000 kyats.

INDULGENCES

Smoking is common among both men and women, cheroots in the villages and among poorer city-dwellers, cigarets among the others. The chewing of betel once was equally common, and betel-boxes have been made of lacquer or beautiful silver. A leaf of the betel-vine is smeared with slaked lime; on it are placed a slice of the nut from the betel palm and a dab of spices; the leaf is rolled together and the whole bit is chewed. The combination is an astringent, necessitating a spittoon for the red juice, and a mild stimulant. A late-nineteenth-century observer compared it to the use of snuff in Europe.

Education has caused some decline in its use; spittoons are not seen in the homes of the educated, the telltale red saliva does not deface halls or stairways of schools or universities as it still does those of some public buildings. The culture seems to see no evil in its use, merely a growing disapproval of its messiness, though the public spitting may be a cause in the spread of tuberculosis.

Opium is something else again. Its use has never been a severe problem in Burma Proper, but its production has always been a matter of concern to public officials. Under the British it was merely controlled. Under independent Burma it is illegal. Raised chiefly by some hill peoples, opium can't be exported through normal channels but can easily be smuggled over the borders to Thailand or China, where it brings high prices. The raisers of the poppy are also among its users, so the problem becomes both social and economic.

For years the Agricultural and Rural Development Corporation has sought without success a crop which would be as financially rewarding to the grower as the poppy. The government is again trying to solve the double problem, setting up clinics to break users of the habit and offering loans so growers can switch to mulberry trees. The mulberry feeds silkworms, but the worms must be killed in the process of unwinding the delicate thread from the cocoons. Burmese Buddhists prize silk but resist the killing; hence, domestic production could be increased if non-Buddhist hill people would take it up.

The switch would have to be voluntary. Policing the hill fields is almost impossible. Yet a dark, sticky ball of raw opium easily moved across the border is worth more than a season's silk, and in the hills opium users draw much less social disapproval than in Burma Proper.

Use of hard liquor came from the West. Mild rice beer and wine are traditional in the hills, as is a toddy from a special palm in the lowland. For the toddy, the giant cluster of palm flowers is slashed off, the juice caught from the stump in an earthenware container and mildly fermented. A night of drinking any of these brings results, though seldom as drastic as what the West means by drunkenness.

Now the situation is changed. Buddhism forbids the use of alcohol; this somewhat controls its use. But a fairly good beer is brewed in Mandalay and the domestic pharmaceutical industry has distilled a "country spirits" resembling a mildly flavored gin. The beer is generally accepted; the spirits have drawn some Buddhist questions but have been defended because they bring a profit to the young industry and provide a pure drink for those who would otherwise drink a local "moonshine." Smuggled foreign whiskies fetch a high price on the black market. Drinkers can turn up in village or city, but there are no statistics on drunkenness and the government does not consider it a problem equal to opium use.

FESTIVALS AND PWES

Far more than sports, far, far more than drinking or even gambling, both village and city cherish the pwe and Buddhist festivals. The two are bracketed intentionally. Just as it is fitting for a family on pilgrimage to eat its rice on some quiet, open space of a pagoda platform, so it is fitting for a religious event to coexist with a secular pwe, often within the pagoda monastery compound itself. Or a father, proud of his son at his shinbyu, will entertain his village with not only a feast but a pwe on the eventful day.

Once it might have been a zat, but a pwe can be shorter, the troupe is smaller and less expensive to hire, and there are many more pwe troupes. The artistry is not as fine as that of a great zat troupe, there is no story involved, but there are the traditional dancers, singers, clowns, and orchestra offering a delightful, sometimes rather bawdy, show which resembles a vaudeville turn or, to be more contemporary, a TV variety show. The star is the *minthami*, the female dancer, supported by several other dancers. The clowns make the jokes, often topical, tease and mock the minthami. All sing, to the accompaniment of the orchestra.

Major orchestral instruments are a circle of drums and a circle of gongs, both tuned to play melodies; a woodwind instrument somewhat loosely described in English as an oboe; a flute, usually made of bamboo and played from the end instead of the side; brass cymbals; and bamboo clappers made from a node of bamboo with a strip of the arc cut down so that it can be clapped rhythmically against the remaining bamboo.

One of the loveliest of Burmese instruments is the harp, its base shaped something like a boat, the deck covered with buffalo hide. Slender wood curves up and over the "boat" and thirteen strings of silk, now often nylon, are strung from the wood curve to the boat. It is the only instrument a woman normally plays. But it is a solo instrument, not a part of the orchestra.

Burmese music is difficult for the western ear to enjoy until it becomes familiar. It lacks a chromatic scale and the harmony of chords. But, since even the drums and gongs are tuned so that they can play melodies, an orchestral selection becomes a blending of melodies in a complex, graceful pattern. Even the martial airs seem as plaintive as the love songs.

The finest music this observer ever heard was in a village where a flutist improvised on his bamboo pipe, accompanied only by bamboo clappers. Almost as charming is the unself-conscious young man wandering down the street in the twilight singing to his absent sweetheart.

To describe Burmese dancing is quite difficult. Even a ten-year-old child may fall absently into the steps of the dance when she hears music, if she thinks no one is watching her. For a top professional, the discipline is nearly as great as for western ballet. The dance is stylized, not fluid. Wrists, elbows, knees are moved effortlessly "against the grain" of the joints in postures that are hopelessly awkward for a western dancer. Part of each dance is done with knees bent, which must place great tension on thigh muscles, and all is performed in the long-skirted, tight-jacketed traditional court costume, for both male and female dancers.

This music and dancing, plus those impudent clowns, make up a pwe, a performance that may last three or four hours, the audience sitting about the pandal, the temporary stage, on their finely woven reed mats. In very recent years a new kind of pwe, probably growing out of the contemporary zat, is sometimes performed at pagoda festivals. Without dancing or singing, actors and actresses in everyday Burmese dress perform in front of a painted backdrop of something as familiar as a city street. The quickly changing skits and audience response indicate it still has a vaudeville quality and is still laced with humor.

But the pwes are only the vessels to catch the joy that spills over from the event itself, whether shinbyu, a single pagoda's festival, or one of the important Buddhist festivals that the whole country shares.

Of these, the most beautiful is the October Festival of Lights at the Full Moon of Thadingyut, which commemorates both the end of Lent and the return of the Buddha to earth from heaven where he had gone to preach to his mother. Because she had died before he reached Enlightenment, she had never heard him preach. It is a dark passage down the stairs from heaven to earth; lights are lit everywhere to guide the Buddha safely back to earth.

He must find his way freely, for Burma turns into a fairyland of lights. Dancing lights from earthen saucers filled with oil and a wick line the veranda railings of the poor. Buildings and some homes are outlined with what Westerners call Christmas-tree lights; those near a lake are reflected in the still waters. Small red and green cellophane lanterns may be purchased at certain monasteries and fitted with candles to hang about a porch or along a driveway. Fire-balloons of thin paper, fitted with a candle which warms the air and sends the balloon aloft, float through the sky in open spaces over villages and small towns. The Rangoon fire department would not appreciate their use in the city.

Before the happy people set out to see the sights, buy a few tidbits from the food-hawkers, stop in this neighborhood and that to watch part of a pwe given on a temporary pandal, they go first to a pagoda. In Rangoon it is preferably the Shwedagon. Here they light candles before one of the shrines and, with hands folded, sit quietly and meditate on the teachings of the Buddha. Many will return again to end the night's gaiety in the same quiet devotionals. The secular and religious may merge but the two are not confused.

The nation's most important festival is the Buddhist New Year and the three-day Water Festival which precedes it, in mid-April, right in the middle of the hottest and driest part of the hot season. There is a ceremonial washing of the hair the day before; in the days of the kings, the ceremonial washing of the monarch's hair was an important event. The Thagya Min, the spirit-king, comes down to earth at midnight the first night to enjoy the festival and to check up a bit on humans. His statue often shows him holding pad and pencil for his note-taking.

In the morning, young girls and young men go in dignified procession to the pagodas for a ceremonial washing of the statues of the Buddha. But once that is ended, dignity is ended for the three-day festival. By the time the girls reach home they are drenched, and the young men aren't precisely dry. Everyone is fair game for all these three days, everyone is wet unless he stays safely indoors. Elders and sayas may be more delicately sprinkled with scented water from silver bowls, but few are accorded such honor. Fortunately the hot sun dries thin garments quickly. The padauk tree is in bloom with its yellow blossoms, and branches are broken off to be taken indoors, their dark green leaves glistening with water, symbol of the freshness, the cleanness of a New Year.

Elders have always complained that each generation was more rowdy at the Water Festival than they were when they were young. Perhaps each has been. In 1969, special supervisors were appointed for Rangoon districts to restrict water waste.

There is always much visiting back and forth; gifts of sweetmeats and special treats are sent to friends' homes. Everyone tries to be particularly good-tempered, honest, and careful in his speech, a good omen for the New Year's beginning. Pandals for pwes are once again erected and the gaiety continues until the Thagya Min returns to heaven and the New Year itself has arrived.

These, and other Buddhist festivals, are what the majority of the country shares, rich and poor, country and city, more intimately than anything else, just as they share Buddhism, the very cornerstone of the nation's life.

10 Conclusion

The economic and political events of Burma's 20-odd years since independence seem to throw a grim, gray air of depression over the story of this newly freed nation. This air is misleading. The Burmese are a tenacious, stubborn people with limitless confidence in their own culture, their own identity, and the culture's ability to survive. This steadfastness threads the centuries of their history from its beginnings. They are sustained in some measure by the long view of history which Buddhism gives them, with its attendant sense of the temporal. But the Burmese are not only tenacious and religious; they're a gay, ebullient people with a quick eye for the irony in life. Their response is not black humor but an earthy laughter. This instinct for survival is their greatest strength as a people, yet it exacerbates their greatest problem, the basic threat to the unity or viability of the nation. (Note here the distinction between "people" and "nation," and recall the earlier discussion of the usage of "Burman" and "Burmese.")

The severity of the economic problems, for all their immediate importance, will pass in time. Burma is, as Ne Win has pointed out, a food-surplus nation, and some 80 per cent of the people still live on the land. In the interim, basic commodity shortages can still be filled "from the outside," or by peddlers who come in over borders or Burmese purchasers who cross borders to bargain their own surpluses for necessities in other nations' bazaars. Now this is called smuggling. Once it was part and parcel of the people's customary commerce. Reports have reached Rangoon that women in some up-country communities which have long been dependent on manufactured textiles have dusted off old looms and renewed old weaving skills. In terms of the nation's reach for development, this kind of activity is a poor solution. But in terms of survival, it is quite logical.

If development is slowed, it will be easy to blame the corrupt inefficiency of commodity distribution, and there could be justification for the correlation. But a partial cause of the slowdown may also be found in the symbolic dichotomy between Mandalay and Rangoon, the tension between the old and the new.

The Burmese individual who studies abroad seldom has trouble in absorbing modern western training, taking what he wishes from the other culture, and still remaining uniquely Burmese. Burma has few expatriates. (Most observers familiar with Burma can name those few, but could never name all those they know who ended their studies abroad with no psychological hangups and no reluctance to return home.) Contrarily, the nation as a whole has had no marked success with blending the Burmese and the foreign, the old and the new. This may be what General Ne Win had in mind when, having sent home the private technicians and private foundations of the West, he explained to an ambassador, "As long as your people stay and do for my people, they will never learn to do for themselves."

General Ne Win's method turned out to be something like throwing the child in the water so he would learn to swim. With no one else there to teach them, the Burmese would presumably be forced to develop the skills needed to run a modern nation—commercially, technically, educationally, and politically—in a way consonant with Burmese culture and the Burmese sense of identity. If the other method was too slow, perhaps the General's method was too traumatic, the tension between the old and the new too great.

No one knows for a certainty what triggers a country into modern development. Some scholars believe that in a traditional society like Burma's, the "crust of custom" must first be broken before the society can move in new directions, consider new ways of doing old tasks. There is some evidence that such movement cannot occur, especially in an agricultural nation, until the country has a fairly strong system of elementary education and eight to ten per cent of the population enrolled in primary schools. Secondary and higher education, even if strong, are not enough. India is often used as an example of a country with strength in both these sectors but without a widespread, sturdy system of elementary education; India has therefore developed with ragged unevenness, capable of manufacturing an atomic bomb, not yet capable of raising her villagers up from abysmal poverty.

If there is truth in this theory, General Ne Win's greatest contribution to Burma's development program may not be in the factories but in the schools. In 1969, over 3.5 million children below 14 were in school, out of a population of almost 27 million. Of importance is regularity of attendance and the number of grades completed. Statistics do not show these facts. But at least a proportion in excess of the magic 10 per cent were enrolled in 1969. In addition, the steady campaign against illiteracy has produced more literate adults. It may not be without significance that newspaper readership had also begun to rise in the rural areas in 1969.

To economic and development problems must, of course, be added the political one as the time approaches when power is returned to the people. What kind of state will be chosen to assume power? Politically minded westerners tend to think that the only satisfactory answer to such a question is a western-style democracy, but this may or may not be true. The earlier Burmese experience may have taught them what they need to know to make such a democracy work. Or it may have turned them in a new direction, as it turned Ne Win.

The lack of skill to make democracy function well on a national scale may be less a measure of a people's immaturity than of their historical inexperience. By the same token, America's use of democracy stems less from virtue than it does from a set of fortuitous historical inheritances. But it must be recognized that any form of self-government does demand skills.

Though the new government may not be cast in a western image, it will surely not be Communism, of the Communist–bloc variety. The long years of antireligious Communist insurgency have set the people and the Sangha against such a government.

If Burma is permitted to choose freely a system that provides the necessary "democratic competitions," that institutionalizes participatory democracy in a way to make the government responsive to the people's will, and that avoids concentrating "the intoxication of power" in a clique, it will hardly matter by what name it is called.

But it must be remembered that General Ne Win in 1962 led the Revolutionary Council in seizing power, against his "most cherished principles," not to impose a system of government but to preserve the nation's unity. This, in his mind, was the major problem in 1962. It was the major problem in 1949 when he became deputy prime minister and turned the rebels back almost from the gates of Rangoon. It was the problem of Bayinnaung as it had been of Alaungpaya and indeed of Anawrahta himself. It is the major problem today, as it will be of any new government.

There is often a tendency to attribute Burma's post-independence problems of all varieties to the villain of colonialism. For proof, comparison is sometimes made between the Thais and Burmese, with the differences between the two peoples, who still show many similarities, attributed to colonialism or the lack of it. The Thais are assured, outgoing, and confident, accepting or rejecting as they wish what the outside world offers. Thus there is growth in the twentieth century, a successful transfer of their early identity to a new world. The Burmese, on the other hand, had their sense of confidence shattered and their social institutions disrupted by colonialism, with grave consequences to their assurance and their ability to cope with the modern era. So the comparison runs. But do the facts authenticate such an explanation or is there another, more likely comparison to be made?

Certainly sixty years of colonialism is not a painless experience to endure. There was no deliberate effort on the part of the colonialists to disrupt or to destroy the social institutions of the Burmese. There was, indeed, some effort to conserve these traditions as in the research into the Dhammathats and the customary laws governing family relations and the attempt to use the hpongyi-chaungs as part of the elementary education system.

But there was also heedless destruction. The colonialists were twice strangers. They saw the Burmese with the eyes of strangers from the West, but they also looked at the country as westerners who believed themselves knowledgeable of Asians. To them, Burma was simply a far-western province of India. The astigmatism of India-knowing distorted their vision. If they had felt they were complete aliens, they might have seen this Southeast Asian country more objectively and might have avoided reducing the Burmese to second-class citizens in their own country.

The waves of immigration from the Indian subcontinent, far from being encouraged, might not have been permitted. India was not the Golden Land and the tools of survival had been sharply honed among its people. The Burmese, in whose land the living had been easier, were no match for them. The sense of exploitation, that abrasive Burmese heritage of colonialism, has been directed quite as much against the Indians and Pakistanis as against the British. (The Chinese in Burma are included now in the list of exploiters, but this emotion is of more recent origin.)

Dr. Hla Myint, senior lecturer at Oxford University, when speaking at the Society of Antiquaries in London in 1963, emphasized the psychological handicaps that a one-time colonial possession must shed before it is free to develop. An authority on economic development in Southeast Asian nations, he was not speaking directly of his own Burma nor did he specify a particular handicap. Yet this almost pathological sensitivity to exploitation is certainly one of those hang-ups from which Burma suffers and Thailand does not.

It sometimes leads Burma into unnecessary bypasses. The Caretaker Government (1958–60), with General Ne Win as Prime Minister, successfully controlled would-be economic exploiters among its merchants with price controls, prices posted on all goods, and a law against the indigenous Asian custom of bargaining. Availability of consumer goods was increased and Defense Services stores were partially opened to the public, these functioning somewhat like a publicly owned utility in the United States, regulating indirectly a privately-owned utility. The system worked. The Revolutionary Council, under the same leader, allowed confidence in its ability to control the merchants to be overwhelmed by that fear of exploitation. The earlier system was never revived though U Ba Nyein has said that nationalization of commodity distribution was not a part of the government's original plans.

Yet even granting the constrictive effect of colonialism on the natural development of Burmese confidence, such reasoning hardly seems sufficient to account for the country's present problems. The Burmese have always been a resilient people. They have recovered in the past from much longer periods of eclipse than their years of colonialism. It seems a questionable assumption that their sense of identity and the shape of their social institutions, molded into their basic outlines eight centuries ago, should be shattered in sixty years.

Comparison with the Thais is legitimate, especially since the Burmese themselves often make the comparison. But I would suggest a different type of comparison to account for some of today's problems, in particular the major one—the lack of unity.

Within the main river valleys of the two countries, each people sought hegemony and unity by assimilating the parts. But the Thais were always assimilating other Thai city-states. Even though there were Khmers or Mons among the people, by the time of assimilation the rulers were Thais. When one city was conquered by another, the conqueror could merge royal families through marriage, merge cultures which varied little, merge loyalties into a single loyalty. It was a king of Sukothai who created the Thai alphabet, and all Thais boast of this, considering it a common part of their culture. Even Chiengmai, which was ruled by both Shans and Burmese, looks upon those periods as rule by foreigners. The people are Thai.

The Burmese couldn't accomplish this. The Mons and Pyus lived in the main valley. The Arakanese and Shans were just beyond the neighboring hills. With the exception of the Pyus, Burmans had opponents for the prize of identity in the land. There were no other Burman power centers in the assimilation days of Pagan, only centers of other peoples.

In Thailand, rebellions less often racked the country and, when they did, they left no residue to embitter modern Thailand. Rebellions were frequent in Burma, leaving behind feelings of bitterness that aren't ended to this day. Over and over, the powerful, exuberant waves of Burman identity were dashed against these other rocks in their effort to flow smoothly over the land and form one unified whole. The task has never been completed.

Both countries also are home to many hill tribes and other minorities. But the Thais number about 80 per cent of their country's total population; the Burman population is only about 55 per cent of the whole. Even when the acclimated Mons and Arakanese are added to this figure and with only the distinct minorities counted as exempt, Burma still has a minority figure totaling over 30 per cent of her population. Thailand has an indigenous minority of no more than 5 per cent. Nor can the Thais of the Thai northeast be equated with the Shans of the Burmese northeast and east. The Shans, who have been opponents of the Burmans, are still separate. The Thais of the northeast are cousins of the Chao Praya valley Thais, country cousins perhaps but still relatives.

The land occupied by the minorities in Thailand is a small portion of the whole; in Burma it is a large portion, a vast area to be policed and, often, subdued. Except for a minor part of the land and the people, Thailand is a nation with a single culture and slight regional differences. If the Burmans are aggressive about their own sense of identity it is because, unlike the Thais, they have had to be. They were always threatened. After eight centuries, this guardedness gets to be a habit.

Modern Burmese tend to blame the British for the divisiveness within their country. They say the British kept them out of the lands of the minorities who were governed separately. This is true. These lands were called the Frontier Areas and were ruled with their own leaders, though under the same governor as Burma Proper. But the Burmese of Burma Proper forget how seldom any of them had gone into the hills (except under arms), and this through three royal dynasties.

There are other differences between the two peoples, but it is no distortion of history to omit them here. The stark clarity of Burma's problem is revealed in the figures. Nor is there need at this point to review again the 20-year story of the indigenous rebels among Shans, Kachins, and Karens and the two groups of Communists. A reminder is necessary that the country is not falling apart because of the rebels, but neither are they so unimportant that they can be ignored. Nevertheless, they are symptoms, not causes, of the basic disunity. What the country has attempted to do about this basic disunity is more important here than the military actions taken against the rebels.

Perhaps out-and-out federalism among equal states might have worked in 1948, but it would have been a wild gamble, ignoring the reality that the states were not equal in power or resources. By 1970, the states were more developed economically and politically; yet the success of federalism was even more improbable than in 1948. The right of secession, for some states, had been written into the 1948 Constitution, to become effective any time after 1958. However wise the provision seemed in 1948, it turned the Union into a trial marriage from which the party to the second part could threaten to withdraw whenever irritations arose, as they were bound to do. In 1960–62, whether for reasons of politics or genuine conviction, U Nu held out the hope to additional groups that they too could have separate states. Some Mons and Arakanese were serious about it. Even the Chins began talking about it. To demand such separateness became the thing to do, as if, somehow, a minority downgraded its own culture unless it did make the demand. And the corollary of secession hovered in the wings.

Such a trial basis made a Union untenable because it weakened the will to make the Union work, replaced the necessary hard work of compromise with an easy escape hatch. Tossing in U Nu's amendment to make Buddhism the state religion only aggravated this sense of separateness among animists, Christians, and even such Buddhists as the Shans who feared the Burmese Sangha's authority over their own monks. It was at this point that the Revolutionary Council staged its coup in the name of unity. To return to federalism in a new constitution, awakening all these old ghosts, would seem a highly improbable course.

The Unionism which the Revolutionary Council has struggled to inculcate in the peoples raises problems of its own. But a singularity of political rights and responsibilities in tandem with mutual respect for cultural plurality has accomplished something no other proposal has done. It has involved the Burmese of Burma Proper. No longer is the Union something by which other peoples attach themselves to the center of power. The ideal is across-the-board cultural equality. No longer is Union Day an occasion when the hill peoples in quaint costumes make a trip to Aung San Stadium in Rangoon to perform their exotic dances for eager photographers and then go home to be forgotten. The major celebration of the day is no longer necessarily held in Rangoon at all.

For the first time ever, as the Burmese say, an article on racial prejudice has appeared in the *Guardian* magazine. U Htin Fatt, the author, believes that prejudice arose in Burma Proper not because of past history but because of chauvinism in the Burmese nationalist movement, whose student leaders ignored or downgraded those who were not Burman-Buddhist. U Htin Fatt himself was of that movement and he writes with touching honesty of the results, feeling, as he says, arnarde, that Burmese hesitancy to embarrass another with one's criticism.

He remembers his childhood when he played with Mons, Arakanese, and Karens, protesting that such matters made no difference at all to the children. There are sad echoes in the words for one of another nation involved in racial problems, who has heard the same protests before in his own country and knows them to be true, knowing equally that to admit them is only a first step to racial harmony.

Maran La Raw, a Kachin anthropologist and a moderate, though a concerned one, wrote as a graduate student in the United States in 1965 that "a lack of complete cultural integration becomes a problem only if complete integration is the expressed objective of the majority." For Burma, the emphasis must not be on cultural integration but on the pluralism which is, to his mind, an alternate policy. But he emphasized strongly that majority and minority interests must coincide since the nation-state is the minimal unit which can survive in the present world.

This seems close enough to Unionism to provide a basis for dialogue, not only between government and minorities but between peoples. It probably comes as a strange idea to Burmans, so sensitive to exploitation, that they can appear as exploiters to those less powerful but just as proud as they. No Burman nationalist publicly shared the pride of the Kachins, for instance, because the Kachins resisted the British until 1935 and resisted the Japanese throughout all the war years. Nor has any Burman nationalist suggested that the Maha Muni image of the Buddha, brought from Arakan to Mandalay as a war trophy by Bodawpaya, be returned to the Arakanese people who made it and treasured it for centuries. Pride is a common denominator among all the people of Burma.

Unionism of the most sensitive variety will not immediately bring all ethnic rebels into the fold. Indeed, some warring groups will actively resist it for reasons of their own. Naw Seng and his shadowy "army" above Lashio near the Chinese border may be counted as one of them. A Kachin officer who mutinied, assumed leadership of the Karen National Defense Organization in central Burma, and fled into China after Taunggyi was recaptured (1949), Naw Seng may be leading dissident ethnic Burmese or dissident Chinese elements. An army of a thousand men or more will not pull down the Burmese government, but they pose a problem for the Burmese army because they can flee across the border into the sanctuary of China. The border is well delineated now, and the Burmese cannot follow. Nor are all ethnic rebels pure patriots; some resemble dacoits, free of the law, doing a little opium smuggling on the side, fighting the Burmese army when it threatens their hideouts. Such problems will persist, perhaps for some time. After all, they began some time ago.

The way to unity and to the survival of Burma as a nation surely lies in the direction of equal rights, equal responsibility, and equal respect. This will be a challenge to the dominant majority who have themselves survived because of their strong Burman-Buddhist culture. But the stakes are high.

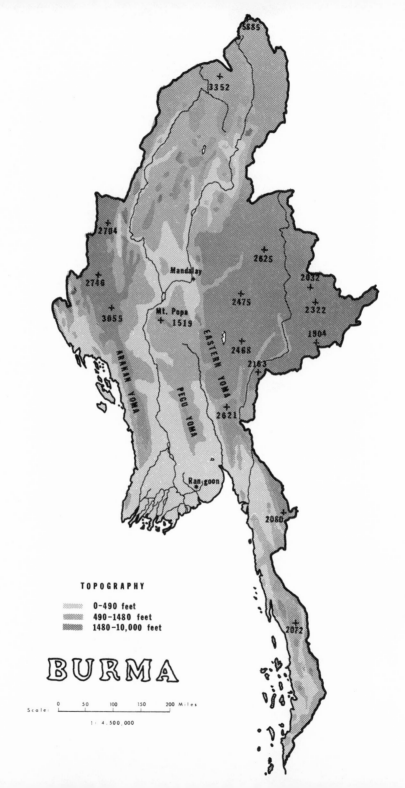

5885

3352

2794

2746

2625

2032

2475

3055

Mandalay

Mt. Popa
1519

2322

1904

2468

2163

EASTERN YOMA

ARAKAN YOMA

PEGU YOMA

2621

Rangoon

2080

TOPOGRAPHY

0-490 feet
490-1480 feet
1480-10,000 feet

2072

BURMA

Scale: 0   50   100   150   200 Miles

1 : 4,500,000

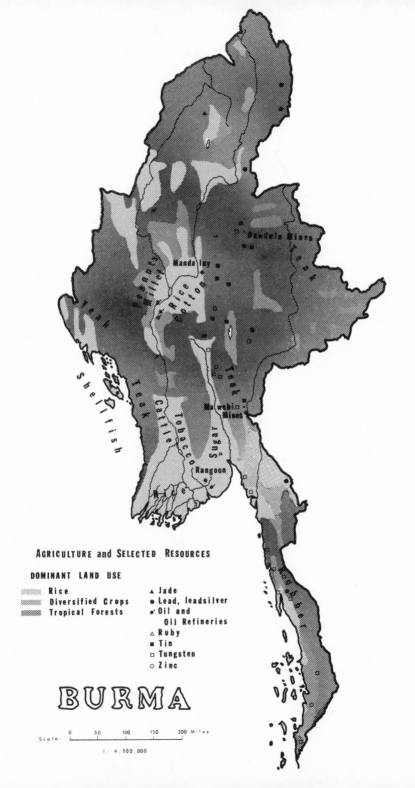

AGRICULTURE and SELECTED RESOURCES

DOMINANT LAND USE

Rice
Diversified Crops
Tropical Forests

▲ Jade
● Lead, leadsilver
⚹ Oil and
 Oil Refineries
△ Ruby
■ Tin
□ Tungsten
○ Zinc

BURMA

Scale: 0   50   100   150   200 Miles

1 : 4,500,000

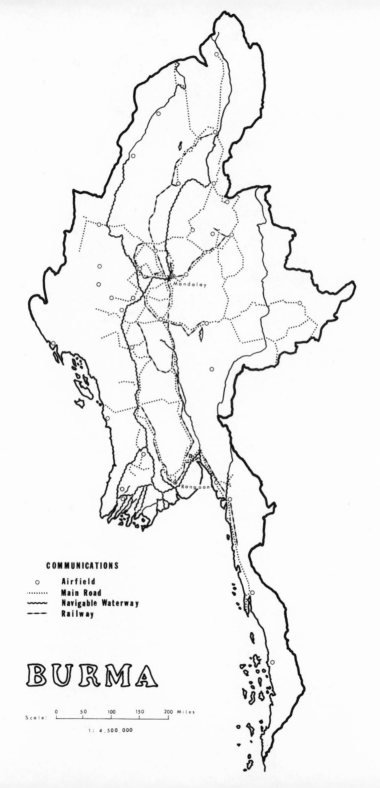

COMMUNICATIONS

○ Airfield
········· Main Road
〜〜 Navigable Waterway
—·—· Railway

BURMA

Scale: 0   50   100   150   200 Miles

1 : 4,500,000

Glossary

ARNARDE—Deep sense of embarrassment at disputing or correcting another person.

BASHA HUT—Small house on stilts with woven bamboo walls and thatched roof.

CHETTYARS—Indian moneylenders.

CHINTHE—Mythical lion, frequently guarding a pagoda entrance.

DAW—Respectful form of address used for a woman. Literally, aunt.

DHAMMATHATS—Treatises of rules that are in accordance with customs and usage, referred to in the settlement of disputes relating to persons or property. Strictly speaking, they are not codes of law.

DUWA—Kachin chieftain.

EINGYI—Woman's blouse.

GAUNG-BAUNG—A kind of headgear, like a turban, worn by important Burmese men.

HINTHE—Mythical bird of Lower Burma.

HLUTDAW—Advisory council to Burmese kings.

HPON—Power, glory.

HPONGYI—Buddhist monk.

HPONGYI-CHAUNG—Monks' school. (Chaung also means monastery.)

HTI—Upper portion of pagoda, sometimes golden or jeweled or

ornamented with small bells that tinkle in the wind. Literally, umbrella.

Ko—Term of address used in speaking to a man of one's own status. Literally, brother.

Lakh—Indian word meaning 100,000, used in Burma particularly in reference to money.

Longyi—Men's or women's skirtlike garment.

Ludu—The common people, ordinary Burmese.

Ma—Usual form of address for girl or woman.

Maung—Usual form of address for boy or man.

Min—King; used after the name, as Mindon Min.

Mintha—Leading actor or dancer.

Minthami—Leading actress or dancer.

Nat—A spirit. Belief in nats is a heritage of earlier animism.

Ngapi—Paste of fish or shrimp prepared by fermentation and pickling in brine.

Parabaik—An old manuscript on soft, sturdy bamboo paper, which has been rubbed with a mixture of charcoal and rice water. Writing was then done with a steatite pencil.

Pwe—A variety show or entertainment. Also, anyein pwe.

Ratu—Classical Burmese verse form.

Sangha—The order of Burmese Buddhist monks.

Sawbwa—Shan chieftain, hereditary ruler of a Shan state.

Saya—Any wise man but especially a teacher or doctor.

Sayadaw—A learned, or senior, monk, head of a monastery.

Shikko—To bow down, kneeling and touching forehead to the ground as a traditional gesture of respect to elders or superiors.

Shinbyu—The ordination or initiation ceremony of a Burmese boy as novice monk.

Stupa—The lower portion of a pagoda, a domelike mound housing relics of the Buddha. From the Sanskrit.

Thakin—Master, lord. Assumed defiantly by young Burmese nationalists as form of address.

Thathanabaing—Head of the Sangha, appointed by each king.

TIPITAKA—The "three baskets" of the sacred Buddhist Scriptures. A Pali word.

TOYWA—Jungle village or any isolated village.

U—Form of address used for a man to show respect either for age or achievement. Literally, uncle.

ZAT—Play or drama based on an early life of the Buddha, or other historical event or legend. PYAZAT—similar to above, but with a contemporary theme.

Bibliography

Brief references made on occasion in the text do not reappear here. The bibliography includes principally the materials on which I placed major reliance in my writing. I drew freely on the files of the *Guardian* magazine (Rangoon) for the years 1967 to early 1970 and also on the government-supplied statistics in the Burma section of the *Far Eastern Economic Review Yearbooks* for the period 1964–70. Other periodical articles and parts of books are interfiled alphabetically below with the larger works consulted.

BA HAN, U. "The Emergence of the Burmese Nation." *Journal of Burma Research Society.* XLVIII, part II (December, 1965): 25–38.

BA MAW, U. *Breakthrough in Burma: Memoirs of a Revolution, 1939–1946.* New Haven, Conn.: Yale University Press, 1968.

Burma Research Society. *Fiftieth Anniversary Publication.* no. 2. Rangoon, 1960. (Selection of articles in history and literature from the files of the Society's *Journal.*)

"Burma Today—36 Page Supplement." *Far Eastern Economic Review* XXVIII, no. 11 (March 17, 1960).

"The Burmese Way to Socialism: The Policy Declaration of the Revolutionary Council." *Burma Weekly* XI (May 3, 1962): 1–2, 8.

CHULA, PRINCE. *Lords of Life: The Paternal Monarchy of Bang-*

kok, 1782–1932, With the Earlier and More Recent History of Thailand. New York: Taplinger, 1960. (Thai history including a Thai view of Burman kings and armies.)

The Glass Palace Chronicle of the Kings of Burma. Translated by Pe Maung Tin and G. H. Luce. Rangoon: University of Rangoon Press, 1960. (First printed, London, 1923.)

HALL, DANIEL GEORGE EDWARD. *A History of South-east Asia.* New York: St. Martin's, 1955.

HTIN AUNG, U. *Burmese Drama: A Study, with Translations of Burmese Plays.* London: Oxford University Press, 1937.

———. *A History of Burma.* New York: Columbia University Press, 1967.

HUKE, ROBERT E. "Geography and Population," chapter III (pp. 65–104), volume I, *Burma.* New Haven, Conn.: Human Relations Area Files, 1956.

KAUNG, U. "A Survey of the History of Education in Burma Before the British Conquest and After." *Journal of Burma Research Society* XLVI, part II (December, 1963): 1–124. (With revised bibliography by his son, U Thaw Kaung.)

KUNSTADTER, PETER, ed. *Southeast Asian Tribes, Minorities and Nations.* 2 vols. Princeton, N.J.: Princeton University Press, 1967.

LEACH, EDMUND RONALD. *Political Systems of Highland Burma: A Study of the Kachin Social Structure.* Boston: Beacon Press, 1965. (First published in 1954.)

LeBAR, FRANK M.; GERALD C. HICKEY; and JOHN K. MUSGRAVE. *Ethnic Groups of Mainland South-east Asia.* New Haven, Conn.: Human Relations Area Files, 1964.

LEHMAN, FREDERICK K. *The Structure of Chin Society: A Tribal People of Burma Adapted to a Non-Western Civilization.* Urbana: University of Illinois Press, 1963.

MAUNG MAUNG, U. *Burma's Constitution.* The Hague: Nijhoff, 1959.

———. *Law and Custom in Burma and the Burmese Family.* The Hague: Nijhoff, 1963.

MI MI KHAING, DAW. *Burmese Family*. Bloomington: Indiana University Press, 1962. (First published, London, 1946.)

NASH, JUNE C. "Living with Nats—An Analysis of Animism in Burma Village Social Relations," in *Anthropological Studies in Theravada Buddhism*, pp. 117–136. New Haven, Conn.: Southeast Asian Studies, Yale University, 1966.

NU, U. *Burma Under the Japanese*. Edited and translated with introduction by J. S. Furnivall. New York: St. Martin's, 1954.

SCOTT, SIR JAMES GEORGE. *Burma: A Handbook of Practical Information*. London: A. Moring, 1906.

SEIN, KENNETH, and J. A. WITHEY. *The Great Po Sein: A Chronicle of the Burmese Theatre*. Bloomington: Indiana University Press, 1966.

TINKER, HUGH. *The Union of Burma: A Study of the First Years of Independence*. 4th ed. London: Oxford University Press, for Royal Institute of International Affairs, 1967.

TRAGER, FRANK N. *Burma: From Kingdom to Republic—A Historical and Political Analysis*. New York: Praeger, 1966.

WOODMAN, DOROTHY. *The Making of Burma*. London: Cresset Press, 1962.

Index

DATE DUE

APR 2 0 1981			
MAY 4 1981			
MAR 1 8 1982			
MAR 3 1 1982			
APR 1 4 1982			
OC 5 '87			